Jump-start
your
legal
research
on Westlaw.

PLI Treatises

PLI's treatises are authored by experts in their field and provide a wealth of information in every relevant legal area. PLI's treatises are updated annually (or as needed) to always reflect the latest developments in your field. Each book purchase includes Basic Upkeep Service. The PLI Library includes:

BANKING & COMMERCIAL LAW

635 Asset-Based Lending $225
626 Bankruptcy Deskbook $250
644 Documenting Secured Transactions $165
608 Equipment Leasing – Leveraged Leasing $350
625 Hillman on Commercial Loan Documentation $165
615 Reinsurance Law $195
643 Structured Finance $185

BUSINESS, CORPORATE & SECURITIES

595 Accountants' Liability $160
661 Advising High Technology Companies $185
5047 Broker-Dealer Regulation $175
616 Corporate Law and Practice $140
601 Corporate Legal Departments $210
9287 Corporate Whistleblowing in the Sarbanes-Oxley Era $195
8136 Directors' and Officers' Liability $195
585 Doing Business Under the Foreign Corrupt Practices Act $170
610 Financial Product Fundamentals $190
4376 GSI's Primer to SEC Research $35
9308 Hedge Fund Regulation $195
627 How to Draft for Corporate Finance $190
7861 Insider Trading $195
596 Investment Adviser Regulation $150
648 Legal Opinions in Business Transactions $185
5519 Mutual Fund Regulation $195
9362 PLI's Guide to Securities Offering Reforms $21
4905 PLI's Guide to the Sarbanes-Oxley Act for Business Professionals $24.95
9256 Pocket MBA: Everything an Attorney Needs to Know About Finance $49
654 The Sarbanes-Oxley Deskbook $325
577 The Securities Law of Public Finance $195
9946 Soderquist on the Securities Laws $195
641 Thinking Like a Writer: A Lawyer's Guide to Effective Writing & Editing $24.95
6589 Variable Annuities and Variable Life Insurance Regulation $195
646 Working with Contracts: What Law School Doesn't Teach You $24.95

EMPLOYMENT

622 Disability Law Deskbook $170
7483 Employment Law Yearbook $190

ESTATE PLANNING AND ELDER LAW

628 Estate Planning & Chapter 14 $140
592 Income Taxation of Estates and Trusts $160
656 Manning on Estate Planning $225

Continued on back...

ESTATE PLANNING AND ELDER LAW *continued*

587 New York Elder Law Handbook $160
617 Stocker and Rikoon on Drawing Wills and Trusts $180
636 Tax Planning with Real Estate $175

IMMIGRATION

599 Immigration Fundamentals $195

INTELLECTUAL PROPERTY

4906 Advertising and Commercial Speech $185
7793 Art Law $225
639 Copyright Law: A Practitioner's Guide $195
580 How to Write a Patent Application $255
658 Landis on Mechanics of Patent Claim Drafting $325
589 Likelihood of Confusion in Trademark Law $195
613 Patent Law $190
629 Patent Licensing $185
638 Patent Litigation $165
619 Sack on Defamation: Libel, Slander, & Related Problems $280
651 Trademark Law $245
7792 Trade Secrets $195
7785 2005 Federal Circuit Yearbook $165
631 Substantial Similarity in Copyright Law $195

LITIGATION

605 Evidence in Negligence Cases $210
649 Federal Bail and Detention Handbook $150
604 Federal Rules of Evidence at a Glance $30
621 How to Handle an Appeal $150
633 Medical Malpractice $185
615 Reinsurance Law $195
5565 Sinclair on Federal Civil Practice $195
641 Thinking Like a Writer: A Lawyer's Guide to Effective Writing & Editing $24.95
653 Trial Handbook $225

REAL ESTATE

642 Commercial Ground Leases $155
8124 Friedman on Contracts and Conveyances of Real Property $350
660 Friedman on Leases $425
584 Holtzschue on Real Estate Contracts $150

TAXATION

636 Tax Planning with Real Estate $175
606 Internal Revenue Service Practice and Procedure Deskbook $200
591 International Tax and Estate Planning $170
624 Langer on Practical International Tax Planning $350
9134 The Circular 230 Deskbook $235

For further information on these titles, visit our website at **www.pli.edu** or call **(800) 260-4PLI**, Monday through Friday, 9am-6pm, Eastern Standard Time.

** Prices are subject to change.*

When ordering please refer to **Source Code: LSF6-AD1**

CORPORATE LAW AND PRACTICE
Course Handbook Series
Number B-1613

Basics of Accounting for Lawyers

What Every Practicing Lawyer Needs to Know

Co-Chairs
Karen Kincaid Balmer
Curtis Burr
Lawrence M. Cirelli

To order this book, call (800) 260-4PLI or fax us at (800) 321-0093. Ask our Customer Service Department for PLI Order Number 11112, Dept. BAV5.

Practising Law Institute
810 Seventh Avenue
New York, New York 10019

"This work is designed to provide practical and useful information on the subject matter covered. However, it is sold with the understanding that the publisher is not engaged in rendering legal, accounting or other professional services. If legal advice or other expert assistance is required, the services of a competent professional should be sought."

Foreword

This course handbook is one of about 200 published each year by the Practising Law Institute.

Its primary function is to serve as an educational supplement to each program. It may also be used as a reference manual by attorneys and related professionals unable to attend the sessions.

The method of reproduction utilized has been chosen to insure that registrants receive these materials as quickly as possible and in the most usable form practical.

The Practising Law Institute wishes to acknowledge its debt and extend its sincere appreciation to the authors who have rendered this valuable service. They exemplify the finest tradition of our profession by sharing their expertise with their colleagues.

Prepared for distribution at the
BASICS OF ACCOUNTING FOR LAWYERS:
WHAT EVERY PRACTICING LAWYER NEEDS TO KNOW
Program
July-August 2007

CONTENTS:

1

UNDERSTANDING GENERALLY ACCEPTED ACCOUNTING PRINCIPLES (GAAP), GENERALLY ACCEPTED AUDITING STANDARDS (GAAS) AND THE ACCOUNTING CYCLE

Patricia A. Woodbury, CPA, CFE

FTI Consulting, Inc.

I. Introduction

A. The SEC system of regulation is based on the concept of full and fair disclosure.

1. The assumption is that investors will be able to make rational and intelligent evaluations of the risk and rewards of a particular investment decision provided they have free and equal access to information about their investment.

2. The free flow of investment information ensures that capital will be allocated efficiently among competing businesses.

3. Financial statements and financial disclosures are some of the most important information provided to investors.

B. The concept of full and fair disclosure as it applies to financial statements means that financial statements must be prepared in accordance with General Accepted Accounting Principles ("GAAP").

1. GAAP consists of conventions, rules, and procedures necessary to define accepted accounting practice at a particular time.

2. GAAP includes not only broad guidelines of general application, but also detailed practices and procedures.

3. Although the SEC has statutory authority to establish GAAP, it chose not to exercise that authority (except in rare circumstances). Instead, the SEC decided to rely on standards promulgated by the private sector.

4. The Financial Accounting Standards Board ("FASB") is currently the principal private sector body responsible for establishing accounting standards.

a. Statements of Financial Accounting Standards (SFASs or FASB Statements)

b. Emerging Issue Task Force Consensus (EITFs)

c. FASB Staff Positions (FSPs)

d. FASB Interpretations (FINs)

e. FASB Technical Bulletins (FTBs)

f. FASB Concept Statements

5. In addition to that established by the FASB since its formation, GAAP also includes other standards.

   a. Accounting Principles Board Opinions established by the predecessor to the FASB (APB Opinions)

   b. Accounting Research Bulletins (ARBs)

   c. AICPA Industry Audit and Accounting Guides

   d. AICPA Statements of Position (SOPs)

   e. AICPA Practice Bulletins

   f. AICPA Accounting interpretations

   g. FASB Staff Qs and As

   h. Industry practices widely recognized and prevalent

   i. AICPA Issues Papers

   j. International Accounting Standards

6. Since there are so many sources of GAAP, the auditing literature has outlined a GAAP hierarchy. This is the order in which GAAP literature should be applied and is especially useful when different principles may be applied to the same transaction.

7. GAAP Hierarchy

GAAP Hierarchy Summary[1]	
A	FASB Statements of Financial Accounting Standards and Interpretations APB Opinions AICPA Accounting Research Bulletins
B	FASB Technical Bulletins AICPA Industry Audit and Accounting Guides AICPA Statements of Position[3]
C	AICPA Accounting Standards Executive Committee Practice Bulletins Consensus positions of the FASB EITF

GAAP Hierarchy Summary[1]	
D	AICPA accounting interpretations "Qs and As" published by the FASB Staff Industry practices widely recognized and prevalent

Other Accounting Literature[2]	
E	FASB Concepts Statements AICPA Issues Papers International Accounting Standards GASB Statements, Interpretations and Technical Bulletins FASAB Statements, Interpretations and Technical Bulletins Pronouncements of other professional associations or regulatory agencies AICPA Technical Practice Aids Accounting textbooks, handbooks, and articles

[1] Per SAS 69 The Meaning of "Present Fairly in Conformity With GAAP"

[2] In the absence of established accounting principles, the auditor may consider other accounting literature, depending on its relevance in the circumstances.

C. Financial statements and other filings by SEC registrants must also comply with:

1. Regulation S-X – The principal accounting regulation of the SEC. It contains substantially all the requirements for financial statements, related footnotes, and supplemental financial schedules required to be included in documents filed with the SEC. Although the basic disclosures and presentations are substantially those required by generally accepted accounting principles, compliance with Regulation S-X may necessitate additional captions on the face of the financial statements, additional footnote disclosures, supplemental schedules, and other information.

2. Accounting Series Releases – The ASRs covered a wide range of accounting and enforcement topics, some of which subsequently became outdated or superseded by other pronouncements. Accordingly, over the years, the SEC rescinded a number of ASRs. In 1982, the ASRs were replaced with Financial Reporting Releases (FRRs) and Accounting and Auditing Enforcement Releases (AAERs).

3. Financial Reporting Releases – The FRRs are designed to communicate the SEC's positions on accounting and auditing principles and practices. They are used to adopt, amend, or interpret rules and regulations relating to accounting and auditing issues or financial statements disclosures.

4. Accounting and Auditing Enforcement Releases – AAERs are public releases issued by the Commission in connection with enforcement actions brought against registrants and accountants.

5. Staff Accounting Bulletins – Staff Accounting Bulletins (SABs) represent interpretations and practices followed by the SEC's Division of Corporation Finance and the Office of the Chief Accountant in connection with the administration of the disclosure requirements of the federal securities laws. SABs are published on a joint basis by the Division of Corporation Finance and the Office of the Chief Accountant. They are not an official part of Regulation S-X and, as stated in the introduction to each SAB, they are not rules of the Commission. The SABs serve an important function, however, in that they provide the SEC with a mechanism for apprising the public of current staff practices and interpretations.

6. Regulation S-K – Regulation S-K describes the registrant-related requirements as to information to be disclosed in documents filed with the SEC. For example, the requirements for Management's Discussion and Analysis, Selected Financial Data, Description of the Business and information related to Executives are Items described in Regulation S-K.

D. SEC forms contain a great deal of information that is useful in interpreting and understanding financial statements. Some commonly used forms are:

1. Form 10-K – Principal form used by most commercial and industrial companies in the United States (and Canada). It must be filed by companies which have registered securities under Section 12 of the 1934 Act and are required by Section 13 to file periodic reports, or which have registered securities under the 1933 Act and are required by Section 15(d) of the 1934 Act to file periodic reports.

2. Form 10-Q – Quarterly report required for each of the first three quarters of the fiscal year. (Filed pursuant to Rule 13a-13 or 15d-13 of the 1934 Act.)

3. Form 8-K – Current report required to be filed when certain significant events occur.

4. Form S-1 – The general form used for the registration of securities for which no other form is authorized or prescribed.

5. Form S-3 – A short form available to registrants which have complied with 1934 Act reporting requirement for at least 36 months and which meet certain market value, trading, or debt-rating tests. The form is available for registering most types of securities, except those issued in an exchange offer, and provides for incorporation by reference of 1934 Act reports filed and to be filed with the SEC.

6. Form S-4 – A form that is used to register shares offered in connection with business combinations as, for example, exchange offers for securities of another entity. The form permits the incorporation by reference of 1934 Act reports based on the concepts introduced in Form S-3.

7. Form S-8 – A form used for the registration of securities to be offered to employees pursuant to option or other employee benefit plans.

8. Form S-11 – Used for the registration of securities issued by real estate investment trusts and securities issued by other registrants whose business is primarily that of acquiring and holding for investment real estate.

9. S-20 – A form used to register standardized options.

10. Form 10 – A form used by registrants for the registration under Section 12(b) or (g) of the 1934 Act of a class of securities for which no other form is prescribed.

11. Form SB-1 – Available for transitional small business registrants to register up to $10 million of securities in any continuous 12-month period. This form is only available for the registration of securities to be sold for cash.

12. Form SB-2 – Used by small business registrants that do not qualify for registering on Form SB-1. It may be used only for securities sold for cash. Revenues and aggregate public float must be less than $25 million.

II. Overriding accounting concepts – basic concepts or assumptions used in the preparation of financial statements.

A. Entity – Financial statements are prepared for the entity, which may be an individual, a partnership, a legal corporation or consolidated group engaged in profit-seeking (in the case of a public company).

B. Accrual accounting – Attempts to record the financial effects on an entity of transactions and other events and circumstances in the periods in which they occur rather than when paid.

C. Historical cost/current value – Transactions are reported at their historical cost. However, GAAP requires certain assets and liabilities to be recorded at market value and the lower of cost or market at the balance sheet date.

D. Going concern – The entity is assumed to be a going concern and will continue to stay in business for the foreseeable future. If the entity is not a going concern and will be liquidating, its assets and liabilities must be reported at their market values rather than historical cost.

E. Market value – The amount that an asset could be sold for or for which a liability could be settled in an arms-length transaction.

F. Income/revenue recognition – Revenue generally is recognized in the financial statements when the earning process is complete or virtually complete and an exchange has taken place.

G. Matching - For the most part, expenses should be matched (reported in the same period) with the revenues they generate.

H. Materiality

1. The magnitude of an omission or misstatement of accounting information that, in light of surrounding circumstances, makes it probable that the judgment of a reasonable person relying on the information would have been changed or influenced by the omission or misstatement.

2. SEC staff provided guidance on Materiality in SAB 99.

3. Read the warning labels on FASB standards.

   "The provisions of this statement need not be applied to immaterial items."

4. Both quantitative and qualitative judgments play a part in any materiality determination.

5. Quantitative Materiality

   a. Usually apply against pretax income but can be used to determine if other items in the financial statements are materially misstated.

   b. Refers to the amount that the numbers in the financial statements are misstated.

6. Qualitative materiality

   a. Relatively small dollar misstatements may be material when fraud is present (*i.e.*, illegal acts by management). Is it probable that the judgment of a reasonable person relying on the information would be changed or influenced?

   b. Must consider the nature and amount of the misstatement. What is material to one company may not be material to another.

   c. Materiality test is applied to misstated items individually and in the aggregate.

I. Substance over form

1. This is an overriding concept that requires that transactions be accounted for in a manner consistent with their economic substance.

2. This means that the particular facts and circumstances concerning the economic substance of a transaction should dictate the accounting.

3. The concept is articulated in the auditing literature in SAS No. 69, par. 6:

   a. "Generally accepted accounting principles recognize the importance of reporting transactions and events in accordance with their substance. The auditor should consider whether the substance of transactions or events differs materially from their form."

   b. Although SAS No. 69 is auditing rather than accounting literature, the concept of "substance over form" is a bedrock concept that underlies GAAP financial statements.

   c. An example of the substance over form concept applied to GAAP is contained in FIN 46R dealing with consolidation. FIN 46 requires that a company that is controlled shall be consolidated with the controlling company. This control may be in the form of ownership interest or may be in the form of contractual or other interest. Therefore, although the legal structure of an organization may indicate control lies elsewhere, if contractual and other indicators point toward control by a registrant, that registrant must consolidate the entity into its financial statements.

J. Related party transactions should be disclosed (FAS No. 57).

K. The economic development brought about by the Industrial Revolution transformed financial reporting to a dynamic science created for the public interests.

III. The accounting system

A. The accounting system provides the information that is needed to prepare the financial statements.

B. While accounting systems differ from company to company, they conceptually work the same way.

C. There are numerous company records but there is a simple logic and rationale to the flow of information through the accounting system.

D. No financial fraud would be successful without some interruption of the flow of information through the company's accounting system.

E. Kinds of company records that exist:

1. Accounts

   a. An account is a document used to record and maintain monetary information from transactions.

   b. Accounts are set up for each item on the balance sheet and income statement.

   c. An account balance is the difference between the total increases in an account and the total decreases in an account.

2. Journal entries

   a. Each transaction is entered as a journal entry to the accounts.

   b. Each journal entry must be balanced – the total of the debit entries must equal the total credit entries. (This means that every transaction affects at least two accounts.)

3. Journals and ledgers

   a. Many transactions are first recorded in a journal.

   b. A general journal is a document used to explain each transaction. This explanation may include the date of the transaction, the accounts to be debited and credited, the amounts of the entries, source documents, justification and authorization of the transaction.

   c. Many companies also have special journals or subsidiary ledgers for the initial recording of transactions. These journals may include Cash Receipts Journals, Cash Disbursements Journals, and Sales Journals.

   d. Special journals or subsidiary ledgers may be updated frequently and are periodically posted to the general ledger.

   e. "Posting" is the process of transferring balances from the subsidiary ledgers to the general ledger.

   f. A general ledger is the entire set of accounts for a company.

g. A trial balance is a schedule that lists all the general ledger account balances at a given point in time.

h. The balance sheet and income statement summarizes information directly from the trial balance.

4. Source Documents

a. Source documents are records that show that a transaction has occurred.

b. Checks, invoices, shipping documents, bills of lading, and bank statements are examples of source documents.

IV. Internal controls

A. "Internal controls" is a system of checks and balances that serves to ensure that accounting entries are accurate and that assets are safeguarded.

B. Elements of an Internal Control System – The Statement on Auditing Standards (SAS No. 55) elaborates on the elements of an internal control system that are outlined below.

1. The Control Environment – The control environment consists of various factors that have the effect of setting up, enhancing, or mitigating the effectiveness of management's policies and procedures. Such factors include:

a. Management's operating style;

b. Organizational structure of the company;

c. The functioning of the board of directors and the audit committee;

d. Methods of assigning responsibility;

e. Internal audit function and management's methods of monitoring and following up on performance;

f. Personnel policies and practices;

g. Other external circumstances such as examinations by banking regulators.

2. The Accounting System – an effective accounting system establishes methods and records so that:

a. Only valid transactions are identified and recorded;

b. Transactions are described on a timely basis and in enough detail to permit proper classification for financial reporting;

c. The value of transactions are measured in a manner that permits recording the proper monetary value in the financial statements;

d. The time period in which a transaction occurred is determined to allow transactions to be recorded in the proper period;

e. Transactions and the related disclosures are properly presented in the financial statements.

3. Control Procedures – Control procedures are policies and procedures established by management that provide reasonable assurance that specific objectives of the company will be achieved. These procedures may be in addition to or a part of the control environment and accounting system. They generally provide the following:

a. Authorization of transactions and activities;

b. Assigning to different people the responsibilities of authorizing transactions (segregation of duties), recording transactions and maintaining the custody of assets to reduce the opportunities for allowing any one person to perpetuate and conceal errors or irregularities;

c. Designing and using adequate documents and records to ensure the proper recording of transactions and events;

d. Safeguards over access to and use of assets and records;

e. Independent checks on performance and proper valuation of recorded amounts.

V. Standards of the Public Company Accounting Oversight Board (PCAOB Standards) and Generally Accepted Auditing Standards (GAAS)

A. PCAOB Standards and GAAS are the standards auditors must use.

B. PCAOB Standards are set by the Public Company Accounting Oversight Board (formed through the Sarbanes-Oxley Act of 2002) and must be followed during public company audits.

C. The basis for the PCAOB Standards is the auditing standards in existence as of April 16, 2003.

D. GAAS is set by the American Institute of Certified Public Accountants and must be followed during non-public company audits.

E. There are many similarities between PCAOB Standards and GAAS.

VI. The Auditor

A. Investors rely extensively on the independent auditor to ensure that financial statements filed with the Commission are prepared in accordance with GAAP.

B. The auditor adds credibility to the financial reporting process.

C. Enforcement actions against auditors help ensure that incompetent or dishonest accountants are either prevented from practicing before the Commission or are forced to undergo additional training or supervision to ensure that they meet professional standards.

D. The four largest accounting firms include the firms of KPMG, Deloitte & Touche, PricewaterhouseCoopers, and Ernst & Young.

E. The second four largest firms consist of Grant Thornton, BDO Seidman, McGladrey & Pullen and Crowe Chizek.

F. Over 98% of all public companies are audited by the largest eight firms.

G. The remaining firms include large regional firms, smaller partnerships and sole practitioners.

VII. Standards of the PCAOB consist of the following ten core standards. The GAAS core standards are similar to the PCAOB standards.

A. General standards

1. The audit is to be performed by a person or persons having adequate technical training and proficiency as an auditor.

2. In all matters relating to the assignment, an independence in mental attitude is to be maintained by the auditor or auditors.

3. Due professional care is to be exercised in the performance of the audit and the preparation of the report.

B. Standards of field work

1. The work is to be adequately planned and assistants, if any, are to be properly supervised.

2. A sufficient understanding of the internal control structure is to be obtained to plan the audit and to determine the nature, timing, and extent of tests to be performed.

3. Sufficient competent evidential matter is to be obtained through inspection, observation, inquiries and confirmations to afford a reasonable basis for an opinion regarding the financial statements under audit.

C. Standards of reporting:

1. The report shall state whether the financial statements are presented in accordance with generally accepted accounting principles.

2. The report shall identify those circumstances in which such principles have not been consistently observed in the current period in relation to the preceding period.

3. Informative disclosures in the financial statements are to be regarded as reasonably adequate unless otherwise stated in the report.

4. The report shall either contain an expression of opinion regarding the financial statements, taken as a whole, or an assertion to the effect that an opinion cannot be expressed. When an overall opinion cannot be expressed, the reasons therefore should be stated. In all cases where an auditor's name is associated with financial statements, the report should contain a clear-cut indication of the character of the auditor's work, if any, and the degree of responsibility the auditor is taking.

VIII. In addition, PCAOB Standards include:

A. PCAOB Rules

1. Rule 3100/3101 – Compliance with professional practice standards and a description of certain terms.

2. Rule 3200T – 3600T – Interim Standards

a. Interim auditing standards

b. Interim attestation standards

c. Interim quality control standards

d. Interim ethics standards

e. Interim independence standards

3. Rule 3700 Advisory Groups

B. PCAOB Standards

1. AS1 – References in auditors' reports to the standards of the PCAOB.

2. AS2 – Audits of internal control over financial reporting performed in conjunction with an audit of financial statements.

3. AS3 – Audit documentation.

4. AS4 – Reporting on whether a previously reported material weakness continues to exist.

C. Additional pronouncements, known as Statements on Auditing Standards ("SAS"), that were issued by the Auditing Standards Board of the American Institute of Certified Public Accountants ("AICPA") to provide additional guidance with respect to auditing responsibilities involving, among other things, errors and irregularities, illegal acts, management representations, analytical procedures and other matters of contemporary importance.

D. For example, the Auditor's responsibilities for the detection of fraud and illegal acts are set forth in SAS 99 (October 2002) and SAS 54 (April 1988).

1. The auditor should design the audit to provide reasonable assurance of detecting errors and irregularities that are material to the financial statements, and

2. Illegal acts having a direct and material effect on the determination of financial statement amounts.

E. It is also important to understand that audit standards, for the most part, only provide general guidance. The actual procedures used by the auditor in conducting the audit are not prescribed. These procedures have been determined over the years by practice and are contained in the various programs prepared by individual accounting firms, text books and other authoritative literature.

IX. The audit report:

A. The auditor, based on a PCAOB Standards audit, issues an opinion or audit report that states whether the financial statements have been prepared in accordance with GAAP and whether the audit was conducted in accordance with PCAOB Standards.

B. The auditor must also issue an opinion regarding management's assessment of internal control over financial reporting. This opinion may be incorporated into the audit report or may be separately presented.

C. The Audit Report may be:

1. Unqualified – states that the financial statements are prepared in accordance with GAAP.

2. Qualified – based on uncertainties relating to the GAAP presentation or limitations in the scope of the audit.

3. Adverse – states that the financial statements do not comply with GAAP.

4. Disclaimer – no opinion is given.

D. The auditor's reporting requirements with respect to audits of registrants are set forth in Regulation S-X Rule 2-02 and AS2.

X. The audit:

A. The primary purpose of the audit is to determine whether the financial statements comply with GAAP.

B. The auditor is required to plan his audit to provide reasonable assurance that errors or irregularities that are material to the financial statements are detected.

C. Management represents explicitly and implicitly that certain things are true about the financial statements. These representations are technically referred to as "assertions."

1. The transactions reported in the financial statements exist and are not fabricated;

2. The amounts reported are not over-or understated;

3. The company actually owns the assets and owes the liabilities that are included in the financial statements;

4. The valuations comply with GAAP; and

5. The amounts in the financial statements are presented and classified properly (*i.e.,* current assets can be liquidated within one year).

D. The auditor's job is to determine if these assertions are true.

E. The auditor does this by performing audit procedures.

F. Audit procedures are used to verify the accuracy of the information contained in the books and records.

G. Audit procedures can be found in text books and in audit programs used by accounting firms. Some examples of audit procedures include:

1. Testing transactions (usually based on a sample) recorded in the books and records to ensure that they are supported by invoices, shipping documents or other source documents.

2. Confirming receivable balances with third party customers to determine if they are recorded in the books at the proper amount.

3. Observing the physical inventory count to ensure that proper procedures are being followed.

4. Inquiries of management and others concerning recorded transactions.

5. Analytical procedures designed to identify anomalies in the amounts reported that might result from errors or irregularities.

H. The auditor <u>does not</u> examine every transaction recorded in the company's books and records.

1. Instead, the auditor tests transactions based on a representative sample.

2. The auditor assumes, absent evidence to the contrary, that the documents examined are authentic.

3. The auditor should not assume that management is unquestionably honest or dishonest.

4. The extent of the testing is determined by the nature of the account and the strength of the internal controls. If internal controls are strong, testing can be less extensive.

I. To summarize:

1. The auditor verifies management assertions concerning the financial statements.

2. This verification is performed using auditing procedures that are, to a large extent, established by general practice.

XI. The structure of the audit staff

A. Engagement partner – Has primary responsibility for ensuring that the audit complies with PCAOB Standards and also usually maintains client relationships, reviews portions of the audit work, signs the audit report, and approves client billings.

B. Concurring partner:

1. Responsibilities differ from accounting firm to accounting firm.

2. PCAOB Standards now require that there be a concurring partner assigned to the audit.

3. Historically, because there was no GAAS requirement for a concurring partner review, the SEC usually authorized enforcement action against a concurring partner only when it could be proven that the partner was aware of the problem that caused the financial statements to be materially misstated but failed to reasonably resolve it.

C. Manager – Conducts the day to day audit. Directly supervises audit personnel and reviews audit work.

D. Senior – Responsible for planning and performance of a part of the audit work assigned by the manager. Reviews the work of juniors assigned to him/her.

E. Juniors (or assistants) – Performs work assigned by the Senior.

XII. Audit working papers:

A. Auditing Standards No. 3, "Auditor Documentation," provides that "audit documentation is the written record of the basis for the auditor's conclusions that provides the support for the auditor's representations, whether those representations are contained in the auditor's report or otherwise."

B. Working papers

1. Record the understanding of the client's business and system of internal control.

2. Document the audit strategy.

3. Document the detailed systems evaluation, transaction reviews, and internal controls.

4. Document procedures performed and evidence obtained related to transactions, account balances and other information presented in the financial statements.

5. Document that the work of any assistants was supervised and reviewed.

6. Document significant findings or issues, actions taken to address them and the basis for the conclusions reached.

7. Provide information for SEC reports, tax returns, and governmental agencies.

8. Serve as a source of information for succeeding audits.

9. In a small engagement, one or two binders may hold all the work papers. In larger engagements one (or more) binders will be devoted to individual audit areas (*e.g.,* "Inventories," "Sales," "Assets," and might reach 50 to 100 binders in total.)

XIII. Some typical working papers include

A. Trial balance – Prepared by the client and lists the ending balances of all ledger accounts. The financial statements are prepared from the trial balance. All underlying working papers are integrated, referenced and summarized into the amounts appearing in the trial balance.

B. Planning memorandum – Discusses the accounting environment of the company and how that environment will impact the specific audit issues of concern along with anticipated problem areas and proposed solutions.

C. Audit program – Contains specific audit procedures to be performed in order to audit a particular account (*i.e.*, cash, accounts receivables, inventories, etc.).

D. Engagement Completion Memos:

1. Summary document that discusses the work done and conclusions reached in each area of the audit. These conclusions are usually included in a document at the front of each audit area and are sometimes referred to as the "lead schedule."

2. At the conclusion of each engagement, an overall summary memorandum (referred to as the Engagement Completion Document in AS3) must be prepared. This document must identify all significant findings or issues and include information necessary to understand the significant findings and issues.

3. Significant findings or issues include:

   a. Complex or unusual transactions

   b. Accounting estimates

   c. Uncertainties related to management assumptions

   d. Matters involving the selection, application or consistency of accounting principles and disclosures

   e. Audit results that indicate

      (1) That the auditor needs to modify audit procedures

      (2) The existence of material misstatements

      (3) Omissions in the financial statements

      (4) The existence of significant deficiencies or material weaknesses in internal control over financial reporting.

   f. Audit adjustments

   g. Disagreements among members of the engagement team or with others consulted on the engagement about final conclusions reached on significant accounting or auditing matters

   h. Circumstances that cause significant difficulty in applying auditing procedures

   i. Significant changes in the assessed level of audit risk for particular audit areas and the auditor's response to those changes

   j. Any matters that could result in modification of the auditor's report

E. Management representation letter contains certain representations of management.

F. Documentation of matters to be communicated to the audit committee

G. Permanent working papers:

1. Working papers for recurring engagements usually contain files that are carried forward from preceding years' audits; these are often referred to as permanent files. The file should include data having continuing use and not subject to frequent change. Examples of such data include copies or abstracts of the certificate of incorporation, bylaws, bond and note indentures, union agreements, important contracts having historical significance, organization charts, the client's accounting policies and procedures, key personnel, and location of plants.

2. The file may also include activity schedules not maintained by the client, for example, schedules of future amortization or depreciation (sometimes referred to as "lapse schedules") and analyses and other working papers that have historical significance, such as analyses of various capital accounts. Audit programs, narrative descriptions of accounting and control systems, flow charts, and internal control questionnaires also are frequently kept in the permanent files.

H. Journal entries – Errors discovered during the audit can be corrected by journal entry.

I. Consolidation working papers – These working papers bring together the trial balances of all subsidiaries and tie the numbers into the financial statements. They can be used to prove that the misstated numbers actually got into the financial statements.

J. Internal control evaluation and testing

K. Relevant accounting literature – Particularly with an unusual accounting issue, the audit staff may include in the work papers copies of (or excerpts from) the accounting pronouncements they intend to apply to a given situation.

L. If the audit staff consults with the firm's National Office and asks for advice as to how to handle an accounting issue, the advice should be included in the work papers.

M. Letters to management – After the audit work is complete, and generally well after the financial statements are filed, the auditors may prepare a letter to the client's management that discusses any problems with the client's internal accounting control or other administrative and operating matters noted during the examination. Issues that are communicated in this manner can range from minor matters that are repeated yearly to the very important.

N. Board of Directors Minutes – The auditors will have collected copies of (or written summaries of) the client's Board of Directors minutes, as well as the minutes of the Audit Committee of the Board of Directors. A senior member of the audit team will have reviewed these minutes, even if they are not initialed. If the audit resolution of an issue seems to conflict with what you know went on at the client company, the Board minutes are an excellent source of determining auditors' awareness of certain events.

O. Analytic Review Documents – In many engagements, the auditors will examine particular figures from the balance sheet or income statement for the past two or three years and analyze why they may have changed.

XIV. Section 10A of the Exchange Act requires direct reporting.

A. Each audit required pursuant to this title of the financial statements of an registrant by a registered public accounting firm shall include:

1. Procedures designed to provide reasonable assurance of detecting illegal acts that would have a direct and material effect on the determination of financial statement amounts

2. Procedures designed to identify related party transactions that are material to the financial statements or otherwise require disclosure therein; and

3. An evaluation of whether there is substantial doubt about the ability of the registrant to continue as a going concern during the ensuing fiscal year.

B. If, while conducting its audit, an accountant becomes aware of information indicating that an illegal act has occurred or may have occurred,

1. An "illegal act" is "any action or omission that violates any law, or any rule or regulation having the force of law."

2. Whether or not material to the financial statements.

C. Then the auditor is required

1. To determine whether it was "likely" that an illegal act has occurred and, if so,

2. Its possible effect on the financial statements (including fines, penalties, damages, and so on).

D. The registrant's management must be informed as soon as practicable.

E. If, after doing further work, the auditor reaches one of the following three conclusions, then it is required, as soon as practicable, to report directly to the Audit Committee or the board of directors in the absence of an Audit Committee.

F. The three conclusions are:

1. The illegal act has a material effect on the registrant's financial statements;

2. Senior management and the board of directors have not taken appropriate remedial action; and

3. The failure of management and the board to take appropriate remedial action is reasonably expected:

a. To warrant either a modification of the audit report, or

b. The accountant's resignation from the audit engagement.

G. If the board receives a report from the auditor that it has reached the three conclusions described above, the board must, within one business day, notify the Commission that it received such a report and describe the substance of the report.

H. If the accountant does not receive a copy of the registrant's notice to the Commission within one business day, then the registered public accounting firm shall:

1. Resign from the engagement; or

2. Furnish to the Commission a copy of the report given to the board (or documentation of any oral report) not later than 1 business day after the accounting firm failed to receive notice

NOTES

NOTES

2

UNDERSTANDING BALANCE SHEETS: ASSETS, LIABILITIES AND STOCKHOLDERS' EQUITY

Christopher J. Rosetti, CPA, CFE

BST Valuation & Litigation Advisors LLC

I. INTRODUCTION

Prior to the standardization of monetary systems, individuals kept track of what was owed to them and what was owed by them by documenting the various items exchanged, for example, four cows, 2 bundles of corn, etc. The development of coinage and standard monetary units paved the way for trade expansion and allowed merchants to account for the exchange of dissimilar assets.

Throughout much of recorded history, a list of assets and liabilities was the paramount measure of an individuals or business's financial position. This list, now called a balance sheet provides information on the resources, obligations and residual (equity) of the business's owners.

The balance sheet was the preeminent financial documents prior to the latter half of the 20th century. Its secondary status was primarily due to the increased emphasis placed on earnings. However, renewed interest in the balance has taken hold as investors and lenders seek to measure the liquidity and financial stability/flexibility of businesses.

II. THE BALANCE SHEET

The Balance Sheet provides information about a firm's solvency. It also provides economic information about an entity's resources (assets), claims against the resources (liabilities) and the remaining claim accruing to the owners (owners' equity). The balance sheet is also known as the Statement of Financial Position, however, the term balance sheet is preferred because it reflects an important aspect of accounting, namely, the statement balances in conformity with the basis accounting equation:

ASSETS = LIABILITIES + OWNERS' EQUITY

Before understanding the equation, we must first understand the key concepts and definitions:

- Assets: Probably future economic benefits obtained or controlled by a particular entity as a result of past transactions of events (Items you posses, own and have rights to).
- Liabilities: Probable future sacrifices of economic benefits arising from present obligations of a particular entity to transfer assets or provide services to other entities in the future as a result of past transactions (Items or amounts owed to vendors or other third parties).
- Owners' Equity: The residual interest in the assets of an entity that remains after its liabilities are deducted.

Another way to illustrate this equation is to think of your home. For example;

Asset = the original cost basis of your house

Liability = your current mortgage balance

Equity = the portion of the cost of the house that is not owed to the bank

To make accounting information understandable and usable, balance sheet items are grouped and arranged according to certain guidelines:

- Assets are listed first and are presented in order or liquidity (or convertibility in to cash), i.e., assets with the least liquidity are listed last. The general classification and presentation order of assets are as follows:
  - Current Assets
    - Cash and short-term investments
    - Receivables
    - Marketable Securities
    - Inventories
    - Prepayments
  - Non-Current Assets
    - Other Investments
    - Property, plant and equipment
    - Intangible assets
    - Other assets
    - Deferred charges
- Liabilities are classified and presented based on time to maturity, thus obligations currently due are listed first. The general classification and presentation order of liabilities are as follows:
  - Current Liabilities
    - Accounts payable
    - Short-term notes payable
    - Unearned income/revenue

    - Accrued Expenses
    - Current portion of long-term debt
  - Non-Current Liabilities
    - Capital Leases
    - Long-term debt
    - Pension and Post-Retirement Obligations
    - Commitments and Contingencies
- Owners' equity items are classified and presented in the order or permanence, thus owner contributions are listed first, while accumulated earnings, which are update regularly, are listed last. The general classification and presentation order of owners' equity are as follows:
  - Contributed (or paid-in) Capital
    - Capital stock
    - Contributed capital in excess of the par value of stock
    - Other contributed capital
  - Retained Earnings

III. CURRENT ASSETS

Current assets include cash and other assets that are reasonably expected to be realized in cash or to be sold or consumed during the normal operating cycle (one year or less). Most companies use one year because the operating cycle may be difficult to measure reliably. With few exceptions, most items appearing on the balance sheet are reflected at historical cost.[1] A few exceptions exist for items that are recorded at the lower of their cost or current market value, or net realizable value.

Cash and short-term investments – Cash in the bank plus investments in money market funds, CDs or other securities that are expected to be liquidated during the year.

---

1. Items acquired via a non-cash transaction are recorded at the prevailing market value of the item acquired.

Receivables – Receivables represent amounts due from customers for the sale of goods or services. They should be reported net or any anticipated reduction because of uncollectible amounts.

Marketable Securities – Includes trading securities, securities held to maturity and securities available for sale. Generally recorded at cost, temporary reductions are reflected in owner's equity while permanent reductions are reflected on the income statement.

Inventories are reported at the lower of cost of market value. In addition, the valuation basis can be in at least two forms (FIFO or LIFO). Manufacturing often distinguish their inventories as follows: raw materials, work in process or finished goods.

Prepaid Expenses – This asset can also be characterized as non-current, depending on when the prepaid expense matures. Prepaid expense are cash outlays made in advanced of receipt of service, i.e., paying your rent in advance. Prepaid expenses are usually characterized as current because a current asset (cash) is used to make the advance. They are also expected to have been used during the current year

IV. NON-CURRENT ASSETS

The important distinction between current and non-current assets is:

1. Non-Current assets are not completely used up in a single operating cycle, and
2. Management plans to retain non-current assets beyond one year from the balance sheet date

Long-term investments are usually shown at their cost, and include:

Investments and other funds – This includes cash set aside for long-term use as needed or other investments, and includes:

- Investments in subsidiaries
- Funds set aside for long-term use, such as bond sinking funds, stock retirement funds or long-term savings deposits
- Cash surrender value of life insurance policies carried by the company

Property, Plant and Equipment (PPE) – This includes operational assets used in operations and items that are depreciable, i.e., generally decline in value over time, including buildings, machinery, and fixtures. Land is also included but reported separately. Land is not subject to depreciation. PPE is recorded at cost.

Intangible Assets – These assets, which include goodwill, patents, copyrights, are reported at their net amortized amount, i.e., cost less dimishment in value since acquired.

Other Assets – These include but are not limited to long-term receivables owed by company officers/employees or idled assets.

Deferred Charges – These items are usually the result of the prepayment of long-term expenses, bond issuance costs, pension costs paid in advance and insurance prepayments.

V. CURRENT LIABILITIES

The difference between current assets and current liabilities is called working capital, and is a measure to gauge a company's liquidity, i.e., its ability to meet short-term obligations.

Current liabilities include those obligations expected to be liquidated using current assets during the year, and they include:

Accounts payable – amounts owed for the purchase of goods or services

Short-term notes payable – promissory notes to pay for goods or services. Due within the year.

Unearned income/revenue – Represents collections in advance of providing a service, such as prepaid rent collected by you, or prepaid subscriptions when the person has the right to cancel and order.

Accrued Expenses – represents obligations due but not yet paid. It does not relate to items purchased for resale of services provided, rather it relates to payroll, interest owed on debt, and the existing portion of property, sales or payroll taxes.

Current portion of long-term debt – That portion of a mortgage or long-term loan that is payable during the year, usually the monthly installments due during the year.

VI. NON-CURRENT LIABILITIES

Capital Leases – Long-term portion of lease payments due after the current year

Long-Term Debt – Amounts owed to investors (after next year) who purchased your bonds or who lent you money in the past

Pension and Post-Retirement Obligations – relate to accumulated pension costs and post-retirement cost (health care) for past employee services rendered. It represents the present value of future obligations.

Commitment and Contingencies – represent other long-term obligation that are due or may be due after one year. There is an uncertainty as to the possible amount of this event or when it will actually occur (usually over one year). We record the liability only if it is probable that the event will occur and we can reasonably estimate the loss amount. Gain contingencies are generally not recognized, and only recognized in the footnotes to the financial statements. Not on the balance sheet.

VII. OWNERS' EQUITY

Capital Stock – This is the par value of stock issued. The stock can be common or preferred.

Contributed Capital in Excess of par Value – represents the difference between the par value of the stock and the amount paid for the stock.

Other Contributed Capital – Generally relates to the sale of Treasury stock, i.e., the excess of the price paid over the acquisition cost. Treasury stock is capital stock repurchased by the company and held by the company.

Retained Earnings – This is the company's net earnings since inception (less dividends paid to stockholders). Many companies in a growth phase do not pay dividends. Retained earnings may be restricted due to contractual obligations relating to bond indentures or for future planned plant expansions. These are signs to the stockholders that not all of the retained earnings are available for dividends.

VIII. MISCELLANEOUS

The term reserve is often used to reflect a reduction of an asset account (usually accounts receivable), estimated liabilities (reserve for warranties) and appropriation of retained earnings (reserve for future plant expansion). Except for the latter example, it should not be used as an account description because it implies, or the reader can infer, that money is set aside somewhere.

When possible, annual balance sheets should be compared to measure the changes between accounts and financial position to help you gauge the companies improved (or decreased) liquidity.

NOTES

3

BALANCE SHEET PRESENTATION

Sonya Andreassen
PricewaterhouseCoopers LLP

This session will cover the basic components of a balance sheet based on US Generally Accepted Accounting Principles (GAAP) including:

- Cash and cash equivalents
- Accounts Receivables
- Prepaid Expenses
- Inventory
- Other assets (tangible and intangible)
- Fixed assets
- Accounts Payable
- Accrued liabilities, including goods received not invoiced (GRNI)
- Debt and other loans/notes
- Reserves and other accruals
- Deferred taxes
- Components of shareholders equity

Definitions and examples will be provided, focusing on areas that would be most relevant to attorneys.

Other US GAAP concepts and terminology will be presented and explained including contra accounts, valuation methods, and assessment of asset impairment, capitalization and accrual accounting.

NOTES

4

INCOME STATEMENT & ITS IMPORTANCE

Glenn Newman, CPA/ABV, CFE, MBA
Robert Gray, CPA/ABV, CFE, FACFEI
Parente Randolph

sociations:
nerican Bar Association

:ensing Executives Society

nerican Institute of Certified
ıblic Accountants *(Business
ıluation/Forensic & Litigation
ırvices Executive
ommittee)*

CPA – Past Chairman –
*aud & Litigation National
onference*

urnal of Accountancy –
litorial Board

ennsylvania Institute of
ertified Public Accountants

ssociation of Certified Fraud
kaminers

ational Bond Claims
ssociation

urety Claims Institute

censes/Certifications:
ertified Public Accountant
Pennsylvania

ertified Fraud Examiner

Glenn Newman, CPA, CFE, MBA

Principal in Charge
Forensic and Litigation Services

Philadelphia office
215.972.2354
gnewman@parentenet.com

Glenn has provided a variety of financial consulting and accounting services to attorneys, insurance companies, governmental agencies and public and private corporations since 1980. Prior to joining Parente Randolph in 1993, he spent approximately nine years with a national accounting firm prior to organizing a boutique litigation consulting firm. He specializes in providing financial consulting analyses related to matters in dispute. Specifically, the majority of the analyses performed involve litigation and/or insurance claims matters.

Glenn has recently completed a three year term for the American Institute of CPA's Forensic and Litigation Services ("FLS") Committee and has been recently elected to serve on its Business Valuation/FLS Executive Committee. The Committee provides professional guidance to CPA practitioners who perform fraud investigations and calculate economic damages.

Glenn is responsible for the firm's Forensic Accounting and Litigation Services group. His current responsibilities include assignment planning, supervision of staff, assistance with interrogatories, and expert witness testimony as required. Responsibilities are carried out through financial and forensic analysis of financial statements and tax returns, general ledgers and other original books of entry, relevant contracts and agreements, and industry data.

Representative assignments on which he has worked include:

- Acquisition Disputes
- Antitrust Matters
- Bankruptcy and Troubled Company Issues
- Business Interruptions
- Construction Defaults and Delays
- Economic Damages
- Fidelity and Surety Losses
- Fraud Investigations
- Healthcare Fraud and Abuse
- Intellectual Property Infringements
- Partnership Disputes
- Products Liability
- Professional Negligence
- Royalty Compliance

Glenn has spoken before professional and educational groups on various aspects of financial analysis, litigation consulting, fraud investigations and economic damages.

Glenn has a Bachelor of Science degree in Accounting from Pennsylvania State University and a Master of Business Administration Economics/Finance from West Chester University. His education has been supplemented by various continuing education courses offered by a variety of professional organizations.

The income statement is a significant scorecard for corporations. Contrary to the balance sheet which measures financial condition or net worth, the income statement provides insight as to "how'd we do." Today's program will address how the income statement fits in among the other traditional financial statements, its relative importance, how management utilizes the data, and how it has been abused.

The income statement measures results of operations for a particular time period, typically a full operating cycle, or one year. It is akin to the remnants of one's checkbook for the year which the mortgage, utilities, car payments, kids' allowance are subtracted from our paycheck and hopefully leaves a balance after Uncle Sam and friends take their bite. The statement goes beyond the mere accounting of transactions. It can be used to compare historical growth, return on investment, and profitability of an entity measured against its peers. Why is that important? Just ask the folks on Wall Street. It is the investing community which judge's operating results and assigns values to a stock price.

There is a reason why the income statement is traditionally the first financial statement presented after the auditor's opinion letter. It is a company's revenue or profit growth, which is eagerly awaited by analysts.

One of the more meaningful measures of a public-traded company is its price-earnings ratio (PE ratio). It is a basic computation that compares the earnings per share to the company's stock price. A stock that is earning $1 per share that sells for $20 on the open market is said to trade at "a 20 multiple", that is 20 times its earnings. That company commands a premium versus another stock earning the same $1 that trades for $10 per share. The second company is likely to have fewer prospects for growth and increased profitability.

Many individual components drive the data that ultimately results in an income statement prepared in accordance with Generally Accepted Accounting Principles. It starts with the product or service that is sold to customers. Different products, different customers and different prices, when recognized, result in net sales or revenues. Revenues, or "top line", is generally what is referred to when we hear that the company did $25 million last year. The $25 million is not the cash in bank, net income, equity or total market value; it is the revenue, or "turnover" as referred to by our friends on the other side of the pond. Measuring revenue is one way analysts and management evaluate a company's prospects.

Profitability, at various levels, differentiates one company from another in the same industry. Flowing downward, the first level of profitability is sometimes not disclosed on an income statement. Specifically, the gross to net sales amount reflects how much the company must discount, or give away its product in order to generate revenues. Whether its returns, rebates, volume discounts, marketing allowances, among others, a large spread between gross and net sales may provide an indicator of future prospects or competitive position. Think of the automotive industry the last several years. It started with discounts for college graduates or military personnel, then evolved to low interest loans, and finally to thousands of dollars in rebates. Each of these items has been accounted for in determining net sales.

Perhaps the single most important indicator included in the income statement is the gross profit margin. The gross profit margin represents the amount left over after considering direct costs such as materials, labor, and certain overhead. These costs are known as costs of goods sold, or COGS in a manufacturing environment. In a law firm COGS would likely include the lawyers' salaries and related benefits. Effectively, these costs are what drive production and ultimately sales. While most COGS costs are variable, that is they increase with increased sales, some may be fixed in nature. For example, heat, light and power necessary to operate a manufacturing plant may be mostly fixed. Accordingly, it is management's goal to run its plant efficiently, as close to capacity as possible, to increase its profit margin.

After the profit margin, also known as "the line," operating costs are presented. These costs are typically combined as selling, general and administrative expenses. These "below the line" costs may be more fixed in nature at specified volumes and include such items as support staff, computer systems, sales commissions, professional fees, insurance, to name a few.

Many times companies which are stagnant seek to grow net income by managing their overhead. This occurs by an analysis of S, G &A. It is common for companies to benchmark their overhead expenses as compared to peers in one's industry. For example, financial institutions need to be run very efficiently to generate profits. That is one reason we see much consolidation in the industry. A bank which has total assets of $25 billion can likely be run as efficiently as one with $50 billion. The elimination of duplicate accounting systems, branches, and websites can result in increased profitability.

It is the thirst for profitability that has unleashed greed in many instances in corporate America. Recent year's headlines concerning Enron, Worldcom, Tyco, HealthSouth, and scores of other entities have resulted in billions of dollars of stock value disappearing almost overnight. The manipulation of earnings and misrepresentation to the investing community has caused the pendulum to swing toward corporate compliance. Sarbanes-Oxley and other regulatory actions have forced public companies to spend significant resources in an attempt to regain confidence in our systems. These costs are not only the professional fees incurred, but the redirection of management focus away from running its business. As in life, a few bad apples spoil things for all.

The common denominator in many of these frauds begins with the Income Statement. Earnings are increased by inflating sales, hiding or misclassifying expenses, or a combination of the two. Because many senior level officers' incentive compensation is based on increased profitability or share price, an inherent conflict of interest may exist. Accordingly, public companies are now required to demonstrate that adequate controls are in place that provides the foundation for the company's financial statements. Regardless of the level of controls, companies are continuously competing to be best in class. A complete and accurate income statement provides the stakeholders (e.g., – the investing public, management, lenders, employees) a useful and necessary tool for basic and advanced decision making.

NOTES

5

STATEMENTS OF INCOME AND COMPREHENSIVE INCOME

Felicia C. Battista

FTI Consulting, Inc.

Statements of Income
and Comprehensive Income
PLI Presentation
July 9, 2007

Felicia C. Battista
FTI Consulting, Inc.
Senior Managing Director
felicia.battista@fticonsulting.com

FTI

Felicia C. Battista

Senior Managing Director - Forensic and Litigation Consulting

felicia.battista@fticonsulting.com

1101 K Street, NW
Suite B100
Washington, D.C. 20005
Tel: (202) 312-9223
Fax: (202) 312-9102

Certifications

Certified Public Accountant

Licensed to practice law in the District of Columbia, the Commonwealth of Pennsylvania, and the Supreme Court of the United States

Education

Bachelor of Business Administration with concentration in accounting from George Washington University

Law Degree from the Columbus School of Law at the Catholic University of America

Felicia C. Battista is a senior managing director in the FTI Forensic and Litigation Consulting practice and is based in Washington, D.C. Felicia has more than 25 years of accounting experience. She began her accounting career in public accounting and held accounting and legal positions in the private sector and with the U.S. Securities and Exchange Commission. Felicia provides expert consulting services to clients in matters of accounting, financial reporting, corporate governance and SEC disclosure requirements and procedures.

Prior to joining FTI, Felicia was Of Counsel at the law firm of Patton Boggs LLP, Washington, D.C., where she advised clients on corporate and securities matters, corporate governance matters, mergers and acquisitions, business transactions, financial services, banking regulatory matters and NASDAQ related matters. Before joining Patton Boggs, Felicia was a Partner at the law firm of Malizia Spidi & Fisch, PC in Washington, D.C.

Felicia spent 10 years at the SEC Division of Corporation Finance. During such time, she reviewed and analyzed documents for accounting and legal compliance for companies in various industries, including financial institutions, retail, mining, oil and gas, pharmaceutical and biotechnology. While at the SEC. Felicia served on the Divison's Financial Institution Task Force from 1991 to 1993 and its Shareholder Proposal Committee in 1993.

Felicia began her accounting career at a major national accounting firm (now Deloitte & Touche LLP). She also held accounting positions with a publicly traded utility company and a privately held real estate development company.

Felicia holds a Bachelor of Business Administration with a concentration in accounting from the George Washington University and a Juris Doctor degree from the Columbus School of Law at the Catholic University of America in Washington, D.C. She is a Certified Public Accountant and is also licensed to practice law in the District of Columbia, the Commonwealth of Pennsylvania and the Supreme Court of the United States.

I. What is an Income Statement?

II. Other Terms Used For Income Statement

III. The Income Statement

  A. Multi Step vs. Single Step

  B. What does "Restated Caption" Mean?

  C. Definitions
    - Revenues
    - Expenses
    - Gains / losses
    - Earnings Per Share

  D. Measurement
    - Revenue
    - Gross vs. Net
    - Expenses

IV. Other Comprehensive Income
  - Definition
  - Presentation

V. Ratio Analysis
  - What information does the Income Statement provide?

NOTES

6

STATEMENT OF CASH FLOWS

Christopher J. Rosetti, CPA, CFE
BST Valuation & Litigation Advisors LLC

I. INTRODUCTION

Earnings per share is a widely used measure of business performance, but operations, and the cash resulting there from must ultimately provide enough cash to pay the bills. Many companies have ceased operations because they could not satisfy their creditors even while reporting positive earnings. Prime Motor Inns is an example, they reported earnings of $77M during 1990 yet filed for bankruptcy the following year. What happened? Many of the firms profit was derived from sales of hotels rather than routine operations. Debt had increased and cash flow from operations was negative. In other words, the firm's line of business was depleting rather than generating cash.

The Statement of Cash Flows provides information relevant to the cash flow conditions of many firms in similar circumstances. The statement contains information useful for assessing future cash flow potential of companies, and it helps explain the difference between earnings, an accrual measure, and cash flow from operations, a cash-basis measure.

For example, Safeway's 1991 earnings of $54.9 million were surpassed by its $337.6 million operating cash flow. The largest item contributing to this difference was $296 million of depreciation and amortization, which are non-cash expenses.

The Statement of Cash Flows also supplies information not disclosed in the income statement, balance sheet or footnotes. For example, how much did Microsoft spend on capital expenditures? How mush did Coca Cola receive when it issued new stock? Answers to these questions can be found in the Statement of Cash Flows.

II. CASH FLOW REPORTING: DEVELOPMENT AND USEFULNESS

The Statement of Cash Flows is a report listing cash inflows and outflows by category. It explains the change in cash during the financial reporting periods. Firms have not always been required to report this information. Prior to 1971 some firms voluntarily disclosed the sources and uses of funds, albeit in a variety of formats.

SFAS #95 issued during 1987 superseded previous reporting requirements and required enterprises to provide a Statement of Cash Flows whenever a balance sheet and income statements are reported. Separate disclosure of operating, investing and financing cash flows is required. As a result, investors and creditors increasingly find cash flow information valuable for assessing an enterprises liquidity and risk.

Beginning in the mid 1970s, an increase in business failures and suits against auditors for not adequately warning of those impending failures contributed to an increased interest in cash flow information. A growing bankruptcy rate as well as general economic indicators, pointed to an overall increase in risk. For example, the average current ratio of US Manufacturing firms fell from 2.7% to 1.7 between 1947 and 1979, suggesting a general deterioration in financial condition.

The WT Grant bankruptcy demonstrates the value of cash flow information in assessing risk. WT Grant filed for bankruptcy during 1978. However, during 1973 Grants common stock was selling 20 times earnings per share, a high level by historical standards (then). Income and working capital provided by operations were positive from 1966 through 1974 and the company paid regular dividends. Yet during the decade before bankruptcy, the company generated almost no cash flow from operations.

A lack of uniformity in format and content also contributed to an increased interest in standardizing cash flow information. Specifically, a firm with strong working capital does not necessarily imply a strong cash flow. A firm with healthy working capital but also large inventories, prepaids and receivables might be in a weak cash position.

Another factor in the trend toward cash flow reporting was the increased complexity of financial accounting principles. Accounting pronouncements on leases, pensions, foreign exchange, tax allocation and investments have made financial statements more complicated. This complexity combined with management's flexibility to choose among several reporting choices allows companies to manipulate earnings; and the lack of a general relationship between earnings and cash flow leads to a preference by many financial statement users for cash flow information.

Accrual accounting matches efforts (costs) and results (revenue). The resulting earnings figure reflects changes in financial position, rather than immediate cash consequences; and users find this information valuable because in the long run profits determine the success of a company.

In the short run however, cash flow information is significant. It indicates whether a borrower will produce sufficient cash to pay its liabilities. Business creditors are interested in the historical record of cash flows and outflows, for the same reason a mortgage lender insists on knowing the borrowers credit history and cash income.

III. USEFULNESS OF CASH FLOW INFORMATION

Many analysts use cash flow information in making recommendations about buying and selling. For example, operating cash flow is a primary performance measure for companies. Investors often avoid companies without free cash flow because the cash flow deficiency must be made up with additional debt or equity financing. Healthy operating cash flows imply financial flexibility.

The cash flow information also provides feedback on past investment decisions, how capital expenditures were financed and the amount of debt issued. The statement of cash flows also helps explain changes in balance sheet accounts, such as increases in long term debt and whether cash was affected.

The purpose of the statement of cash flow is to provide relevant information about cash receipts and disbursements. Cash flow information helps user's assess:

1. A firm's ability to generate cash.
2. A firm's ability to meet future obligations.
3. The reasons for the difference between income and associated cash flows.
4. The effect of cash and noncash investing and financing activates on a firms' financial position.

By listing cash flows in meaningful categories and disclosing significant noncash investing and financing activities, the Statement of Cash Flows details the cash consequences of operations and changes in the balance sheet accounts arising from investing and financing activities.

The basis for understanding the Statement of Cash Flows is cash and cash equivalents – highly liquid, short-term securities readily convertible into cash[1]. Cash and cash equivalents are normally combined for balance sheet reporting. The Statement of Cash Flows summarizes the change in cash and cash equivalents during the reporting period, usually a year.

SFAS #95 requires reporting the change in cash and cash equivalents as an item that reconciles the beginning and ending balances of cash and cash equivalents.

---

1. Generally items with a maturity of three months or less.

IV. CASH FLOW CATEGORIES

All cash inflows and outflows are categorized into one of three categories:

1. Operating
2. Investing
3. Financing

The classification is important for evaluating past cash flows and predicting future flows. For example, the ability of a firm to generate positive cash flow from operations is critical for survival. A firm cannot indefinitely sell its assets or incur additional debt if it is not operating successfully. The classification enables the users to distinguish between repetitive ongoing activities and long-term strategic changes.

Operating cash flows are associated with producing and delivery goods and/or providing services. Operating cash flows generally include:

Inflows:

- Receipts from customers
- Interest received
- Dividends received
- Tax refunds
- Refunds from suppliers
- Receipts form lawsuits
- Insurance proceeds
- Proceeds from the sale of selling securities

Outflows:

- Payments to suppliers
- Payments to employees
- Interest payments
- Tax payments
- Prepayment of expenses
- Payments of leases
- Lawsuits

- Payments on debt
- Purchases of trading securities
- Payments of fines and penalties
- Charitable contributions

The association with income is the reason for classifying these flows as operating

Investing cash flows are associated with investing in and disposing of plant assets and certain debt and equity securities, making and collecting loans, and other strategic activities. This category is important for identifying a firm's growth plans. Capital expenditures and acquisitions of subsidiaries are important strategic decisions for a firm. This category includes:

Inflows:

- Proceeds from the sale of plant assets
- Proceeds from sales and maturities of debt and equity securities not classified as cash equivalents
- Collections of principal amounts of loan
- Sale of real estate

Outflows:

- Payments to purchase plant assets
- Purchases of debt or equity instrument not classified as cash equivalents
- Loans made to other parties
- Payments to purchase real estate

The difference between investing cash flows and outflows is net cash inflow (outflow) from investing activities. A fundamental difference between operating and investing cash flows is the anticipated benefit period. Operating pertains to the short-run while investing relates to the long-run.

Financing cash flows:

Financing cash flows are associated with obtaining resources from owners and providing a return on their investment, borrowing money and repaying principal. Frequently long-term debt or owners equity accounts are involved in the transactions that give rise to financing cash flows. Examples of financing cash flows include:

Inflows:

- Proceeds from stock issuance
- Proceeds from bond issuance
- Proceeds of loans from financial institutions

Outflows:

- Payments to purchase treasury stock
- Payments to retire bonds
- Dividends paid
- Principal payments on loans from financial institutions
- Payments on capital leases

The difference between the financing cash inflows and outflows is net cash inflow (outflow) from financing activities.

SFAS #95 also requires the reporting of significant noncash investing and financing activities in a supporting schedule or footnote. Common noncash transactions include bond retirements using stock, settlement of debt by transferring noncash assets and the incurrence of capitalized lease obligations.

The format of the SCF is as follows:

Cash flows from operating activities

Add/subtract cash flows from investing activities

Add/subtract cash flows from financing activities

Equals net increase (decrease) in cash

Add cash at the beginning of the year

Equals cash at the end of the year

NOTES

NOTES

7

UNDERSTANDING THE STATEMENT OF CASH FLOWS

Mark Ryan V. Pineda, CPA

Odenberg, Ullakko, Muranishi & Co. LLP

I. CASH FLOW STATEMENT

A cash flow statement is a financial report that tells the reader the source of a company's cash and how it was spent over a specified time period. This is an important indicator of financial soundness because it is possible for a company to show profits while not having enough cash to sustain operations. A cash flow statement counters the ambiguity regarding a company's solvency that various accrual accounting measures create. It also categorizes the sources and uses of cash to provide the reader with an understanding of the amount of cash a company generates and uses in its operations, as opposed to the amount of cash provided by sources outside the company, such as borrowed funds or funds from stockholders. The cash flow statement also tells the reader how much money was spent for items that do not appear on the income statement, such as loan repayments, long-term asset purchases, and payment of cash dividends.

II. DEVELOPMENT OF THE REPORTING STANDARD

In November 1987, the **Financial Accounting Standards Board (FASB)** adopted Statement of Financial Accounting Standards No. 95 – "Statement of Cash Flows". FASB 95 requires that a full set of financial statements includes a cash flow statement as the fourth required financial statement (along with a **balance sheet, income statement,** and **statement of stockholder's equity**). This statement established standards for cash flow reporting, and superseded the Accounting Principles Board (APB) Opinion No. 19, "Reporting Changes in Financial Position". APB Opinion No. 19, adopted in March 1971, had permitted, but did not require, enterprises to report cash flow information in a statement of changes in financial position, also commonly known as a funds statement. There was no required format or universally accepted definitions for categories in the statement, however, and the term "funds" itself was not sufficiently defined. Hence, the statement referred to changes in funds, but what constituted those funds differed across companies. Among the ambiguities, some firms defined funds as cash, some used cash and short-term investments, some used quick assets, and some used working capital. While it was widely recognized that the funds statement provided valuable and relevant information, the lack of consistency in format and focus from one firm to another was part of the reason that the FASB eventually took up the matter and, with extensive commentary from accountants and other interested parties, adopted the standards espoused in FASB 95. The standard, which took effect in 1988, discouraged use of the word "funds" in cash flow statements because the term had been cloaked in so much ambiguity.

III. REQUIREMENTS FOR CASH FLOW STATEMENTS

FASB 95 requires "that a statement of cash flows classify cash receipts and payments according to whether they stem from operating, investing, or financing activities". It also provides that the statement of cash flows may be prepared under either the direct or indirect method, and provides examples of how to prepare statements using each method.

Under the FASB standard, the core concept, cash, is defined as "cash and cash equivalents." Cash includes currency and bank deposits, whereas cash equivalents include other highly liquid investments like U.S. Treasury bills, money market accounts, and commercial paper. Other sorts of investments such as stocks, bonds, futures contracts, and so forth are not considered cash.

IV. CLASSIFICATIONS OF CASH RECEIPTS AND PAYMENTS

Nearly all business transactions completed during the fiscal year impact cash flow in one way or another, and in summary form they are factored into the year's cash flow statement. Exactly where on the statement depends on the nature of the transaction. As previously noted, the three essential categories of cash flow are operating activities, investing activities, and financing activities. The components of each of these are addressed as follows:

A. Operating Activities

Operating activities are the bread-and-butter transactions that keep the business running. Most notably, they include incoming revenue from the sale of goods or services and most kinds of outgoing payments. Cash flow from operating activities doesn't include principal paid on or received from loans, and only includes transactions that were completed during the period. This simply means that an operating transaction is not considered cash flow until the cash is actually received or paid, as opposed to just being recorded as accounts receivable or payable. In general, if an activity would appear on the company's income statement, it would be a candidate for the operating section of the cash flow statement. Net changes in balance sheet categories from period to period also represent cash flow; thus, a net decrease in accounts receivable from year to year normally suggests an increase in cash flow for that period.

Sometimes goods or services are paid for, prior to the period in which the benefit is matched or recognized to revenue. This results in a deferred or prepaid expense. Items such as insurance premiums that are paid in advance of the coverage period are classified as prepaid. Sometimes goods or services are received and used by the company before they are paid for, such as telephone service or merchandise inventory. These items are called accrued expenses, or payables, and are recognized on the income statement as an expense before the cash flow occurs. The cash flows statements present the true cash changes resulting from these transactions.

B. Investing Activities

Investment cash flow results from (1) the purchase or sale of property and equipment, (2) the purchase or sale of securities and related investments, and (3) loans made to other businesses. It includes only the principal or book value of the investment. Interest and depreciation are classified as operating cash flow, as are net gains or losses on investments. Because of these distinctions, cash flow from investment activities is typically more complex to calculate than that from other categories.

C. Financing Activities

Financing activities consist of transactions affecting a company's liabilities and shareholder equity. Mainly involving how the company obtains capital and enhances the value of its stock, they include such things as issuing bonds, payments on debt, paying dividends, and issuing and buying back stock.

V. METHODS OF PREPARING A CASH FLOW STATEMENT

FASB Statement No. 95 allows the preparer a choice of the direct or the indirect method of cash flow statement presentation, although the FASB prefers the direct method. The difference lies in the presentation of the operating cash flow information.

A. Direct Method

Companies that use the direct method are required, at a minimum, to report separately the following classes of operating cash receipts and payments:

Receipts:

1. Cash collected from customers
2. Interest and dividends received
3. Other operating cash receipts, if any

Payments:

1. Cash paid to employees and suppliers of goods or services (including suppliers of insurance, advertising, etc.)
2. Interest paid
3. Income taxes paid
4. Other operating cash payments, if any

Companies are encouraged to further break down any operating cash receipts and payments that they consider meaningful.

B. Indirect Method

The indirect method, by contrast, reports operating cash flow based on changes in the balance sheet (the distribution of assets and liabilities) from period to period as they relate to net income. Thus, instead of reporting the total cash received from customers, an indirect statement only lists the change in cash received from the previous period. The net cash flow reported should be the same as in the direct method, but in the indirect method the level of detail tends to be less.

The key elements of the operating activities section using the indirect method are as follows:

1. Net income
2. Depreciation and amortization
3. Deferred income taxes
4. Interest income
5. Change in accounts receivable
6. Change in accounts payable
7. Change in inventories
8. Net gains from sale of investments or assets

A few additional categories are used in some circumstances. Each category is either added or subtracted from net income depending on whether it corresponds to an inflow or outflow of cash. When all of these factors are combined, they equal the net operating cash flow for the period.

As an alternative, some cash flow statements using the indirect method report operating cash flow as a single line item and present the reconciliation details elsewhere in a supplementary schedule. According to FASB standards, the direct method also requires a supplementary schedule that essentially incorporates the indirect measures into the statement. Due to this added burden, the majority of companies tend to use the indirect method only, despite the FASB's stated preference for the direct. Exhibit I shows a sample statement of cash flows from the using the indirect method.

Regardless of whether the direct or the indirect method is used, the operating section of the cash flow statement ends with net cash provided (used) by operating activities. This is the most important line item on the cash flow statement. A company has to generate enough cash from operations to sustain its business activity. If a company continually needs to borrow or obtain additional investor capitalization to survive, the company's long-term existence is in jeopardy.

The presentation of the investing and financing sections of the statement is the same in each method.

VI. BALANCE SHEET ACCOUNTS AND CASH FLOW

Every balance sheet account reflects specific activity. There are only a few distinctive transactions that affect each account. Following are examples of some of the common changes in balance sheet accounts that register as cash flow.

Accounts receivable increases when the company sells merchandise or does a service on credit, and decreases when the customer pays its bill. Accounts receivable is associated with sales or revenue on an income statement. The change in accounts receivable or the cash collected from customers is classified as an operating activity.

Inventory increases when the company buys merchandise for resale or use in its manufacturing process, and decreases when the merchandise is sold. Inventory is associated with the income statement account cost of goods sold (COGS). The change in inventory or the cash paid for inventory purchases is classified as an operating activity.

Prepaid insurance increases when the company pays insurance premiums covering future periods and decreases when the time period of coverage expires. The change in prepaid or the amount paid for insurance is classified as an operating activity.

Land, building, and equipment accounts increase when the company purchases additional assets and decrease when the assets are sold. The only time the income statement is affected is when the asset is sold at a price higher or lower than book value, at which time a gain or loss on sale of assets appears on the income statement. The amount of cash used or received from the purchase or sale of such assets is classified as an investing activity. The gain or loss is reported as operating cash flow.

Accumulated depreciation increases as the building and equipment depreciates and decreases when building and equipment is sold. Depreciation expense does not appear on a cash flow statement presented using the direct method. Depreciation expense is added back to net income on a cash flow statement presented using the indirect method, since the depreciation caused net income to decrease during the period but did not affect cash.

Goodwill increases when the parent company acquires a subsidiary for more than the fair market value of its net assets. Goodwill amortizes over a time period not to exceed 40 years. Goodwill is associated with amortization expense on the income statement. Amortization expense appears in the operating section of a cash flow statement prepared using the indirect method. Amortization expense does not appear on a cash flow statement prepared using the direct method.

Notes payable increases when the company borrows money, and decreases when the company repays the funds borrowed. Since only the principal appears on the balance sheet, there is no impact on the income statement for repaying the principal component of the note. Notes payable appears in the financing section of a cash flow section.

Premiums and discounts on bonds are amortized through bond interest expense. There is no cash flow associated with the amortization of bond discounts or premiums. Therefore, there will always be an adjustment in the operating section of the cash flow statement prepared using the indirect method for premium or discount amortization. Premium or discount amortization will not appear on a cash flow statement prepared using the direct method.

Common stock and preferred stock increase when additional stock is sold to investors, and decrease when stock is retired. There is no income statement impact for stock transactions. The cash flow associated with stock sales and repurchases appears in the financing section.

Retained earnings increase when the company earns profit and decreases when the company suffers a loss or declares dividends. The profit or loss appears as the first line of the operating section of the cash flow statement. The dividends appear in the financing section when they are paid.

VII. SIGNIFICANT NONCASH TRANSACTIONS

Non-cash transactions are not incorporated in the statement of cash flows, but often they need to be disclosed elsewhere in financial statements. Examples of these types of transactions include:

- converting bonds to stock
- acquiring assets by assuming liabilities

If there are only a few such transactions, it may be convenient to include them on the same page as the statement of cash flows, in a separate schedule at the bottom of the statement. Otherwise, the transactions may be reported elsewhere in the financial statements, clearly referenced to the statement of cash flows.

Other events that are generally not reported in conjunction with the statement of cash include stock dividends, stock splits, and appropriation of retained earnings. These items are generally reported on a statement of retained earnings or schedules and notes pertaining to changes in capital accounts.

VIII. SEC COMMENTS ON CASH FLOWS OF REGISTRANTS

IX. CASES

Sample Company - EXHIBIT 1
Statement of Cash Flows (Indirect Method)

CASH FLOWS FROM OPERATIONS:	
Net income	$ 2,300,000
Items not requiring current use of cash:	
Depreciation and amortization	300,000
Compensation expense on stock options	150,000
Impairment of long-lived assets	700,000
Changes in assets and liabilities:	
Increase in accounts receivable, net	(150,000)
Decrease in inventory	284,000
Increase in prepaid expenses	1,800,000
Decrease in accounts payable and accrued liabilities	(800,000)
CASH PROVIDED BY OPERATING ACTIVITIES	4,584,000
CASH FLOWS FROM INVESTING ACTIVITIES	
Acquisitions of property and equipment	(75,000)
Sale of property and equipment	1,600,000
Purchases of investments in securities	(500,000)
Sale of investments in securities	2,975,000
Acquisition of business	(9,800,000)
Investment in and advances to joint ventures	(3,500,000)
CASH USED FOR INVESTMENTS	(300,000)

CASH FLOWS FROM FINANCING ACTIVITIES:	
Issuance of common stock, net of expenses	300,000
Repurchase of preferred stock	(500,000)
Repayment of long-term debt	(325,000)
Line of credit borrowings, net	2,000,000
Payment of dividends to stockholders	(325,000)
CASH PROVIDED BY FINANCING ACTIVITIES	1,150,000
INCREASE IN CASH AND CASH EQUIVALENTS	5,434,000
CASH AND CASH EQUIVALENTS, BEGINNING OF YEAR	4,450,000
CASH AND CASH EQUIVALENTS, END OF YEAR	$ 9,884,000
Supplemental cash flows disclosure:	
Interest paid during the year	$ 375,000
Income taxes paid during the year	$ 150,000
Supplemental non-cash activities:	
Debt converted to common stock	$ 180,000
Acquisition of business with debt and common stock	$ 130,000
Acquisition of equipment with capital lease obligation	$ 150,000
Sale of assets for note receivable	$ 158,000

NOTES

NOTES

8

NOTES TO THE FINANCIAL STATEMENTS

Shirley Hudler, CPA, CFE

UHY Advisors FLVS, Inc.

Reprinted from the PLI Course Handbook, *Basics of Accounting & Finance: What Every Practicing Lawyer Needs to Know — Summer 2006* (Order #8650).

Biographical Information

Name: **Shirley Hudler**

Position/Title: Senior Manager
Forensic, Litigation and Valuation Services

Firm or Place of Business: UHY Mann Frankfort Stein & Lipp Advisors, Inc.

Primary Areas of Practice: Securities Class Action related to Accounting Improprieties

Work History: Corporate Finance, Energy

Professional Memberships:
Association of Certified Fraud Examiners
Association for Corporate Growth, Houston Chapter

WHY READ THE FOOTNOTES?

- An integral part of the financial statements
- Meant to provide a detailed description of a company's practices and policies related to its accounting methods
- The fine print that explains the financial information presented in the financial statements
- Required by GAAP but no prescribed format

GOALS OF THE FOOTNOTES

- Transparency
- Clarity
- Comparability
- Simplicity

6

RESOURCES

- FASB
- AICPA
- SEC

HOW ARE THE FOOTNOTES ORGANIZED?

Summary of Significant Accounting Policies

- ❍ Restatements
- ❍ Basis of Consolidation
- ❍ Revenue Recognition
- ❍ Depreciation and Amortization
- ❍ Goodwill
- ❍ Inventories
- ❍ Allowance for Losses on Receivables
- ❍ Use of Estimates
- ❍ EPS
- ❍ Accounting Changes

Detailed Disclosures

- ❍ Acquisitions and Divestitures
- ❍ Debt and Capitalization
- ❍ Pension Benefits
- ❍ Stock Options
- ❍ Related Party
- ❍ Minority Interests in Equity of Consolidated Affiliates
- ❍ Deferred Taxes
- ❍ Guarantees and Commitments
- ❍ Losses and Contingencies
- ❍ Derivatives
- ❍ Securitizations
- ❍ Subsequent Events

AREAS OF CONCERN

REPORT PURSUANT TO SECTION 704 OF SARBANES-OXLEY

- Improper Revenue Recognition
- Improper Expense Recognition
- Improper Accounting for Business Combinations
- Inadequate Management's Discussion and Analysis
- Failure to Disclose Related-Party Transactions
- Improper Use of Off-Balance Sheet Arrangements
- Improper Use of non-GAAP Financial Measures

DISCUSSION OF RED FLAGS

SOME REAL LIFE EXAMPLES

NOTES

NOTES

9

ACCOUNTANTS AS FACT AND EXPERT WITNESSES

John P. Woods

Inspector General

New York City Department of Investigation

Table of Contents

Accountants can be critical witnesses in civil litigation as defendants or plaintiffs, employees or agents of parties, or fact or expert witnesses. Such testimony will usually be as to matters and concepts, which are unfamiliar to virtually all jurors and to most lawyers and judges. Thus, a substantial amount of time will have to be spent by the attorney in understanding the relevant accounting principles, becoming familiar with the relevant documents, identifying the pertinent points to be made and then figuring out how to convey those points to the jury and the court. None of this is easy. This article will provide some suggestions as to how to proceed in the discovery and investigation phase of the case and then later in trial preparation and at trial.

DEPOSITION PREPARATION AND PRACTICE

There are four main circumstances under which attorneys conduct depositions of accountants. The attorney can depose or defend the deposition of a fact witness who is an accountant, e.g., a company's CFO or internal or external auditor or, alternatively, take or defend the deposition of an accountant who is an expert in a case. There is considerable overlap in the preparation for any of these four types of depositions[1] but the attorney's goals and the techniques used for those goals will vary.

I. GENERAL CONSIDERATIONS ABOUT DEPOSITIONS

Depositions are one of the most time intensive litigation events and usually play a critical role in the resolution of the case whether by trial, settlement or dismissal after motion practice. Two dynamics are going on simultaneously. The questioner is seeking to obtain information which the party being deposed is either willing or reluctant to disclose. Second, the attorney and the witness are each seeking to establish a certain degree of psychological dominance over each other for purposes of negotiation or a potential trial. The first consideration relates mostly to the substance of the questions asked while the second relates to the manner in which the questions are asked and answered.

Depositions are generally used: (a) to obtain information to make a motion; (b) to freeze the witness' story; (c) to assess the witness' demeanor and credibility; and (d) for trial impeachment. Generally, you don't want to depose witnesses before you have in hand all the relevant documents. Otherwise, a key document may come to light later and you will have already conducted your deposition. In some large and complex cases, you may wish to schedule preliminary depositions of key witnesses so that you can ascertain what kind of records the company keeps, how the records are generated, where these records are kept, and who the custodian of the records is and to identify key witnesses. If you conduct such depositions, you should make their limited purpose clear on the record and leave the deposition open.

Unlike trial testimony which needs to be in a logical order so that the finder of fact can understand what happened, a deposition can jump around and need not take things in their logical order. Doing this may cause the witness to stumble.

Before you take a deposition, consider what you want to accomplish. You may want to get specific factual admissions to set up a summary judgment motion. You may want to encourage the witness to make statements you can prove are false so you can impeach the witness at trial. You may want to get your opponent's witness, whether factual or expert, to adopt as much of your factual theory as possible. You always want to get

---

1. As discussed *infra* in greater detail, the information gathered in the discovery and investigation phase provides the basis for direct and cross examination.

the witness' story and evaluate the witness's disposition and credibility for trial. Be prepared to be surprised and to follow the testimony where it leads.

Finally, the taking and defending of a deposition is one of the first heavily labor intensive activities which your adversary will have to perform after filing the complaint. If you represent the defendant and, after investigating the case, the case appears appropriate for settlement, serious consideration should be given to trying to settle before depositions are taken. If the case is in federal court, a Rule 68 offer may be appropriate, particularly if the case is brought under a statute with a fee shifting provision. An early settlement will save your client legal and court reporter fees and will likely be cheaper since the lawyer will not have as much of his own time to factor into the plaintiff's demand.

II. GENERAL TECHNIQUES APPLICABLE TO ALL DEPOSITIONS

A. Taking a Deposition

1. Make sure that you, your adversary, and the court reporter all have the same "standard stips."
2. Try to use the same reporter throughout a series of depositions, so that the reporter becomes familiar with the names and terms relevant to the case.
3. Make friends with the reporter who may be able to give you a read on the credibility of the witnesses.
4. If it's your deposition, you control the court reporter. Don't allow your adversary to go on or off the record without your consent. If there are substantive discussions about privileges, keep them on the record or, at the least, summarize them when the parties go back on the record.
5. Bring at least four copies of each exhibit (one marked-up copy from which to ask questions, one copy for your adversary, one copy to be marked as an exhibit and shown to the witness, and one extra).
6. For convenience, if you are conducting a series of depositions in a case with numerous documents, mark the exhibits in the first deposition, and continue to use them with the same letter or number marking in subsequent depositions.

7. Once a document is marked, always refer to it thereafter by the exhibit number. Otherwise, the record you are making may get confused.

8. Ascertain who prepared a document and how and when it was prepared.

9. Ascertain who received a document and how and when it was received and whether any action was taken. Who relied upon the document?

10. Ascertain whether the document is accurate and, if it is inaccurate whether the inaccuracy was ever corrected. Who relied upon the inaccurate information? For what purpose and to what effect? If the inaccuracy was not corrected, then you can attack the witness for leaving others with information known to be incorrect.

11. In many jurisdictions, parties, witnesses, and potential witnesses can attend a deposition. Make sure their appearance is noted on the record and that they do not improperly influence the proceedings.

12. Unless you know that your adversary will be calling the witness at trial, do not depose (and thereby preserve the testimony of) non-party witnesses whom you know will not be helpful to your case. Similarly, if you have a witness who is friendly and will be available for trial, then there is usually no reason to depose that witness.

13. If you have reason to believe that a witness's demeanor when asked questions will be poor, you may want to consider preserving it by videotaping it.

14. Have a list of topic areas as to which you intend to ask questions. You should have your documents keyed to your questions so that the deposition goes faster.

15. If necessary write out your questions but, other than technical questions, DO NOT READ your questions.

16. LISTEN TO and OBSERVE the witness as he or she answers questions. Pick up on body language and discomfort about answering certain questions. Don't have your head down reading your notes. At least once, look the witness in the eye.

17. Be prepared to depart from the planned order of your questions, but make sure that you cover all of the ground you planned.

18. Ask the good, the bad, and the ugly about the case. Testimony unfavorable to your client will not go away because you ignore the topic. You just won't know what it is and won't have locked the story down.

19. Find out what the witness does not know. If the complaint makes broad accusations, ascertain whether the witness knows the factual basis for those accusations. If the witness does not know, ask who would know.

20. If you represent multiple defendants, ascertain the basis for the claims against each individual defendant.

21. Always ascertain what the witness has done to prepare for the deposition, i.e., who has he or she spoken to, and what documents has he or she reviewed.

22. Unlike at trial, don't be afraid to ask questions you don't know the answer to. That's the whole purpose of a deposition.

23. If a document's admissibility at trial may be uncertain, use the deposition to lay a foundation from the testifying witness. You can then be sure of being able to use the document in a summary judgment motion or at trial.

24. Surround loaded questions with innocuous ones, so plaintiff thinks you are just on a fishing expedition.

25. If a blank space is left in the transcript for the witness to later fill in information not known at the deposition, don't forget about it. Pester your adversary if the information sought is at all material.

26. If opposing counsel objects incessantly, ask counsel to state the basis for the objection.

27. Neither make nor allow your adversary to make speaking objections, which provide the witness with the answer to the question. (E.g., "The witness already testified the light was green when he went through the intersection.") If your adversary does this, state on the record that he or she has made a speaking objection and, if it continues, call the Court.

28. If a witness claims not to remember something, ask whether there is anything anywhere on the earth which would refresh his recollection. Ask whether there are any documents anywhere which would contain the information. (This is to avoid sudden miracu-

lous revivals of memory at trial). Ask if the witness knows who else might have the information. If it is something the witness ought to remember, ask if this is the kind of thing that the witness might forget.

29. If the witness does not know something, ascertain who would know it.

30. Conversely, if the witness's memory is too good (i.e., the weather on a particular day ten years earlier), see if the witness remembers other unlikely things.

31. If a witness is giving you evasive answers, keep asking the question until you get an answer. Rephrase the question and ask it in a different way. Consider the form of the answer you need to get to use either for a motion or for cross at trial

32. If the witness keeps answering with irrelevant and non-responsive material, put that on the record, instruct the witness not to do that and, if necessary, convert the question into a yes/no answer and then follow up.

33. Don't let a witness give you vague time-lines as to key events. Refresh his or her recollection with documents. Get the witness to give his or best estimate as to when something occurred. Ask what season an event occurred in. Did it occur before or after some other event? If so, how much long after?

34. Ask the same critical question in different ways at different times to see if the witness gives different answers. Don't abuse this.

35. Don't ask the witness if he or she "recalls" something, unless you really are interested in their recollection rather than the facts.

36. You can put psychological pressure on a witness by pausing after they gave their answer to see if they add something else.

37. If you are questioning as to a technical area, make sure you use technical terms correctly. Otherwise, the answers you get may not be what you think they are.

38. If the witness uses a technical term, get the witness to define the term. "Just so we're all talking about the same thing, what do you mean by ____________?"

39. If you get a key answer that you were looking for, quit while ahead without signaling the answer's significance. If you have to go back to the same area, casually incorporate the answer into your other questions.

40. Don't assume that the witness only knows about the area in which the witness is employed, or as to which the witness is known to have knowledge. The witness may have seen other things which are pertinent or had conversations with other parties or key witnesses. Ask.

41. Nail down the basis on which a witness knows something. Personal knowledge? A document (if so, what document)? Hearsay?

42. If a witness does not know something, ask if the witness knows who might know the answer to the question.

43. Find out what was the normal way something was done and then ask if there was a departure from the normal procedure and, if so, in what way and why.

44. If a witness discloses the existence of documents of whose existence you were unaware, call for their production and don't forget to follow up with a letter asking for the document or with a formal document demand. If the document may be significant, leave the deposition open for renewed questioning after the document is produced.

45. Do not allow conferences to be initiated by counsel while a question is pending, unless there is a possible privilege objection.

46. If your adversary regularly initiates conferences after the witness answers a loaded question, put the fact of the conference and perhaps its duration on the record, and then ask the witness whether he or she wants to change his or her answer after consultation with counsel.

47. If possible, save the loaded and difficult questions for the afternoon when the witness and his or her counsel are tired.

48. If a witness has a tendency to exaggerate, encourage the witness to do so.

49. One of the perennial questions is whether to confront an adverse witness with key documents or evidence at the deposition or whether to save the impeachment for trial. That question must be

answered case by case. By disclosing the impeachment material, you lose the effect of surprise at trial. On the other hand, the opposing party may still find out that you have the material before trial. The pre-trial order may even require identification and exchange of impeachment exhibits. By confronting the witness with the impeachment material earlier, you may trap the witness into answering before he or she can concoct an explanation. You may also find that there is an innocent explanation for something you think is suspicious. A variation that can provide you with the best of both worlds is to hit the witness hard with some of the impeachment while hinting that you have other impeachment you are saving for trial. This will make the witness nervous and may even lead to some pre-emptive honesty by an otherwise dishonest witness. Another consideration is that most commercial cases do not go to trial. They are typically disposed of by motion or settlement. Thus, a jury may never actually see the devastating piece of impeachment. That evidence may, on the other hand, considerably improve your bargaining position in a settlement negotiation. If you are going to end up disclosing the fact or document anyhow, then you are probably better off asking questions about it at the deposition.

50. Sometimes, if the deposition appears to be proceeding in an amiable fashion, a witness can be lulled into saying things he or she would not otherwise say. Alternatively, you may want to conduct more of a hostile deposition if it will intimidate the witness for a future trial or make the opposing party more reasonable on settlement.

51. If the deposition is getting out of control, or the witness is refusing to answer pertinent questions, call the Magistrate or the Judge and get a ruling. Ascertain in advance the judge's practices or preferences for resolving discovery disputes and bring the number of Chambers to the deposition with you. If the deposition is becoming unmanageable, call immediately. Otherwise, save your questions up for the end of the day. Have the court reporter mark the transcript areas where a ruling is sought, so that the read back can be done efficiently. Don't call over trivia. Put the conference with the Magistrate/Judge on the record.

B. Defending a Deposition

1. As discussed *infra*, never let a witness be deposed without thoroughly preparing the witness.
2. Let your witness know what the themes of your case are, so that the witness can weave them into testimony.
3. Have your witness review relevant non-privileged documents no longer than a week before the deposition. Again, unless your adversary is incompetent, producing a witness whose memory is impaired and deliberately not refreshed will just result in the deposition being adjourned.
4. Tell your witness not to discuss the substance of the witness's testimony with others, especially other defendants.
5. If the form but not the substance of your adversary's questions is improper, object, but let the witness answer the question. You can move at trial to exclude the question.
6. Generally, don't be an obstructionist.
7. Don't have hallway or bathroom conferences which include others whose presence waives attorney client privilege.
8. Object if your adversary poses a question which is contrary to fact and, if your adversary has a history of doing this, warn your client in advance.
9. If you have a choice of who to provide as a witness, pick the most articulate witness who will follow your instructions.
10. Do not deliberately produce a witness who has no knowledge. That will likely only delay things. You can sometimes get a little bit of an idea what your adversary is after by asking him or her what she is looking for in the deposition, so that you can provide the most knowledgeable witness.
11. Objections to form (i.e., leading, assumes facts not in evidence, misstates prior testimony, seeks a legal conclusion, or inadequate foundation) must be made at the deposition.
12. Other types of objections (attorney client privilege, attorney work product, confidential business secret, trade secret, and relevance) are preserved but should be made at the deposition together with, if necessary, an instruction not to answer.

13. When instructing your witness not to answer, be prepared to explain your reasoning to a magistrate or judge.

14. One technique to avoid a direction not to answer is to suggest alternative questions to your adversary. You may be able to subtly steer your adversary away from a sensitive area.

15. Try to avoid having your witness testify as to his or her recollection of what a document says without having the document before him or her.

16. Make sure your witness is not cut off and gets to complete his or her statement.

17. Monitor your witness' physical and mental condition and get a break if necessary. If necessary, adjourn the deposition. (That tactic should be used sparingly because it gives your adversary another shot at your witness and time to think of additional questions.)

18. Keep a list as you go along of areas you want to clear up at the end of your adversary's questioning.

19. Another issue to be decided on a case-by-case basis is what to do when the opposing counsel has elicited answers, which are factually correct but misleading or confusing. This can happen when questioning counsel uses technical terms inaccurately and elicits answers which mean something other than what counsel thinks. Letting the answers stand may leave your adversary with an incorrect understanding of the facts which may work to your advantage. Conversely, it may cause additional work and confusion in motion practice or at trial. The key question is whether the correct testimony can hurt you. If it can't hurt you, then probably the better practice is to clear up the mistake.

20. If your witness makes a mistake and you know it is a mistake, clean it up at the first opportunity.

21. If your witness lies, correct it at the first possible opportunity. Under DR 7-102, (22 NYCRR 1200.33(a)(4)), an attorney cannot "knowingly use perjured testimony or false evidence."

22. Train your witness not to look at you for the answers.

23. If you have any reason to suspect that the witness being deposed will not be available at trial (e.g., ill health, plans to move out of the jurisdiction, imminent mental breakdown), then you should be sure to elicit all testimony which you will need even if your adversary does not do so.

III. PREPARATION FOR THE DEFENSE OF A DEPOSITION OF AN ACCOUNTANT WHO IS A FACT WITNESS

Several things need to be done before any accounting deposition. These include: educating the lawyer as to the accounting issues, interviewing the witness, investigating your client and witness, preparing the witness for the deposition

A. Education of the Lawyer

Unless the attorney has a significant background with accounting issues, the attorney will need to spend considerable time becoming educated as to accounting principles and as to how those principles were applied by his client. The attorney needs to learn how financial record keeping and reporting works (GAAP is nowhere near as rigid as lawyers tend to think. There are often many different ways to do the same thing legitimately). The attorney must also become familiar with the proper technical use of accounting terms. If you use a technical term incorrectly, the witness can be giving you an entirely different answer than you think you are getting.

This self-education can be done by (1) attending courses for lawyers which explain accounting principles; (2) reviewing texts which explain accounting principles; or (3) getting an accountant to teach the outlines of the subject as applicable to your case. As the lawyer begins to understand the relevant accounting issues, the lawyer should give thought to how the same understanding can be imparted to judges and jurors.

B. Determining Whether an Expert Is Necessary and Obtaining and Consulting with an Appropriate Expert

If accounting issues are going to be significant in a case, then a decision should be made early on as to whether an independent expert should be retained and whether that expert should be retained as a "consulting" or a "testifying" expert. That distinction can become critical because communications with a consulting expert will generally be protected as work product, while, at least in federal court, communications with a testifying expert will be subject to disclosure.

If the case needs an expert and warrants the expense, the expert should be retained at the earliest possible moment rather than at the close of discovery. An expert can be useful or necessary where the in-house accountant or the regular auditor is likely to be subject to attack or where it is useful to get an independent opinion.

The expert can:

1. provide an independent view of the evidence;
2. identify the accounting issues on both sides of the case;
3. advise the attorney as to the appropriate documents to seek in discovery;
4. evaluate the documents obtained, suggest appropriate witnesses to depose, and additional documents to request in discovery or to subpoena from third parties;
5. help prepare for and possibly attend depositions of the adverse party's witnesses, including making sure that your questions are technically correct;
6. interpret answers at the depositions of the adverse party's witnesses and suggest appropriate follow-up questions;
7. provide expert reports and testimony;
8. perform analyses not previously done and
9. help prepare questioning at trial.

C. Investigation of Your Client's Witnesses and Evidence

Before your fact witness is deposed, the attorney needs to conduct an intensive investigation of his own side of the case.[2] This is a critical part of, not just the discovery process, but evaluation of your case and trial preparation. In this process, you may identify witnesses who do not end up being deposed but who will be called at trial. Keep track of

2. It is also important to investigate opposing counsel. Basic information can be often obtained through Martindale-Hubbell and/or the firm's web site. You can get some idea about opposing counsel's level of skill and expertise by running his or her name through WESTLAW and/or LEXIS and looking for reported cases. Findlaw also allows for a search of legal professionals but the results are not necessarily complete or reliable. However, the best sense you will likely get of opposing counsel's style and tactics will be through other lawyers who have dealt with him or her on comparable cases. Such information will be critical in advising your witness as to what to expect.

such witnesses.[3] If any of them appear likely not to be available for trial, they you may want to do a deposition to preserve the witness's testimony.

1. All relevant documents should be identified, obtained, and reviewed.

2. Prior to the deposition, review the documents with the in-house accountant (and your expert if you have one) and have them explain the documents until you understand them completely.

3. If the facts are complicated, prepare a chronology which reflects all known information and states the source of each entry. Update this as you acquire new information. This will sometimes connect seemingly unrelated events. Be over inclusive in listing facts rather than under inclusive. You may recognize later that certain facts are important which originally did not seem to matter.

4. Conduct thorough interviews of your own witnesses, not just for their technical competency but also to learn their personal backgrounds.

5. Find out who actually did the work. What was the role of the witness in the accounting process? Did the witness prepare key documents or did someone else? Did the witness have involvement with respect to the critical area in the lawsuit?

6. Interview others in the reporting chain, preferably without their supervisors being present.

7. If a potential witness cannot prove a positive fact, consider whether the witness can prove a negative (e.g., there was no departure from normal procedures, an individual acted normally, etc.).

8. Who initially created the set up for the books and records?

9. If there are adjusting journal entries which seem out of the ordinary, either individually or in volume, ask about them and keep asking until you understand.

---

3. You should maintain a contact list for all key individuals in a case. Obtain home and office telephone numbers, private cell phone numbers, and home and office e-mail addresses. Tell the witness you will not contact him away from the office unless it is an emergency. Ask the witness to let you know if he is moving, retiring, or changing jobs.

10. Who decided what reporting principles to adopt? When? Why?
11. Were those reporting principles changed? When? Why? What notice of the change was provided? What effect did the change have on the financial statements?
12. Did the company ever depart from its normal reporting principles? If so, why? Is that indicated anywhere? If not, why not?
13. Did the company consult with its external auditors before making crucial decisions? If not, why not?
14. Did the company consult with its in house or external counsel before making crucial decisions? If not, why not?
15. Who exactly made the critical decisions? Impress on your witness that avoiding responsibility which clearly belongs to the witness is usually a poor tactic. It is better to acknowledge making the decision and explain why the decision was made. If necessary, admit that it was a good faith mistake.
16. Find out the good and the bad about your client and your witnesses.
17. Run the same sort of background check on your own people as you would on opposing witnesses and experts.
18. Ask the witness if there is anything which would be damaging either to the case or to them personally if the opposing party found it out.
19. Ask if there is anything you didn't ask about which the witness thinks might have some importance.
20. If it turns out your own witnesses are not being frank with you, then you have to reevaluate your case. This is an area where your retained expert can be helpful.

D. Preparing Your Fact Witness to Be Deposed

No witness should ever be deposed without being thoroughly prepped in advance. The witness should be made comfortable with the deposition process. The deposition preparation should include being shown relevant non-privileged documents and refreshing the witness's recollection without unethically planting testimony. The witness should be asked as many times as necessary the specific questions which you anticipate the witness will be asked, so as to make sure that the testimony comes out crisply and accurately. You should also give your witness an idea of opposing counsel's style and usual tactics.

Generic advice to any witness would include:

1. TELL THE TRUTH.
2. Impress on the witness the importance of the proceeding. Large sums of money could change hands and the witness could go to jail for deliberately lying.
3. Listen to the question you are asked.
4. Answer the question you are asked, not some other question.
5. If a question calls for a yes/no answer, but cannot be answered that way, say so.
6. Do not guess. If you do not know the answer to something or you do not remember the answer, say so.
7. If you have to hedge an answer by saying "to the best of my recollection," then do so, but do not abuse this.
8. If you do not understand a question asked by anyone, say so, and ask for it to be rephrased.
9. If you are changing or correcting prior testimony, be up front about it and indicate the reason for the change.
10. Don't think out loud.
11. Do not speculate or offer theories.
12. Do not lose your cool even if the other lawyer baits you.
13. Tell your lawyer everything you know about the case, including things which are unflattering or which you think may not be relevant.
14. If you don't remember something, say so. There is no shame in not initially remembering something. If something will refresh your memory, ask for it.
15. Listen for objections. If your lawyer objects, don't answer until you hear whether the lawyer is directing you not to answer. If the lawyer says, "objection but you can answer," then answer the question.
16. Listen to the colloquy.
17. Review all prior testimony and reports before testifying. If your present recollection is different, tell your lawyer before testimony.

18. Ask for a question to be read back by the court reporter if you get distracted or confused by colloquy.

19. Take advantage of breaks to use the bathroom but be careful of using it as a conference room.

20. Do not have off the record conversations about the case with opposing counsel or parties.

21. Do not talk about the case in earshot of opposing counsel or parties.

22. Advise your lawyer of anything positive or negative in your personal background.

23. Do not relax by having a few beers at lunch. Do not have a heavy lunch; it may put you to sleep for testimony in the afternoon.

24. If asked whether you have discussed the case with anyone, the answer, of course, is that you have discussed the case with your lawyer and probably others.

25. If asked what your lawyer told you to say, reply that he or she told you to tell the truth (assuming that he or she did).

26. Always be respectful to everyone. Refer to others as "Mr." or "Ms." or by their title. Don't get overtly hostile to opposing counsel — even if you are provoked.

27. The opposing counsel is not your friend.

28. Do not be a wise guy or a comedian. The witticism will likely read differently on a cold record.

29. Turn off your cell phone/pager/blackberry.

30. Take as long as you need to think about an answer or to examine a document. Don't get rushed because there is a pause in the proceedings. If you need to read all of a lengthy document, read it all no matter how long it takes.

31. Anticipate questions on cross-examination as to the normal procedures used. If you departed from those procedures, be prepared to explain why.

32. Don't use slang or jargon.

33. Try to avoid stilted language.

IV. PREPARATION TO TAKE THE DEPOSITION OF AN ACCOUNTANT FACT WITNESS

Proper preparation to take the deposition of a fact witness who is an accountant has a number of components. These include: (1) obtaining all the relevant documents; (2) investigating the company which is a party to the action; (3) investigating the witness and the accounting firm which employs him or her; and (4) formulating what you want out of the deposition and figuring out how you will get it.

A. Obtaining the Proper Documents

Before conducting any deposition, it is imperative to have in hand all the relevant documents. Getting the documents you need involves crafting the document demand and evaluating the documents when you get them.

1. What to Ask for and Why You Want It

This is an incomplete list of the types of documents that an examining attorney will generally want. When these documents are obtained, they should be reviewed with an expert and additional documents may also be requested.

1. **Year-end financial statements** and **supporting schedules**.
2. **Internal and external audits** of the company.
3. **Audit work papers** - They will show how the accountant reached his or her conclusions. You will need to have them reviewed by your own accountant.
4. **Tax returns** for the relevant time period and several preceding and succeeding years. Tax returns of not for profit organizations are public records. Tax returns can be compared with financial statements and supporting schedules for discrepancies.
5. **General ledger** - The central control book for the organization. It breaks down all costs and income for a year by account.
6. **Subsidiary ledgers** - They will tell you the costs and income by customer or by account and all the details of the expenditures or income.
7. **Accounts payable** – Amounts due to each vendor or supplier. Payment is expected within the current year

8. **Accounts receivable** – Amounts due to the company from the sale of its goods and services. Collection is expected within the current year.

9. **Aging schedule** – This groups accounts receivable by how old they are. It tells whether there are old accounts which likely will not be collected upon.

10. **Cash disbursements journal** - Similar to a check resister. It will list all checks and expenditures in sequential order and the amounts and the date of the expenditure.

11. **Bank statements** – Will list all income and expenditure and full population of everything passing through the account. It also provides a check of accuracy of general ledger entries since it is prepared independently of the company.

12. **Cancelled checks** - They will disclose the bank accounts of expenditures and where the money went.

13. **Debit/credit memos** – Wire transfers, usually includes the larger transactions.

14. **Invoices**

15. **Requisitions for payment**

2. How to Ask for It

1. Consult with your expert to ask for the right documents and then to follow up with additional demands if appropriate.

2. Have your expert get you publicly available documents, such as 990's if the company at issue is a not for profit or a charity.

3. Subpoenas can and should be issued by counsel pursuant to F.R.C.P. 45(a)(3), New York C.P.L.R. 3120(1)[4] and 735 Ill. Code Civil Procedure § 1101[5] to require third parties to produce documents for copying and inspection. The scope of the material which can be subpoenaed under F.R.C.P. 45 is as broad as that permitted under Rule 26 discovery. See 9 Moore's Federal Practice – Civil § 45.02; see Bouwkamp v. CSX Corp., 2007 U.S. Dist. LEXIS 2834, *5-6 (N.D. Ind. 2007) ("objecting party must show with specificity that the request is improper); Kodish v. Oakbrook Terrace Fire Protection District, 235 F.R.D. 447, 450 (N.D. Ill. 2006); Graham v. Casey's Gen Stores, Inc., 206 F.R.D. 251, 253 (S.D. Ind. 2002) (party opposing production had burden of showing that subpoena was "overly broad, unduly burdensome, or not relevant").

4. As a general matter, third party documents should be subpoenaed as early in the process as possible for multiple reasons. First, the third party's records may be more complete or significantly different from those submitted by the opposing party. Second, waiting until the end of the case may put you up against the record custodian's document retention policies. Third, in October 2004, 12 USCS §§ 5001-5018, otherwise known as the "Check Clearing for the 21st Century Act" or the "Check 21 Act," went into effect. This converts some checks into electronic instruments and effects bank retention of the fronts and backs of checks. The back of the check contains the endorsement history of the check and is critical for tracing where the money went. Fourth, the courts and commentators have generally held that a party's ability to serve a Rule 45 subpoena without leave of court ends with the close of fact discovery. See e.g., Dodson v. CBS Broadcasting Inc., 2005 U.S. Dist. LEXIS 30126, *3-5 (S.D.N.Y. 2005); Mortgage Info. Services v. Kitchens, 210 F.R.D. 562, 566-567 (W.D.N.C. 2002); Dryer v. GACS, Inc., 204 F.R.D. 120, 122 (N.D. Ind. 2001); Alder v. United States, 190 F.R.D. 281, 282-284 (D. Mass. 2000); see also 9 Moore's Federal Practice – Civil § 45.02.

---

4. C.P.L.R. 3120(1) provides in relevant part:

 1. After commencement of an action, any party may serve on any other party a notice or on any other person a subpoena duces tecum:

    (i) to produce and permit the party seeking discovery, or someone acting on his or her behalf, to inspect, copy, test or photograph any designated documents or any things which are in the possession, custody or control of the party or person served; or

    ***

 2. The notice or subpoena duces tecum shall specify the time, which shall be not less than twenty days after service of the notice or subpoena,. . .and, in the case of an inspection, copying, testing or photographing, shall set forth the items to be inspected, copied, tested or photographed by individual item or by category, and shall describe each item and category with reasonable particularity.

 3. The party issuing a subpoena duces tecum as provided hereinabove shall at the same time serve a copy of the subpoena upon all other parties and, within five days of compliance therewith, in whole or in part, give to each party notice that the items produced in response thereto are available for inspection and copying, specifying the time and place thereof.

5. Needless to say, F.R.C.P. 45(b)(1) requires that "prior notice of any commanded production of documents. . .before trial shall be served on each party" in accordance with FRCP Rule 5(b). C.P.L.R. §§ 2303(a) also requires that a copy of the subpoena be served on your adversary. Federal[6], New York[7], and Illinois[8] law allow for sanctions for failure to provide notice.

6. If you are subpoenaing documents from a neutral or friendly third party, speak to the party with the documents or their counsel and ask how to make things easy for all concerned. If you explain what you are looking for, you can frequently narrow the scope of your subpoena and get an agreement accepting service of the subpoena by fax or e-mail.

7. In New York practice since September 1, 2003, under CPLR. § 3122-a, where copies of non-party business records are delivered pursuant to a discovery subpoena, the non-party will also be required to sign a sworn certification attesting to the fact that the documents being produced are correct copies of "business records" which have been prepared in accordance with the evidentiary standards set forth in CPLR § 4518(a).

---

5. Sec. 2-1101 provides in relevant part:

> Subpoenas. The clerk of any court in which an action is pending shall, from time to time, issue subpoenas for those witnesses and to those counties in the State as may be required by either party. Every clerk who shall refuse so to do shall be guilty of a petty offense and fined any sum not to exceed $100. An order of court is not required to obtain the issuance by the clerk of a subpoena duces tecum. For good cause shown, the court on motion may quash or modify any subpoena or, in the case of a subpoena duces tecum, condition the denial of the motion upon payment in advance by the person in whose behalf the subpoena is issued of the reasonable expense of producing any item therein specified.

In People ex. Re. Fisher v. Carey, 77 Ill.2d 259, 265 (1979), the Illinois Supreme Court held that as distinct from discovery, which is the parties' procedure, a subpoena is a judicial process or court writ so that subpoenaed materials should be delivered directly to the court. The court, then, determines the relevance and materiality of the subpoenaed materials, whether they are privileged, and whether the subpoena is unreasonable or oppressive. See generally Illinois Jurisprudence, Civil Procedure 9:14

6. See e.g., Murphy v. Board of Educ. of Rochester Sch. Dist., 196 F.R.D. 220, 222-223 (W.D.N.Y. 2000) (exercising its inherent sanctioning power, court imposed sanctions in form of attorneys' fees and costs on plaintiff's counsel, who issued 12 subpoenas without prior notice to opposing parties); Spencer v. Steinman, 179 F.R.D. 484, 487-489 (E.D. Pa. 1998) (plaintiff's counsel was ordered to pay counsel fees incurred by defendant in bringing violation of prior notice requirement to court's attention).

This certification will qualify the non-party business records for admission at trial in the same manner as for hospital records under CPLR § 2306, and the personal appearance of a non-party foundation witness will not be necessary. Within five days of compliance with the subpoena, the party issuing the subpoena is required by CPLR 3120(3) to notify the other parties that the items produced will be available for inspection and copying, advising as to the time and place of such inspection and copying.

8. Any party intending to seek admission of certified records is required under CPLR § 3122(c) to give notice at least thirty days before trial and to specify the place where the documents can be inspected. No later than ten days before trial, an adverse party can object to the proposed use of certified business records, stating the basis for the objection and, in any event, the party retains the right to object to the admission of such records for reasons other than lack of authentication.

9. Get the documents well enough in advance of the deposition, so that your expert can analyze them for you.

---

7. For a true horror story involving abuse of the subpoena power including failure to serve a notice on an adversary see In re Beiny, 129 A.D.2d 126, 517 N.Y.S.2d 474 (1st Dep't 1987), motion for leave to reargue, renew, or appeal denied, 132 A.D.2d 190, 522 N.Y.S.2d 511. (1st Dep't 1987), motion for leave to appeal dismissed, 71 N.Y.2d 994, 529 N.Y.S.2d 277 (1988). In Beiny, a Sullivan and Cromwell associate served a deposition subpoena, seeking documents on the custodian of the records of a defunct law firm which had represented an adverse party. Accompanying the subpoena was a letter which misrepresented the status of the party represented by Sullivan and Cromwell. The deposition subpoena (which had never been served on the adverse party) was withdrawn after counsel was provided with the originals of the documents – most of which were privileged. Sullivan and Cromwell then used the documents at a deposition, refused to say where it had obtained them, and refused to return the originals unless it was given some concessions. The First Department of the New York Appellate Division took an extremely dim view of this process. It not only upheld an order finding almost all the documents privileged and stricken from the case but, using particularly scathing language, it removed Sullivan and Cromwell from the case and referred the attorneys to the Departmental Disciplinary Committee for investigation. See also In re Estate of Kochovos, 140 A.D.2d 180, 181, 528 N.Y.S.2d 37, 38 (1st Dep't 1988) (use of subpoenas duces tecum without notice to obtain documents from third parties was a "deceptive practice" and "covert discovery [which] warrants severe criticism"); but see Di Marco v. Sparks, 212 A.D.2d 965, 965, 624 N.Y.S.2d 692, 693 (4th Dep't 1995) (declining to strike non privileged documents which could have been otherwise obtained properly).

10. Ask for the documents for a period before and after the periods that at issue in the lawsuit so that you have a baseline and can see whether there were any changes.

11. Ask for the data in electronic form. This will make it much easier to review it and put it into your own database.

12. If the company's continuing accounting practices or finances are at issue, make the discovery demand a continuing one.

13. If you have a theory of the case at the point of the deposition, be careful not to disclose it in the way you frame your discovery demand.

---

8. See e.g. People v. Walley, 215 Ill. App. 3d 971, 575 N.E.2d 596 (Ill. App. Ct. 2 Dist. 1991), app. den. 142 Ill. 2d 663, 584 N.E.2d 138 (1991) (upholding grant of motion to quash where (1) subpoena duces tecum provided for extrajudicial delivery and inspection of materials; (2) defendant was denied an opportunity to challenge the issuance of the subpoena since he was not made aware of what materials were sought in the subpoena until after they were obtained by the State; and (3) the subpoena was issued for a date when no court hearing was scheduled or held.); In re Reimann, 217 Ill. App. 3d 270, 576 N.E.2d 944 (Ill. App. Ct. 5 Dist. 1991) (Subpoenas were improper where they were neither returnable to court nor accompanied by a notice to take the deposition of the custodian of the records.); See also People v. Smith, 259 Ill. App. 3d 492, 631 N.E.2d 738 (Ill. App. Ct. 4th Dist. 1994); c.f. People v. Hathaway, 263 Ill. App. 3d 426, 635 N.E.2d 148 (Ill. App. Ct. 4th Dist. 1994).

B. Investigation of the Opposing Party, It's Accountant, and the Firm Which Employs the Accountant

Investigation is a critical, and often neglected, part of the attorney's job in any litigation. At the latest, before the start of depositions, the attorney needs to have thoroughly acquainted himself with all the information publicly available about: (1) the plaintiff company; (2) its record of previous performance; (3) its principals; (4) the key employees involved in the project at issue; (5) any witnesses; and (6) any predecessor companies. Changes in technology over the last ten years have made massive amounts of information available though the Internet. Where appropriate, private investigators can gather additional information. The deposition then provides an opportunity to fill in any missing spaces and to see whether the witness is truthful.

1. Run LEXIS/NEXUS searches on the plaintiff company and any predecessor companies, its principals, the key employees involved in the project, any witnesses, and the accountant witness and his or her firm. This should include a newspaper search (click on "NYNEWS"). One suggested Lexis/Nexis approach is the following: On the main menu page entitled "Lexis, Nexis Total Research System" (this is the page that says "Look for a Source") click on "Guided Search Forms" on the red tool bar at the top of the page. Then click on "Person Locater" and "Public Records" (as well as other options on the page that may interest you, such as "Business Locator" and "Asset Locator"). After you click on "Person Locator," then fill in the requested information (although it is not necessary to have all of the requested information, such as social security number). After you click on "Public Records," you should click on "State Group Files" and look for the Combined Public Records of the relevant State. A search of the "New York Combined Public Records" option will allow you to simultaneously search over thirty databases including "NY Bankruptcy Filings," "NY Judgment and Lien Filings," "NY Uniform Commercial Code Lien Filings," "NY Federal & State Tax Liens," and "NY Property Records."

2. Go to the appropriate public records site to get the underlying documentation disclosed by your LEXIS search if it seems significant.

3. Run the names of the opposing company and any predecessor companies, its principals, the key employees involved in the project, any witnesses, and the accountant witness and his or her firm through the PACER system's national U.S. Party/Case Index, http://pacer.uspci.uscourts.gov/, and for any districts where the company has a significant history, see e.g. https://ecf.ilnd.uscourts.gov/cgi-bin/iquery.pl; https://ecf.nyed.uscourts.gov/cgi-bin/iquery.pl; https://ecf.nysd.uscourts.gov/cgi-bin/iquery.pl; to see if there are federal lawsuits and, if so, get the court papers. With Electronic Court Filing, the more recent documents can now be downloaded.

4. Run the names of the opposing company, and any predecessor companies, its principals, the key employees involved in the project, any witnesses, and the accountant witness and his or her firm through E-Law or Court Alert or an equivalent service for the last 15 years.

5. Have an ISO (Insurance Services Bureau) search done. Some law firms or government offices subscribe to this service. This search results will tell you if the plaintiff in your case has brought a claim against an insurance company or a governmental entity even if the claim did not develop into a lawsuit. It will give you some basic information about that claim, including the type of claim, date of occurrence, the defendant, the claimed injuries, and attorneys for claimant and defendant. You can than use this information to perform further investigations and for surprise in a deposition or at trial.

6. Check the websites of the opposing corporation and the accounting firm to see what information is included. It may have a photo of individuals you are interested in. Check for advertisements and company information listed on the internet.

7. Have a DMV search done. These searches provide you with a goldmine of information including the address of the witness, the driving history of the witness, and the registration history of vehicles owned by the witness. This search is especially useful in locating witnesses.

8. Publicly available databases run by New York City can contain useful information as to particular NYC locations which are tied to a party you are interested in. The Buildings Information System ("BIS"), http://www. nyc.gov/buildings, will enable you to research and verify if the subject holds any other licenses with the Department of Buildings, if there any other company names, partner information, business locations and to research the addresses in question. An Administrative Enforcement Unit ("AEU") violations search, http://10.217.254.108/aeu/aeu.asp, will find copies and information about Notices of Violation and Environmental Control Board (ECB) violations. ACRIS "Automated City Register Information System": will provide access to find property owned by a person, tax information, copies of records, etc.
http://a836-acris.nyc.gov/Scripts/Coverpage.dll/index. The New York City Housing Preservation and Development ("HPD") web-

site, http://167.153.4.71/hpd online/provide_address.aspx, can be used to check for HPD violations issued to a location. The Vendex website allows the user to verify if a vendor is doing business with New York City or has been barred from doing business with the City of New York http://www.nyc.gov/html/biz search/. The federal Debarment List is at http://eplsarnet/gov,

9. The New York State, Department of State website allows access to search for Corporation, Business Entities, and Notary Public information on their database, http://appsext5.dos.state.ny.us/corp_public/corpsearch.entity_search_entry.

10. The U.S. Department of Labor, Occupational Safety and Health Administration ("OSHA") website enables the user to search for OSHA enforcement inspections by the name of the establishment. http://www.osha.gov/pls/imis/establishment.html

11. Property Shark, http://www.propertyshark.com/mason/index.html, shows a photograph of the address, the number of stories, judgments against the property, the amount of space at the location that is used for commercial/residential/garage, zoning, the market value of the location, and names associated with telephone numbers registered at the location, etc.

12. Online Reverse lookup for phone numbers is at http://yellowpages.com/Index.aspx

13. Run all relevant names through Google and Dogpile and other data bases.

14. Run names of younger subjects through relationship data bases such as www.MySpace.com, www.Facebook.com and www.friendster.com

15. Amazon.com has a feature by which you can search through the text of books. See if the firm (or the individual accountant) is mentioned anywhere.

16. Run a Dunn and Bradstreet on the company at: www.dnb.com.

17. If the company is publicly traded, check the SEC at www.sec.com and http://www.sec.gov/edgar/searchedgar/webusers.html.

18. Other sites with potential financial information are Hoovers at www.hoovers.com and Yahoo at finance.yahoo.com.

19. Specialized web sites have interesting information. The Federal Bureau of Prisons has a web site, http://www.bop.gov/, which allows you to search to see if a named individual has been in federal prison since 1982. The database of the New York State Department of Correctional Services, http://nysdocs.docs.state.ny.us allows you to search the New York prison system back to the early 1970's. For other similar data bases, see http://www.state.ar.us/doc/inmate_info/index.html (Arkansas data base); http://www.dc.state.fl.us/AppCommon/ Florida Corrections Offender Network); central.classification@mail.dc.state.fl.us. (Florida Inmate Population Information Search); http://www.dcor.state.ga.us/GDC/OffenderQuery/jsp/OffQryForm.jsp?Institution= (Georgia inmate Query); https://www.accessidaho.org/public/corr/offender/search.html (Idaho Inmate Locator); http://www.idoc.state.il.us/subsections/search/default.asp (Ill. Inmate Search Database) http://www.in.gov/serv/ind correction_ofs;(Indiana);\http://www.dc.state.ks.us./kasper2/defaultz.asp (Kansas Inmate Locator); http://www.state.mi.us/mdoc/asp/otis2.html (Michigan Offender Tracking Information System); http://info.doc.state.mn.us/publicviewer/main.asp (Minnesota Inmate Locator Database); https://www6.state.nj.us/DOC_Inmate/inmatesearch.jsp (New Jersey Offender Search Engine); http://webapps6.doc.state.nc.us/apps/offender/menu1 (N.C. Dep't of Correction Public Access Information System); http://docapp8.doc.state.ok.us/servlet/page?_pageid=395&_dad=portal30&_schema=PORTAL30 (Oklahoma Inmate Locator); http://www.cor.state.pa.us/inmatelocatorweb/ (Penn.. Inmate Locator); http://www.tennesseeanytime.org/foil/foil_index.jsp;jsessionid=aPF40VHOpSBc (Tennessee Felony Offender Information Lookup); http://www.tdcj.state.tx.us/offender_information.htm (Texas Offender Information Center); http://www.doc.state.vt.us/offender/ (Vermont Inmate Locator); http://www2.vipnet.org/cgi-bin/vadoc/doc.cgi (Virginia Inmate Status Information).

20. Licensure in New York can be checked on line at http://www.op.nysed.gov/opsearches.htm. The screen will tell you the community in which the CPA resides and the status of his or her licensure. In New York, professional misconduct in all the professions (except that by physicians, physician assistants, and specialist assistants) is investigated and prosecuted by the New York State Education Department's Office of the Professions. The Board of Regents, which also has responsibility for licensure in all the professions, is responsible for the final disposition of all disciplinary matters except those involving the medical professions. The web address http://www.op.nysed.gov/rasearch.htm provides for on line license verifications, including disciplinary actions back to January 1, 1994. In Illinois, licensure and disciplinary history can be searched on line at http://www.idfpr.com/dpr/licenselookup/results.asp.

21. The web site for the American Institute of Certified Public Accountants is http://www.aicpa.org/index.htm. The New York State Society of Certified Public Accountants also has a database which provides information. It can be found at http://www.nysscpa.org/leadership/directory.asp. A counterpart website in Illinois is at http://www.icpas.org/icpas/index.asp.z

22. If the company is a not for profit, then its tax returns (Form 990) are public documents. In some cases they will be available on the company's web site.

23. Non profit organizations in New York have to file substantial amounts of information with the Attorney General. That information is publicly available.

24. Information on 6,000,000 not for profit organizations and charities can be found at http://www.guidestar.org/.

25. If appropriate, obtain the company's incorporation papers from the Secretary of State or its equivalent.

26. Ascertain whether the company has ever forfeited the right to do business in the state of incorporation for non-payment of taxes (in New York for failure to pay franchise taxes).

27. Check for conflicts of interest which can occur in different ways. See. AICPA Rules 101 (independence), 102 (integrity and objectivity), 102-2 (conflict of interest), "Principles of Professional

Conduct", "Section 55, Article IV." For example, does the accountant or a family member have any ownership in the entity which the accountant is certifying?

C. Topic Areas for Questions

CAVEAT: The topics listed below are by no means exhaustive. Each case requires particularized attention, and the person taking the deposition must listen to the answers given by the witness, then follow up on new and unexpected material. Do not read your questions to the witness. Engage in a dialogue which you control.

1. General Pedigree of Witness

1. Name;
2. Aliases or nicknames;
3. Date and place of Birth;
4. Citizenship or immigration status; check immigration status on entry into U.S.;
5. Social Security No.;
6. Marriages and children and their employment if old enough;
7. Present address;
8. All previous addresses;
9. All education;
10. All non accounting jobs: - Dates of employment, type of work performed, reason for leaving, names of supervisors (subpoena recent records if witness is critical); ascertain if witness was ever fired or asked to resign. If so, find out why;
11. Military service - When, where, in whose army, commendations, rank at discharge, court-martials or non-judicial punishment, overseas service;
12. Prior lawsuits - Who, where, parties, type of claim, result of lawsuit, did witness testify, names of attorneys;
13. Prior testimony in any forum or any case on any topic;
14. All arrests, convictions - Obtain plaintiff's version of events of each case. (If the witness denies doing something he or she plead guilty to or was convicted of doing, that denial may itself

provide another basis for cross-examination). Obtain the certificate of conviction and the court files, and

15. Medical history - Psychiatric treatment, surgery, etc.

2. *Witness' Professional Pedigree*

1. Education;
2. Academic honors;
3. Professional honors or awards;
4. Licenses and their status – ever suspended, etc;
5. How many times witness took CPA exam;
6. Any other types of certification e.g., Certified Fraud Examiner; board certification;
7. Publications;
8. Lectures or panel discussions;
9. Seminars attended;
10. Periodicals customarily read;
11. Training or expertise in certain specialty areas e.g., government contracting, not for profit organizations;
12. Have negative comments ever been made about the accountant in peer review? If so, what were they and how did the accountant react to them?
13. Have complaints ever been made to regulatory boards against the accountant? Find out whether the accountant has ever been charged for disciplinary action. And, if so, how frequently, for what, and with what result?

3. *Pedigree of Witness' Firm*

1. Is the witness a solo practitioner? In a partnership? A corporation?
2. Where does your witness fit into things? Associate? Partner? Salaried employee?
3. How is your witness compensated?
4. Who does the witness report to?

5. Who reports to the witness?
6. Who does the witness' evaluation?
7. If the employer is a corporation, what kind of corporation is it? (Business Corporation? Not for profit? Subchapter S?)
8. When and where was company incorporated?
9. What are the family relationships of stockholders, officers, directors of the company whose finances are in issue to the accountant?
10. To the accountant's superiors?
11. Has the firm ever sued anyone else or been sued? If so, find out when, where, and why. Contact the other lawyer. You may be able to share useful information.
12. Has the firm ever filed for bankruptcy?
13. Has the firm ever been sanctioned or penalized in any way by any governmental or regulatory body? If so, when? By whom and for what?

4. Structure and Pedigree of the Company Whose Finances Are at Issue

Companies like individuals have pedigrees. If adequate information has not been elicited from other witnesses, then an in-house accountant fact witness can be a source of information and should be asked pertinent questions about the company's structure, ownership, etc. This is obviously going to be more fruitful where the company is not a massive publicly traded organization.

1. When and where was the company incorporated?
2. What kind of corporation is it? (Business Corporation? Not for profit? Subchapter S?)
3. Does the company have any affiliates? If so, who and what is their role? How much independence do they have? (Profits and losses can be spread around this way).
4. Who were principals of company at incorporation?
5. Who are principals today?
6. When and how did that change?

7. Who provided the financing to start the company up? How much money? What terms?

8. Any affiliations with organized crime?

9. What companies had principals been associated with before? (Look for prior history of defaults, fraud, and bankruptcy).

10. Who have been the stockholders throughout the history of the company?

11. Who are the stockholders today? How many shares of stock were issued, and who holds them? Are there shares which have not been issued?

12. Who have been the corporate officers throughout the history of the company?

13. Who are the corporate officers today? What are the duties and authority of each officer? Who has authority to contract for the company?

14. Who are the key employees responsible for the day to day running of the company? What are their responsibilities and how are they compensated?

15. How are the stockholders and corporate officers compensated?

16. If there is a recovery in this action, who will stand to gain financially?

17. What are the family relationships of stockholders, officers, directors, and key employees? Look for fronts, (e.g., 20 year-old son suddenly becomes president of new company after father's indictment), funding coming from suspect sources (e.g., indicted father makes "gift" to son of start-up financing) or continuity with the suspect entity (e.g., new corporation has same employees, office space and officers)

18. Has the company ever sued anyone else or been sued? If so find out when, where, and why. Contact the other lawyer. You may be able to share useful information.

19. Has the company ever filed for bankruptcy?

20. What records does the company keep? Where are those records? Did the company ever issue bylaws? Where are the stock certificates and minutes books reflecting shareholders' and directors' meetings? Are there minutes of stockholders' meetings?

21. If the records have been lost by the usual means (i.e., the Four Horsemen of Litigation — burglary, fire, flood, and moving), check to see if those incidents can be verified (insurance claims, police reports). Possibly, ask at trial for a spoliation hearing and/or an adverse inference.
22. Have the company or its principals, directors, officers, or key employees ever been convicted of a crime?
23. Was the company ever publicly traded?
24. Has the company ever forfeited the right to do business in the state of incorporation (e.g., for non-payment of taxes)?
25. Is the company union or non-union?
26. Which local? Since when?
27. When was the last Collective Bargaining Agreement?
28. Have there been issues with payments to welfare funds?
29. Ever sued over it?

5. In House Accountant's Role

1. How long has he or she been working for the company?
2. What is his or her title?
3. What was the witness's title when he or she was hired?
4. What is the salary differential between now and then?
5. Did the accountant come from an accounting firm which had previously been providing services to the party? If so, when, under what circumstances, and how recently?
6. Where does the accountant stand in the company hierarchy?
7. Who does he or she report to?
8. Who reports to the accountant?
9. How does the reporting chain work?
10. Are there oral or written reports?
11. Salary?
12. Has the accountant received salary increases over the years? How much? How often?

13. Is salary contingent on how well company does?
14. Does the accountant receive year-end bonuses?
15. Based on what?
16. What are his or her relationships with corporate owners, officers, and other key people, e.g., family, friendship?
17. Do they socialize after work?
18. Has the in-house accountant ever been asked to change anything by the management?
19. If so, what? When? Who? Was it changed? What was the reason for the change?
20. Was the original finding in error?
21. Was the change something which benefited the company's stock value?
22. Or tax payments?
23. Ascertain whether the accountant has been fired or disciplined anywhere else.
24. If so, where, when, and why?
25. What kind of financial records does the company maintain, including profit and loss statements, balance sheets, general ledgers, disbursement and purchase journals, year-end financial statements and annual reports, invoices, checks, check registers and bank statements, internal and independent audit reports, and accounts receivable and payable?
26. What is the witness' role with respect to the preparation and review of these documents?
27. Does the company use a fiscal year or a calendar year?
28. What are the names of the employees who do the entry of the data?
29. What are their qualifications?
30. How much turnover is there?
31. Are all of the financial reporting systems operative and accurate during all the relevant time periods?

32. Who is responsible for routine journal entries? For non-routine journal entries?

33. If it is a cash business, what controls exist over the cash?

34. Have any audits been qualified?

35. Have there been material weaknesses?

36. What have previous audits disclosed as weaknesses or deficiencies?

37. What and how is petty cash used?

38. Who approves pretty cash expenditures

39. What computer program is used for the books and records?

40. Who does the data entry?

41. Are there any employees who have been discharged during the relevant time period? Disgruntled former employees may have material information. See e.g. Niesig v. Team 1, 76 N.Y.2d 363, 559 N.Y.S.2d 493 (1990) as to which employees can be contacted *ex parte*.

42. Has the company had any extremely bad or good years? If so, when and what were the circumstances? What caused the change?

43. What about affiliates?

44. Are there any new affiliates during the relevant time periods?

45. Any new business areas or markedly increased business areas?

46. Any segments of the business which were discontinued? Why? When?

6. External Auditor's Role

1. How much does the accountant get paid from doing the audit or preparing the company's financial statements?

2. Does he or she work for any related companies?

3. Any companies with same owners and officers?

4. Does he or she have any family ties or ties of friendship with the ownership or management?

5. What percentage of accountant's income each year is attributable to business from the Company?

6. Has that changed over time? Increased or decreased?

7. Who does the actual auditing work?

8. Junior accountants?

9. Are they CPA's?

10. How much experience do they have in general?

11. In the industry in which they are conducting the audit?

12. If they miss something, then will you of necessity miss it?

13. Has the external auditor ever been asked to change anything by the management?

14. If so, what? When? Who? Was it changed? What was the reason for the change? Large receivables? Large payables? Intercompany officer loans? Unrecovered accruals? Cost allocation methods?

15. Was the original finding in error?

16. Was the change something which benefited the company's stock value?

17. Or tax payments?

7. If Something Is Wrong, Was It an Error or an Irregularity?

1. An "error" is the result of an unintentional mistake, typically a mathematical mistake, a mistake in the application of accounting principles, an oversight or misuse of facts that existed at the time the financial statements were prepared.

2. An "irregularity" is the result of management's intentional misleading of investors or others relying on a financial statement or an audit. This may be the basis for a fraud claim.

3. Ascertain whether you are dealing with an error or an irregularity.

4. Did management attempt to conceal facts or disrupt the audit process?

5. How serious is the misstatement? Intent to mislead may make an irregularity material where an error of the same magnitude may not be material.
6. Were material accounting errors or irregularities discovered in previously issued financial statements corrected or restated?
7. Is there an indication that documents are being back dated, altered, or forged?
8. Are stories changing?
9. Were accounting policies changed at a convenient time?
10. Are key employees personally benefiting?
11. Was the misstatement discovered through the company's own system of financial control or by outsiders?
12. Did the organization act appropriately?
13. Did the company act promptly on the information or stall?
14. What steps did the organization take to ensure competent and independent investigation and review of relevant facts?
15. Did the organization retain independent outside counsel and determine the need for independent auditors or forensic accountants?
16. Was a "litigation hold" put in place to ensure proper document preservation?
17. Was an independent committee of independent and disinterested board members set up to oversee any investigation?
18. Was the scope of the investigation improperly limited?
19. Were employees encouraged to cooperate with the investigation?
20. What happened to wrongdoers? Were they fired, referred for prosecution or retained in place, allowed to retire or promoted?
21. Did the company restate its financials?

8. *Incident Specific Questions*

In some cases, what happened at a particular meeting or encounter will be a significant part of the witness's testimony. You should obtain <u>all</u> the details of this meeting or encounter.

1. What were the facts leading up to the event?
2. Where was the witness?
3. Any consumption of alcohol or drugs (legal or illegal)?
4. Anything which would impair that witness' ability to perceive or to relate accurately what happened;
5. Who was with the witness when the event took place?
6. Location of the event;
7. Date and time;
8. Duration of total event and of each significant portion of event (Possibly have witness indicate on record when same amount of time has passed as incident took and put that time on the record);
9. Every time plaintiff gestures or gesticulates, describe very carefully what plaintiff did (e.g.: "Let the record reflect that plaintiff held both arms straight up, pointing toward the ceiling.");
10. Distances at each important stage of events - Estimate in terms of something in deposition room, and then have counsel stipulate to distance (or, better yet, bring a tape measure);
11. Environmental conditions - Visibility, noise, rain, snow or sunshine, temperature, wind, location of street lights; Were the lighting conditions brighter than in the deposition room or the court room than when the incident took place? Was there enough light to read by? You can get the U.S. weather report, which will have much of this information;
12. Noise levels – Was the conversation shouted or whispered? Was there background noise? If so, what (subway, airplane, crying baby)? How loud and how long? Was the entire conversation audible?
13. Description of persons not identified by name - Gender, age, height, clothing, color of hair, weight, facial hair, etc.;

14. As to those identified by name, how does the witness know their name?
15. What each individual, including non-defendants, did at every stage of the incident;
16. Where each person present, including non-defendants, was in relationship to plaintiff and to each other at each stage of the incident;
17. What each person at scene said and tone of voice, and
18. How incident ended.

9. Damages

In many cases, the Comptroller or Chief Financial Officer of a company will present the plaintiff's testimony as to damages.

1. Was the accountant involved in calculating damages in this case?
2. If so, what was the accountant's role?
3. Has the accountant been involved in calculating damages in other cases?
4. Which ones?
5. For this plaintiff or for others?
6. What methods did the accountant use in other cases?
7. Were the same methods used here?
8. What other methods were considered or rejected?
9. Did the accountant testify in those other cases?
10. Under the other methods which were not used, did the damages come out differently? Higher or lower?
11. Were alternate calculations used?
12. Does the accountant have any training or expertise in calculating damages?
13. In assessing intangible assets?
14. Did the accountant refer to any books or sources before making the damage calculation? If so, which books or sources?

15. Did the accountant follow the methodology suggested in the book or other source?
16. Did the accountant consult with anyone before making the damage calculation? If so , who? What did that person say?
17. Was management involved in the damage calculation?
18. Who specifically in management?
19. What were that person's qualifications?
20. Did management suggest a methodology to follow?
21. Was that methodology followed?
22. Was counsel involved in calculating the damages?
23. Did counsel suggest a methodology to follow?
24. Was that methodology followed?
25. Is the damage methodology used one which is generally accepted in the accounting or legal professions?
26. If there is a claim of lost future business, identify the specific business lost, all previous business with the same party, profit ratios on past business, and all written or oral communications which bear on the loss of business;
27. If there is a claim of expenses incurred, ask for bills or invoices and cancelled checks.
28. Ascertain who paid the bills and if the bills were paid at all.
29. If there is a claim for delay or extra work damages, itemize each claim and find how the damages on each specific claim were calculated. Portions of a claim may be subject to attack.
30. If there is a claim for lost earnings, ask for tax returns and financial statements for three years before incident.
31. As to future damages, ascertain whether the company was having any kind of decline in business or income before the alleged event causing the injury. If so, what does the plaintiff attribute that decline to?
32. Does the witness acknowledge that any part of the decline was due to forces unrelated to the defendant's actions (e.g., the national or local economy, trends in the market or industry, new technology, etc)?

33. What steps were taken by plaintiff to mitigate damages? When were those steps taken?

34. Was any part of the damage mitigated?

35. Why was the plaintiff unable to mitigate all the damages?

V. DEFENDING THE DEPOSITION OF AN OPPOSING ACCOUNTING EXPERT

F.R.C.P. Rule 26(a)(2)(A) mandates that "a party shall disclose to other parties the identity of any person who may be used at trial to present evidence" under the expert witness provisions of the Federal Rules of Evidence (F.R.E. Rules 702, 703 and 705). F.R.C.P Rule 26(a)(2)(B) specifies that accompanying the identification of the expert will be a written report:

> (B) Except as otherwise stipulated or directed by the court, this disclosure shall, with respect to a witness who is retained or specially employed to provide expert testimony in the case or whose duties as an employee of the party regularly involve giving expert testimony, be accompanied by a written report prepared and signed by the witness. The report shall contain a complete statement of all opinions to be expressed and the basis and reasons therefore the data or other information considered by the witness in forming the opinions; any exhibits to be used as a summary of or support for the opinions; the qualifications of the witness, including a list of all publications authored by the witness in the last ten years; the compensation to be paid for the study and testimony; and a listing of any other cases in which the witness has testified as an expert at trial or by deposition with the preceding four years.

Under the Federal Rules, the expert will not be deposed until all the requirements of Rule 26(a)(2)(B) have been satisfied and failure to comply can result in preclusion. F.R.C.P. Rule 37(c)(1).

The New York CPLR is somewhat less demanding. Under §3101(d)(1), "upon request, each party shall identify each person whom the party expects to call as an expert witness at trial and shall disclose in reasonable detail the subject matter on which each expert is expected to testify, the substance of the facts and opinions on which each expert is expected to testify, the qualifications of each expert witness, and a summary of the grounds for each expert's opinion."

In a very real sense, the preparation for the defense of the deposition of your expert accountant begins when you retain the accountant and continues through the drafting of the expert report.

A. Selecting Your Expert

1. One of the advantages of retaining an independent expert is that the expert's independence, or at least appearance of independence, gives greater weight to the expert's report and testimony. Be wary of forfeiting that independence by retaining an expert with too many ties to either counsel or client.

2. Consider using a consulting expert who will not testify and then a testifying expert. The consulting expert's findings will be covered by work product and/or attorney client privileges until and unless the expert becomes a testifying expert.

3. Make sure that the firm conducts a thorough search for conflicts before retention.

4. In selecting your expert, you should consider ability to testify in addition to the witness's technical qualifications.

5. If your expert works as part of a team, determine which team member will make the best witness.

6. Before retaining the expert, do a background search similar to that which you would do on hostile witnesses.

7. Keep the letter retaining the expert neutral and uninformative. Don't disclose your factual and legal theories of the case. Be wary that the document might have to be produced.

8. It is important to avoid future disputes with your expert by giving some thought as to the terms of the engagement and preparing a retainer agreement which reflects those terms. The agreement should set out both side's understanding as to: (1) whether the accountant will be testifying or consulting or both; (2) whether the accountant will be expected to prepare an expert report and be deposed; (3) whether the accountant will be compensated by a flat sum or an hourly rate; (4) whether there will be a cap on the expert's fee; and (5) what happens if the case settles before the expert completes agreed upon tasks.

9. Give your expert a fair and balanced view of the factual and legal allegations. Provide the expert with the complaint, any other detailed pleadings, relevant documents on both sides, deposition excerpts, and all key documents. This is important for many reasons. First, it will avoid an attack on the expert's report as being

the product of a biased and limited view of the facts. Second, if your expert is not given an unvarnished view of the facts, then the expert's advice to you will be less reliable. It may be that you will want to settle quickly, based upon what your expert tells you. Third, if given all the facts, the expert will be better able to provide you with a reality check.

B. Reviewing the Expert Report

1. Avoid substantive written communications with your expert which may end up being disclosed. Make your comments orally. Be wary of e-mail communications as to the substance of the report.

2. Don't give your expert privileged material. It may become discoverable.

3. Assume that anything given to the expert may end up being disclosed. The billings by the expert may end up being discoverable and should also not disclose legal theories.

4. Read the expert report carefully to make sure: (a) it is comprehensible; (b) it is accurate; (c) it addresses all the necessary issues; (d) complies with all the requirements of Fed. R. Civ. P. 26(a)(2)(B); and (e) covers all the critical issues in the case.

5. If the expert's normal practice is to retain drafts or notes, advise the expert not to destroy them.

6. Assume that all drafts will be discoverable. For a discussion of the developing law as the discoverability of drafts, etc., see Easton & Romines, Dealing with Draft Dodgers: Automatic Production of Drafts of Expert Witness Reports, 22 Rev. Litig. 355 (2003).

7. Do not pressure your expert to depart from his or her normal methodology. See EEOC v. Rockwell Int'l Corp., 60 F. Supp. 2d 791, 797 (N.D. Ill. 1999) (excluding expert testimony where a review of two drafts of the expert report and the expert's testimony indicated that the expert was directed by retaining counsel to employ principles that contradicted his normal methodology.)[9]

---

9. Even if such pressure does not lead to the exclusion of the expert report, the revelation of the pressure will likely be highly damaging to the credibility of the expert, and, even more importantly, to the credibility of counsel.

8. Always think on the offensive. Even if your expert is being responsive to the other party's expert report, consider whether there are things you want your expert to say affirmatively about your theory of the case.

9. Do not write the report or portions of it yourself. The Rule contemplates some involvement by counsel. The 1993 Advisory Committee Notes to Rule 26(a)(2)(B) states that the Rule "does not preclude counsel from providing assistance to experts in preparing the reports, and indeed with experts such as automobile mechanics, this assistance may be needed. Nevertheless, the report, which is intended to set forth the substance of the direct examination, should be written in a manner that reflects the testimony to be given by the witness, and it must be signed by the witness."

   Involvement by the lawyer may not by itself bar the admission of the report, see Isom v. Howmedica, Inc., 2002 U.S. Dist. LEXIS 9114, *2-3 (N.D. Ill. 2002) (report not excluded where lawyer served as the "scrivener" for conclusions reached by the expert based upon the expert's study of the relevant data). However, courts have excluded reports written by someone other than the expert. See Butera v. District of Columbia, 235 F.3d 637, 661-662 (D.C. Cir. 2001) (upholding district court's exclusion of an expert report which had been written by counsel for defendants); In re Jackson Nat'l Life Ins. Co. Premium Litig., 2000 U.S. Dist. LEXIS 1318 (W.D. Mich. 2000), affirming, 1997 U.S. Dist. LEXIS 15914 (W.D. Mich. 1997) (in excluding expert testimony where "undeniable substantial similarities between [the expert's] report and the report of another expert prepared with assistance from the same counsel in an unrelated case, demonstrate that counsel's participation so exceeded the bounds of legitimate 'assistance' as to negate the possibility that [the expert] actually prepared his own report within the meaning of Rule 26(a)(2). Plaintiffs' failure to furnish defendant with a report prepared by [the expert] constitutes a violation of Rule 26(a)(2)."); Manning v. Crockett, 1999 U.S. Dist. LEXIS 7966, * 8-9 (N.D. Ill. 1999) ("Allowing an expert to sign a report drafted entirely by counsel without prior substantive input from an expert would read the word 'prepared' completely out of the rule." The district court found that a report, purportedly prepared by the expert pursuant to Rule 26 which "virtually mirrors the allegations" in the complaint, "right down to the repetition of a typographical error from the complaint" did not comply with Rule 26(a).) Moreover, there is a considerable risk that, even if a report prepared by counsel or someone else is not excluded from evidence, the jury could still devalue such a report heavily.

10. Make sure that in a real sense the expert report is the work product of your expert and not something that was prepared by someone else in his firm which he merely signed.
11. Anticipate weakness in the report and attacks from the opposing expert. Play the Devil's Advocate and have responses ready.

C. Preparing the Expert Witness

The same preparation procedure, which was applicable to fact witnesses, should also be followed with respect to an expert witness with some additional considerations.

1. Even if the witness has testified numerous times before, it still pays to give your standard "witness prep" speech.
2. Make sure your witness rereads the report and supporting documentation shortly before the deposition.
3. Ask your witness what things he is most concerned about answering and figure out how to answer the question truthfully, accurately, and with the best view for your client's position.
4. Ask your witness whether there is anything in the professional literature which criticizes the approach the expert has taken. If there is, prepare your expert to address it.

VI. TAKING THE DEPOSITION OF AN OPPOSING ACCOUNTING EXPERT

Generally, the expert should not be deposed until after all the factual evidence has been disclosed. It should never be forgotten that expert witnesses are witnesses like all other witnesses. Bear in mind that experts can also be cross-examined in the same manner as other witnesses. Thus, evidence which would effect the credibility of a non-expert witness, e.g., evidence of bad acts admissible under F.R.E. 608(b) or of conviction of a crime, should be inquired into.

Consideration should also be given as to whether the case warrants the substantial expenditures which expert depositions can incur. In federal court, under F.R.C.P. Rule 26(b)(4)(c), "unless manifest injustice would result, the court shall require that the party seeking discovery pay the expert a reasonable fee for time spent in responding to discovery", including "a fair portion of the fees and expenses reasonably incurred" by the opposing party in "obtaining facts and opinions from the expert". See e.g., EEOC v. Johnson & Higgins, Inc., 1999 U.S. Dist. LEXIS 478, *2 (S.D.N.Y. Jan. 20, 1999); Itar-Tass Russian News Agency v. Russian Kurier, 1996 U.S. Dist. LEXIS 12442 *4-5 (S.D.N.Y. Aug. 26, 1996) (expert's travel and preparation time for aborted deposition); Kruzits v. Okuma Machine Tool, Inc., 1996 U.S. Dist. LEXIS 6617 (E.D. Pa. 1996); Lancaster v. Lord, 1993 U.S. Dist. LEXIS 3986, (S.D.N.Y. 1993); McHale v. Westcott, 893 F. Supp. 143, 151 (N.D.N.Y. 1995) (time spent reviewing files and waiting at deposition); American Steel Products Corp. v. Penn Central Corp., 110 F.R.D. 151, 153 (S.D.N.Y. 1986).

A. Preparation for the Deposition

1. Plan the deposition out with your expert. Ask him why the other expert is wrong. Read and study the expert's writings in the relevant area to see if something in those writings can be used for impeachment.

2. Have your expert look for articles and research that will show the error or bias of the other expert.

3. Inspect the expert's resume and report. Look for gaps in employment or education.

4. Check out the expert's qualifications to make sure the expert is not overstating them.

5. If the case warrants it and your client can afford it, have your expert present for the deposition.

6. Ask your expert what he knows about the other party's expert. Professional gossip may even be useful.

7. If the expert testimony is novel, you may want to request a Daubert hearing.

8. If the expert testifies a great deal, try to find old transcripts. These will help you to anticipate the expert's presentation of his conclusions and may show how the witness was effectively cross-examined before.

9. Call up the lawyers in other cases to see what they thought was effective and ineffective.

10. Run jury verdict, LEXIS, and newspaper searches on your expert and their experts to find out about them. (E.g., Conrad Berenson, a prominent New York plaintiff's economist, was heavily criticized in a published opinion by Judge Leval, now on the Second Circuit).

11. Subpoena from the expert or serve a document demand on counsel for all documents relating to the engagement, including but not limited to the retention agreement, billing and payment records, communications with others about the engagement, and prior drafts of the report.

B. Areas for Questioning at the Deposition

Your goal is to pin the expert's opinion down by establishing all the facts found and/or considered and the expert's methodology and assumptions. You probably will not be able to establish facts to keep the expert from being qualified.

1. How Did the Expert Come to Be Retained

1. Who contacted the witness? A party or counsel for a party?
2. What was the expert told? About the case? About the position the expert was being asked to take?
3. Were there other experts who were retained?
4. Who retained the expert? A party or counsel for a party?
5. How did the person who retained the expert come to hear of the expert?
6. When was the expert retained?
7. Did the expert perform any functions other than writing the report? If so, what?
8. Was there a pre-existing relationship with the party?
9. Or the party's counsel?
10. Had the expert previously prepared reports for the plaintiff's counsel?
11. How often? In what kinds of case? How much money was the expert paid in the other cases?

12. If the expert had never been retained as expert before, why now?
13. Did the expert express any uncertainty when retained?
14. How much is the expert being paid for the report? For the deposition testimony? For trial?
15. What are the financial arrangements?
16. Did the expert perform any other services?
17. Has the expert already been paid in full? Make sure that the expert's recovery is not realistically based upon the plaintiff winning its case, i.e., unless the plaintiff wins, plaintiff will not be able to pay the expert's fee.
18. Is the expert charging his or her normal rate? If less than usual, why?
19. Are there hours which were expended but which were not billed?
20. Or which will only be billed later?
21. Find out if the expert testifies for both plaintiffs and defendants.
22. Ask how much money the expert makes per year testifying in general and then how much testifying for one side. How does this compare with what the expert earns at his or her "day job"?

2. The Expert's Background

1. Ask the same pedigree questions which would be asked of any fact witness. Don't assume that because a witness has a professional degree and a license and testifies as an expert that the witness has nothing to hide.
2. As with other witnesses, an expert can be impeached by showing that he has an ideological or financial interest in the outcome.
3. Mark the expert's CV as an exhibit and go over it line by line. Look for gaps in education or employment.
4. Get the witness to acknowledge that the CV is complete and does not leave out anything.

5. If the CV is not current, ask what is not reflected in it and call for the production of a current CV.

6. Go over not just the ten-year period covered in the federal report but go back to the beginning of the expert's career.

7. If the expert is employed by a firm, how large is the firm? Is it just a corporate name for the expert and the expert's spouse?

8. In what areas does the expert consider himself to be an expert? Are there areas where the expert does not consider himself to have expertise?

9. Has the expert kept current in his field? If so, how?

10. What courses has the expert taken?

11. Has the expert taught any courses? If so, when, where and what courses?

12. What textbooks and other material did the expert use and refer to in his classes? (Such books may provide impeachment if the expert's opinion is different from the books.)

13. Is the expert a member of any societies or professional groups or professional committees? If so, what are the qualifications for memberships? What role, if any, does the expert play in the society?

14. What speeches has the expert given? On what topics?

15. Has the witness ever been qualified as an expert in any court? If so, when, what court, and on what topic?

16. Has any court ever refused to qualify the witness as an expert? If so, when, what court, on what topic and why?

17. Does the expert actually practice his profession any more or just primarily serve as an expert?

3. The Preparation of the Report

1. When did the expert start work on the report?

2. When did the expert finish the report?

3. How many hours did it take to prepare the report?

4. How much time was spent on each task?

5. How much on each section of the report?
6. What kind of detail is reflected in the work papers?
7. Who actually did the work of preparing the report?
8. Was counsel provided with a draft?
9. Did counsel come back with an alternate draft?
10. How many drafts were there?
11. Were the drafts preserved? If not, why not?
12. What was the difference between the drafts?
13. Was the expert asked <u>not to</u> consider anything?
14. Was the expert asked to disregard any materials or not to maintain certain types of materials?
15. Was anything significant taken out of the draft? If so, why?
16. Did counsel suggest any language? If so, what language? Was it accepted? If yes, when and why? If not, why?
17. If more than one person worked on preparing the report, what are the qualifications of each person?
18. How closely did the expert monitor their work?
19. What percentage of the time did the others spend performing the work?
20. Is the expert familiar with the basis of their findings as set forth in their report?
21. What percentage of the report did the expert himself do or review?
22. Did the expert have a normal practice with respect to taking notes?
23. What kinds of things does the expert normally make notes of?
24. Are those notes typically retained? Were they retained here? If not, why not?
25. Did the expert, or anyone else working on the report, take notes?
26. What was the significance of the notes?

27. What other opinions, besides those given in your report, did the expert arrive at during the course of your work on this case?

28. Why aren't they set out in the report?

29. Were there earlier drafts?

30. Did the drafts have different conclusion as to any portion of the report?

31. Or different reasons for the same conclusions?

32. Is expert familiar with all terms as they are used in the report?

33. Where term has a meaning which can vary, e.g., "accurate", to what percentage is it "accurate"?

34. What testing was done? Why were those items selected for testing? Why not others?

35. Ascertain whether the testing is sufficient in volume and in the areas tested for the conclusions that are being drawn.

4. *The Scope of the Report*

1. What is the "scope of the engagement"?

2. What was the expert asked to do? This can be significant because the "scope of the engagement" can be limited in a way to make the report skewed.

3. What documents were provided to the expert?

4. Were there documents which were requested but never provided? If so, what documents and why were they not provided?

5. Who determined what documents would be reviewed?

6. Did the expert interview anyone? If so, who?

7. Who determined whom the expert would interview?

8. Were there individuals the expert wanted to interview but was not allowed to speak to? Who and why did the expert want to talk to them

9. What standard is the report done to? Audit, review, compilation?

10. What procedures were agreed to with respect to the preparation of the report? Were all those procedures followed?

11. See if the expert would agree that access to more information is always better.

12. Was exculpatory evidence or information included in the report? If not, why not?

13. Could additional information have changed the result of the result?

14. Are there facts which the expert has not formed an opinion on? If not, why not?

15. Is the opinion expressed in the report preliminary or final?

16. When will it be final?

5. Assumptions

1. Did the expert start off with any assumptions? Factual or technical? (Your expert should help you figure out which assumptions are inarguable and which are subject to dispute)

2. If so, what were they?

3. Where did the assumptions come from?

4. Did the expert check them out?

5. Does the expert really know if the assumption is correct?

6. Why did the expert find it necessary to make those assumptions?

7. Were there alternative assumptions that the expert decided not to make?

8. On what grounds did the expert select the assumptions you made and reject the alternatives?

9. Did the expert examine the impact those alternatives would have made on the case?

10. Were the assumptions which the expert declined to make neutral or favorable to one party or the other?

11. Was any reliance placed upon representations of management? If so, what?

12. What assumptions were made in the report?

13. Are they set out explicitly anywhere? If not, why not?

6. *Factual Basis for the Report*

1. Where did the expert get his facts?
2. From independent inquiry or from what the party who had retained him told him?
3. Is it the norm to make an independent inquiry in the expert's profession?
4. Did the expert consider the possibility that the person giving the expert the information might not be reliable?
5. Might be biased?
6. Or interested in the outcome?
7. Or simply dishonest?
8. How much money is being sought here?
9. Did the expert consider that such an amount of money might cause people on either side of a dispute to misrepresent the facts?
10. If the expert's opinion is based, in whole or in part, upon information given him by a party, get the expert to acknowledge that, if the party has lied or is mistaken, his expert opinion or some portion of it is no longer valid or is less certain.
11. If some information the expert was given is provably false, confront the expert with it and see what effect he says it has on his testimony.

7. *Things Not Completed*

1. Has the expert completed his work on this project?
2. Is there anything else the expert contemplates doing?
3. Why wasn't it done before?
4. Get the expert and counsel to agree to provide you with the relevant documents when the additional work is done.
5. Does the expert intend to do additional work? Why? When? Is his opinion reliant upon those results?
6. Can those results change his opinion?

8. Things Not Done

1. Highlight tests or observations that your expert did, that the opposing expert did not do.
2. Why didn't the expert do those things?
3. Was the cost of this extra work the reason why it was not done?
4. Whose decision was it? The expert's, counsel's or the client's?
5. Was this discussed with any of them?
6. What did they say?
7. Was cost a component of the decision to not conduct these additional tasks?
8. Would conducting these additional tasks have added further strength to the report?
9. Could conducting these additional tasks change the conclusions?
10. Did the expert review depositions, interview individuals with knowledge, etc.? If not, why not?

9. The Substance of the Report

1. Go over the expert's report in detail, if necessary, sentence by sentence.
2. Ask what each key statement means and what it is backed up by.
3. Did the expert consider any other findings?
4. Break the expert's opinion up into its components. Thus, if the jury discredits one of the factual components, the whole opinion may collapse.
5. If the expert's opinion turns upon his or her judgment, ask the witness whether he or she could be wrong. If the expert says no, ask if the expert has ever been wrong in the past. If the expert says he or she has never been wrong, you can point out his arrogance to the jury in summation. If the expert says he or she has been wrong, you can argue to the jury later that, since the expert has been wrong before, the expert could be wrong now.

6. Are the conclusions reached in accordance with GAAP? GAS?
7. Possibly ask whether this is an issue upon which reasonable experts might disagree.

10. Learned Treatises

An expert can be impeached by being confronted with contrary statements in learned treatises and the like. Whether to impeach the witness with the treatise at the deposition is a tactical choice like other similar pieces of impeachment material. How important is at the time the deposition is taken to get the expert to adopt the position of the treatise? How much other impeachment material do you have?

1. Is the expert familiar with other experts in this field who have analyzed the type of issue the expert is opining on?
2. Has the expert looked at the approach that those experts used?
3. What treatises, etc., does the expert consider to be reliable?
4. Authoritative? If you get lucky, the expert will mention the treatise you are waiting to impeach the expert with.
5. Before showing the excerpt of a treatise to the expert, get the expert to acknowledge that the treatise etc is regarded an authoritative source.
6. Is the expert familiar with the treatise?
7. Has the expert used the treatise?
8. Is the treatise in the expert's library?

11. Agreement or Disagreement with Your Expert

One of the more useful things you can accomplish in the deposition of an expert witness is to narrow or eliminate the disagreements between the expert and your expert.

1. Does the expert have any dispute with your expert's qualifications or reputation?
2. Does the expert acknowledge the validity of the sources of information used by your expert? If not, what should your expert have relied upon?
3. On what points does the expert disagree with what your expert did?

4. Did the opposing expert have access to more information than your expert had?

5. Are there errors in your expert's methodology, results, conclusions, or opinions?

6. If so, what other experts would support your conclusions?

7. Would all experts agree with you?

8. Is this something on which reasonable experts in the field could disagree?

12. *Daubert Issues*

Until the Supreme Court's 1993 decision in Daubert v. Merrell Dow Pharmaceuticals, Inc., 509 U.S. 579, 593-95, 113 S.Ct. 2786, 2796 (1993), the principal test for the admissibility of expert proof was derived from Frye v. United States, 293 F. 1013, 1014 (D.C. Cir. 1923) and turned upon whether the "thing from which the deduction is made must be sufficiently established to have gained general acceptance in the particular field in which it belongs."

However, the Federal Rules of Evidence enacted a different standard. Pursuant to F.R.E. 702, to be admissible, expert testimony must be based upon "sufficient facts and data" and must be the result of "reliable principles and methods" and those principles and methods must have been reliably applied to the facts of the case. In Daubert, the Supreme Court held that F.R.E. 702 superseded Frye and imposed its own standard.[10] In Kumho Tire Co. v. Carmichael, 526 U.S. 137, 143 L. Ed. 2d 238, 119 S. Ct. 1167 (1999), the Court

10. Frye is far from dead. In New York, even after Daubert, the stricter Frye "general acceptance" test continued to be applied in cases where the issue was the reliability and admissibility of novel scientific evidence. See e.g., People v Wernick, 89 N.Y.2d 111, 115, 674 N.E.2d 322, 324, 651 N.Y.S.2d 392, 394 (1996); Zito v. Zabarsky, 28 A.D.3d 42, 812 N.Y. Supp 2d (2d Dep't 2006); Styles v. GMC, 20 A.D.3d 338,799 N.Y.S.2d 38 (1st Dep't 2005). Where, however, the evidence is not scientific or novel, the Frye analysis has not been applied. See People v Persuad, 244 A.D.2d 577, 665 N.Y.S.2d 671 (2d Dep't 1997), app. den. 91 N.Y.2d 976, 672 N.Y.S.2d 855 (1998); Wahl v. American Honda Motor Company, 181 Misc. 2d 396, 693 N.Y.S.2d 875 (Sup. Ct. Suffolk County 1999).

In Illinois, the "law is unequivocal: the exclusive test for the admission of expert testimony is governed by the standard first expressed" in Frye. Donaldson v. Cent. Ill. Pub. Serv. Co., 199 Ill. 2d 63, 77, 767 N.E.2d 314 (Ill. 2002) (rejecting "Frye-plus-reliability" standard); see also Agnew v. Shaw, 355 Ill. App. 3d 981, 823 N.E.2d 1046 (1st Dist. 2005)

held that the district court's Daubert gate keeping functions were applicable, not just to scientific proof, but to all forms of expert testimony.

Under Daubert, prime considerations include (1) whether the analysis can be and has been tested; (2) whether the analysis has been subjected to peer review and publication; (3) the known or potential error rate and existence of standards for control; and (4) whether the analysis has achieved general acceptance in the relevant scientific community. Daubert v. Merrell Dow Pharmaceuticals, Inc., 509 U.S. 579, 593-95, 113 S.Ct. 2786, 2796 (1993); Nimely v. City of New York, 414 F.3d 381 (2d Cir 2005); Amorgianos v. AMTRAK, 303 F.3d 256, 266 (2d Cir. 2002). Other pertinent considerations include (1) whether the testimonial theories grow naturally out of research by the expert independent of the litigation or, rather, have been developed expressly for the litigation; (2) whether the expert has unjustifiably extrapolated from accepted premises to unfounded conclusions; (3) whether obvious alternate explanations have been satisfactorily accounted for; (4) whether the expert has been as careful here as in his standard professional work outside of this testimony; and (5) whether the field of expertise claimed by the expert is known to reach reliable results for the type of opinion the expert seeks to give. Fed. R. Evid. 702 Advisory Committee's Notes (2000).

Where a court, in its duty as gatekeeper, concludes that proposed expert testimony fails to meet operative standards, the court is obliged to exclude the testimony, Amorgianos v. AMTRAK, 303 F.3d at 266, and can do so on summary judgment motion and without conducting a hearing. See Nelson v. Tennessee Gas Pipeline Co., 243 F.3d 244 (6th Cir.), cert. denied, 534 U.S. 822, 122 S.Ct. 56 (2001); United States v. Alatorre, 222 F.3d 1098 (9th Cir. 2000); Fayniarz v. Nike, Inc., 2002 U.S. Dist LEXIS 15825 (S.D.N.Y. 2003); Astra Aktiebolag v. Andrx Pharmaceuticals, Inc., 222 F.Supp.2d 423 (S.D.N.Y. 2002); Colon v. Bic USA, Inc., 199 F.Supp.2d 53, 70 (S.D.N.Y. 2001).

If the expert's testimony is sufficiently novel, you should use the deposition to develop the basis for a Daubert objection either on summary judgment or in an *in limine* motion.

1. Has the expert's method of analysis has been subjected to peer review and publication?

2. If not, why not?
3. If so, in what publications?
4. What was the substance of the peer commentary?
5. Was the theory greeted with support? How wide was the support?
6. Were there critics? Who? What did they say?
7. Is the expert currently preparing something for peer review publication?
8. Has the expert's method of analysis been used in any other case?
9. Does the expert contemplate using it anywhere else? If so, where?
10. Has it been used outside the judicial context?
11. Was the expert's method of analysis developed solely for this case?
12. Did the expert's method of analysis grow naturally out of research by the expert independent of the litigation?
13. Does the expert's method of analysis include subjective features? If so, what?
14. Can the expert's method of analysis be tested?
15. How would it be tested?
16. Did the expert do any testing before writing the report?
17. What is the known error rate?
18. How was this calculated?
19. What is the potential error rate?
20. How was this calculated?
21. What control standards exist?
22. Who designed them?
23. What safeguards are there against mistakes?
24. Are there any uncertainties in the expert's method of analysis?

25. Has the expert's method of analysis achieved general acceptance in the accounting field?

26. On what is that claim based?

PRE-TRIAL PREPARATION AND TRIAL

I. PLANNING FOR TRIAL

The work done in investigation and discovery provides the foundation for direct and cross–examination. What you failed to do earlier you may regret later.

A. Strategy

Accounting concepts are complex, and part of the attorney's job is to teach the jurors what they need to know and then show why that is relevant. You should consider well in advance of trial precisely what it is you want the jury to understand and precisely how you will educate the jury. These considerations will inform your tactical choices.

1. Tell the jurors in your opening that you will teach them all they will need to know to fairly decide the case but no more than that.

2. What exactly do the jurors need to know? Do they need to have a broad understanding of accounting principles or just enough to know that the other party has done wrong?

3. Do the jurors need to understand the accounting issues at the beginning of your case or can that evidence be saved for later?

4. Will you or your adversary go first? What is your adversary going to do?

5. Will your adversary try to educate the jury or to minimize the issues?

6. What will you do if your adversary goes first and confuses the jurors and the court? Do you wait until your case to clear things up?

7. How will you integrate your teaching into your whole case? Will you teach your concepts in the opening, the summation and through the witnesses?

8. How much of your case (or the principles you need the jury to understand) can you get in through your adversary's expert?

9. How much of your case (or the principles you need the jury to understand) was conceded by your adversary's expert at his or her deposition?

10. How much of the opposing expert's testimony can you get out of the case either through Daubert or an in limine motion?

11. What are the key areas of disagreement between your expert and your adversary's expert?

12. What approach will you take on cross against the opposing expert? Is the opposing expert personable and is the jury likely to resent attacks that are too harsh? Or is the opposing expert obnoxious and arrogant, so that the jury will enjoy seeking him or her taken down a peg. That will determine the approach of your cross.

13. Do want or need (and can you afford) to have your expert sit with you through the opposing expert's testimony with you?

B. Use of Trial Consultants

The use of jury consultants goes back to the "Harrisburg Seven" trial in 1971 and is increasingly common in large stakes cases where the parties have the financial resources.[11] Jury consultants have backgrounds (frequently at the Ph.D. level) in Sociology, Psychology and Statistics, as well as law degrees. The services which they provide go far beyond merely helping to select a jury and include: (1) surveying the community to ascertain community attitudes about the parties or key issues; (2) ascertaining jurors' concerns and attitudes through the use of focus groups or mock trials; (3) assisting in the preparation of witness testimony; (4) designing voir dire questions and/or jury questionnaires; (5) assisting in the actual selection of jurors; (6) providing "shadow" jurors; and (7) preparing, testing and coordinating trial graphics. Consultants also provide an objective assessment of the liability and potential damages in a case.

There is surprisingly little case law or even scholarly discussion as the extent to which communications between jury consultants, counsel and parties and witnesses are protected. In In re Cendant Corp. Sec. Litig., 343 F.3d 658 (3d Cir. 2003), the defendant had retained a jury consultant as a non-testifying expert on trial strategy and deposition practice. At the deposition, opposing counsel inquired into the substance of the communications between the witness and the expert and as to any documentation the witness had seen. The Special Master allowed inquiry into whether the witness had met with the consultant and the duration of that meeting, but held that inquiry into the substance of the communication and any documents were barred by the attorney client and work product privileges. The district court reversed the Special Master, holding that neither was applicable. On appeal, the Third Circuit reversed the district court, holding that the information was protected by work product privilege.[12] The Court reasoned that Rule 26(b)(3) "establishes two tiers of protection: first, work prepared in anticipation of litigation by an attorney or his agent is discoverable only upon a showing of need and hardship; second, 'core' or 'opinion' work product that encompasses the 'mental impressions, conclusions, opinion, or legal theories of an attorney or other representative of a party concerning the litigation'" is "generally afforded near absolute protection from discovery." Id. at 663. The interactions with the trial consultant would be discoverable only upon a "showing of rare and exceptional circumstances." Id. Thus, "litigation consultants retained to aid in witness preparation may qualify as non-attorneys who are protected by the work product doctrine." Id. The circuit court did however allow inquiry into whether the testimony had been rehearsed. Id. at 668.

---

11. For some of the literature addressing the use of jury or litigation consultants see: Comment: A Jury of Your Peers?: How Jury Consulting May Actually Help Trial Lawyers Resolve Constitutional Limitations Imposed on the Selection of Juries, 41 Cal. W. L. Rev. 479 (2005); Comment: A Process Right Due? Examining Whether A Capital Defendant Has A Due Process Right To A Jury Selection Expert, 53 Am. U.L. Rev. 1143 (2004); Note: Witness Preparation and the Trial Consulting Industry, 17 Geo. J. Legal Ethics 947 (2004); Ratcliff, Using Trial Consultants: What Practitioners Need To Know, 4 J. Legal Advoc. & Prac. 32 (2002); Yarbrough, The Jury Consultant - Friend or Foe of Justice, 54 S.M.U. L. Rev. 1885(2001); Bocchino, Robson and Solomon, What Juries Want To Hear II: Reverse Engineering the Verdict, 74 Temple L. Rev. 177 (2001); Bocchino and Solomon, What Juries Want to Hear: Methods for Developing Persuasive Case Theory, 67 Tenn. L. Rev. 543(2000); Kagehiro & Frediani, Do I Need Jury Research?, 223 N.Y.L.J. 7, at 1 (2000). Note: Twelve Carefully Selected Not So Angry Men: Are Jury Consultants Destroying the American Legal System?, 32 Suffolk U. L. Rev. 463 (1999); Strier, Essay: Paying The Piper: Proposed Reforms Of The Increasingly Bountiful But Controversial Profession Of Trial Consulting, 44 S.D. L. Rev. 699 (1998); Oliver, False Alarm: Can Trial Consultants Ruin Juries?, 18 Trial Dipl. J. 1 (1996); Greene, Does It Matter if it Doesn't Matter? An Appraisal of Mock Jury Research, 19 Trial Dipl. J. 13 (1996); Singer, Focusing On Jury Focus Groups, 19 Trial Dipl. J. 321 (1996); Genevie & Sebolt, Jury Consulting Assists Defense Counsel in Assisted Suicide Trail, Inside Litig. 19 (1994).

1. **Surveys**, particularly of community attitudes involving prominent individuals or hot button issues, are expensive and not necessarily reliable because of the possibility that they can be skewed by just a relatively small number of aberrant responses and because after after-occurring events may drastically change community attitudes (e.g., New Yorkers' attitudes towards Mayor Giuliani on September 12, 2001 as opposed to September 10, 2001).

2. This research can, however, be used to develop "hot questions" which will reveal attitudes of the real jurors.

3. Typically, jury consultants conduct "deliberation research" through the use of **focus groups and mock trials**. A focus group of 30 or more individuals likely to be similar to the jury pool is assembled. The simulated jurors are told how important their function is, and are required to sign a confidentiality agreement. The potential jurors are paid for their time, transported to the location where the focus group will take place and fed lunch. A focus group in the New York area will likely cost in the vicinity of $60,000 which includes two sessions with different groups of simulated jurors.

4. To give you a true reading, the deck should be stacked against you, i.e. evidentiary rulings which could go either way will be made against you; the other side's best case should be presented to the jury, and graphics which are at least as good as yours will be given to the "jurors."

5. Typically, either the lawyers or consultants will deliver "cloppenings" - a combination closing and opening - to the simulated jurors. The initial "cloppenings" are summaries of each sides' positions delivered with a minimum of rhetoric. The simulated jurors are then given instructions as to the law and "deliberate" to a verdict.

---

12. The court did not reach the attorney client privilege issue, although Judge Garth issued a concurring opinion expressing the view that the attorney-client privilege was implicated in communications between the witness, counsel and the trial consultant, Id. at 668; see also Davis & Beisecker, Discovering Trial Consultant Work Product: A New Way to Borrow An Adversary's Wits?, 17 Am. J. Trial Advoc. 581, 626-27 (1994).

6. The simulated jurors' fill out questionnaires, their "deliberations" are monitored, recorded and analyzed by the consultants[13] and used to identify "themes", successful and unsuccessful arguments, the jurors' hierarchy of case issues, juror questions and concerns, and facts which the lawyers think are legally insignificant but which are emotionally significant to real jurors. Trial graphics are also tried out and evaluated.

7. The data will disclose which types of jurors are likely to have prejudices (which they may not even be consciously aware of). The consultant will look to create general "profiles" of jurors with attitudes, experiences and beliefs adverse or receptive to your theory of the case.

8. "Losing" at the focus group is still valuable because it discloses your adversary's best themes and arguments.

9. After the first go around, the attorney's presentations are refined based on what was learned from the initial focus groups and the process is repeated before another set of simulated jurors. Language used by the simulated jurors will be used by counsel in the next presentation and before the real jurors. The second presentation is more likely to be predictive.

10. A "mock trial" is a more elaborate and time-consuming process with the actual witnesses. Since it is more realistic, it can be expected to be more predictive. It is also significantly more expensive and requires a significantly greater investment of attorney and witness time.

11. Based on their deliberation research, jury consultants will help prepare **jury voir dire questions** designed to elicit biases and which contain the hot questions and other questions which will plant the attorney's key case themes with the jury. In state court, the trial attorney will ask the questions. In federal court, the trial attorney submits the questions to the judge who then asks whatever questions the judge considers appropriate.

---

13. In some settings, the simulated jurors indicate their reactions electronically as the case is presented to them. This allows tracking of which portions of the presentation are the most effective.

12. Helping with the **<u>preparation of individual witness testimony</u>** is another task which can be performed by a jury consultant. This can be done by having the witness "testify" in front of a focus group of mock jurors whose comments are then analyzed.

13. The attorney has an ethical duty to insure that the jury consultant does not engage in witness preparation which would be unethical for the attorney. Under the Model Rules, <u>see</u> Model Rules 8.4. and 5.3, the lawyer can be held liable if a consultant violates Model Rule 3.4(b) which precludes an attorney from falsifying evidence or counseling a witness to testify falsely.

14. Careful thought must be given to using the jury consultant in this capacity because any improvement in the witness's performance can be wiped out if the jury discovers the extent of the preparation. Many lawyers will inquire in their cross as to how much time the witness spent preparing for his testimony and who helped prepare the witness. As noted above, the Third Circuit held in <u>Cendant</u>, 343 F.3d at 668, that the witness could be asked whether his testimony was "practiced or rehearsed."

15. Another task which jury consultants can perform is to prepare **<u>jury questionnaires</u>** for those cases where the court allows their use. The questions are phrased to elicit attitudes and prejudices. Assuming there is time, the consultant can input the data from these completed questionnaires and obtain an individual rating for each prospective juror. The consultant can then create a face sheet for each juror, which bears the overall rating and key comments about that person for use by the trial team during voir dire.

16. **<u>Helping with the actual selection</u>**. Jury consultants prefer to refer to this process as "deselection" – the elimination, one way or another, of unfavorable jurors, leaving neutral or favorable jurors. Jury consultants can also help to identify leaders and followers, as well as jurors, who particularly want to be on a jury because of some private agenda of their own.

17. Jury consultants help draft jury interrogatories or special verdict forms designed to lead the jurors to the proper analysis of the law and facts.

18. Jury consultants can also provide **<u>shadow jurors</u>** who have similar demographics to the actual jurors and who will attend the actual trial and provide their impressions daily to trial counsel. The trial team can then make adjustments to the presentation of its case.

19. Needless to say, the use of shadow jurors is quite expensive and risks alienating the actual jury if they catch on. In addition, interactions between shadow jurors and real jurors can create appellate issues. See e.g., Mercado v. Warner-Lambert Co., 106 S.W.3d 393 (Tex. Ct. App. 2003) (Court properly denied a request for a mistrial where shadow juror asked real juror for a cigarette and a quarter for a soft drink but did not discuss the case and the shadow juror did not know which party had retained him.)

C. Use of Graphics

Almost all jurors have grown up watching television and are used to taking in information visually and in short bites. Thus, visual presentations of demonstrative evidence are helpful ways of presenting complex concepts to the jurors. Graphics can be presented on boards, through PowerPoint slides or through sophisticated audio-visual techniques. They can be prepared by the lawyer, the expert, or by retained firms which provide courtroom graphics. Generally, you get what you pay for. Graphics can be used on opening, closing and direct testimony in a number of contexts. If focus groups or mock trials are conducted, the graphics should be tested out and adjusted based on the research findings. Courtroom technologists can also be retained to present the graphics smoothly.

Accounting testimony is an area where graphics will frequently be a good investment. The jurors will have to absorb new and difficult concepts and terms and apply them to numerous documents.

1. Graphics can be designed to show how a **process** works i.e., the human body, financial controls, construction techniques.

2. **Departures from accepted process** can also be shown after the proper process has been shown. Key bits of deposition or trial testimony can then be popped up to offer the opposing party's admissions or other damaging testimony.

3. **Definitions of relevant terms** can be put onto a board and possibly left in constant view of the jury so that they can use it for reference. Presumably, the parties should be able to agree on neutral definitions.

4. The organizational **table** of a complex entity can be shown either on a board or in a dynamic graphic, and you can then show where individuals are with respect to the entire organization and/or with respect to each other. It is also possible on the computer graphic to pop up pictures of the individuals.

5. Where a party is trying to establish causation through temporal proximity, a **time line** can be used either to prove or to disprove causation by showing intervening events or previous patterns of conduct.

6. **Reconstructions of events** can be prepared in accident cases or police shootings.

7. **Side by side comparisons of documents or testimony** can also be effective when the two versions are brought up together with the key sections highlighted.

8. It is also possible to show **contract expectations** and whether they have been met.

II. DIRECT AND REDIRECT EXAMINATION OF ACCOUNTANT FACT AND EXPERT WITNESSES

A. Witness Preparation

No witness should ever be put on the stand at trial without being thoroughly prepped in advance. The trial preparation should include a full run through of the specific questions which you expect to ask the witness on direct in the order in which you expect to ask the questions. The witness should be prepared for cross-examination by being given a nasty mock cross-examination which approximates your adversary's style. The witness should be asked misleading and improper questions so as to learn to recognize them.[14]

You should also prepare the witness not to be intimidated by the courtroom setting or by the presence of the judge. If possible, let the witness see the courtroom while it is empty. Most of the advice given to the witness in preparation for the deposition should be repeated with the following additions:

1. TELL THE TRUTH: [You can never say this too often to any witness you are putting on in any setting.]

2. Don't forget you are trying to explain things to a jury which knows nothing about the facts at issue and has none of your specialized knowledge.

3. Listen for objections, especially on cross. If your lawyer objects, say nothing until the court rules on the objection.

---

14. The preparation should, however, not be such as to intimidate your own witness.

4. Maintain eye contact with the fact finder (whether judge or jury). Turn in your chair to address them, look them in the eye as you answer the question, and then turn back to the questioner.

5. Keep in mind the purpose of your testimony. On cross-examination, you may be able to repeat your direct testimony if opposing counsel asks the wrong question.

6. Be prepared to use charts, diagrams, etc. If the witness will be using PowerPoint graphics, rehearse the presentation until it goes smoothly.

7. Show up dressed appropriately. Men should wear a business suit and tie. Women should wear appropriate business attire.

8. If asked whether you have discussed the case with anyone, the answer, of course, is that you have discussed the case with the lawyer and probably others. If asked what the lawyer told you to say, reply that he told you to tell the truth (assuming that he did).

9. Don't get rushed because there is a pause in the proceedings and everyone in the courtroom is looking at you as you review evidence. If you need to read all of a lengthy document, read it all, no matter how long it takes. Don't be afraid to tell the judge you need time. The judge will probably give the jurors a break.

10. Always be respectful to everyone. Refer to others as "Mr." or "Ms." or by their title. Don't become hostile toward opposing counsel or the Court.

11. Stick to the themes of your testimony. Where appropriate, incorporate those themes into your answer on cross.

B. Direct and Redirect Examination of Accountant Fact Witnesses

1. Order of Witnesses

Accounting testimony will rarely be riveting. Thus, you should give thought to where you want to put the testimony in the presentation of your case. Are the accounting issues at the core of the case or important but relatively peripheral? Do the jurors need to learn it early in the case?

1. Plan the order of your witnesses. Ideally, you want to start and end your case with strong witnesses. However, you will find, particularly in long and complex cases, that witnesses are not available when you want them, so you have to adapt.

2. Don't start or end a day with a weak witness.

3. If your case is complex, then try to present factually related witnesses together to make it easier for the jury to follow.

4. If you have a number of witnesses who will be telling emotional stories, spread them out through the trial. Use them to breakup technical or boring testimony.

5. If possible, couple testimony from the accounting expert who explains what was done wrong with a fact witness (e.g., a shareholder or pensioner) who can personalize the consequences of the wrongdoing.

6. If your witness will be testifying to something which will surprise your adversary, schedule the testimony, so that your adversary will have less time to respond to it. (i.e., Don't introduce it late on Friday afternoon.)

7. If possible, have witnesses testify to events in chronological order.

8. Ask the court to apply the "rule on witnesses", and to exclude witnesses from hearing testimony. <u>See</u> F.R.E. 615. However, both sides will be able to keep their expert in the courtroom to help with cross examination.

2. Techniques for the Presentation of Testimony on Direct Examination

1. Avoid leading – Use the phrase "Tell the jury, what, if anything, happened then?" Get into the habit of <u>not</u> asking leading questions on direct, even where you can get away with it.

2. Leading questions, <u>see</u> F.R.E. 611(c), can be used:

   a. To elicit preliminary matters;

   b. To elicit non-controversial or undisputed facts;

   c. To elicit inconsequential facts;

   d. To switch to a new topic: "Directing your attention to. . . ."; "Did there come a time when. . .?";

   e. With a hostile witness or a witness called by your adversary. This can include your own client if called as a witness by your adversary;

f. When the witness has difficulty in speaking due to some physical or psychological problem;

g. To contradict statements made by another witness, e.g., "Mr. Smith has said you sought a bribe from him. Is that true?";

h. To refresh a witness's recollection.

3. With fact witnesses, generally use the "double direct" technique as opposed to narrative. Ask the witness a general question which will elicit the general story, then back up and go over the details of the story. Your questions can themselves repeat the story: "Directing you attention back to the point where the plaintiff offered you a bribe, was anyone else present?"

4. The best order for the testimony of a fact witness on direct is usually to elicit positive pedigree facts about the witness, a description of the relevant organizational facts and the witness's role, followed by a chronological statement of events. Try to start and end strong.

5. Humanize your witnesses, whether fact or expert. Elicit the witness's background, family history, education, and professional accomplishments. You want the jury to see the witness as a human being. Look for facts which will either impress the jurors and/or which, will enable the jurors to empathize with the witness.

6. Keep an eye on the clock. Pick strategic portions in the testimony for breaks, lunch, and end of day and end of week. Try to leave the jury something to think about at each break.

7. If a witness can't answer a question on cross with a yes/no answer, then the witness should say that he can't. On redirect, ask him to explain why he could not.

3. Qualifying the Expert to Testify

1. An expert can draw expert conclusions only if the Court certifies the witness as an expert.

2. The party opposing qualifying the witness can ask for a voir dire, which is an open court hearing in front of the jury on the expert's qualifications. Your witness should be prepared for this.

3. The voir dire examination can be used to keep the witness from being qualified (which will rarely be successful), or to limit the effect of his testimony by: a) showing that the witness is not expert in certain areas (where your expert will testify); or b) by getting the witness to acknowledge your witness as more pre-eminent.

4. Usually, the real purpose for voir dire examination is not so much to exclude the expert but to get in some early cross and to undermine the expert before the expert even gives substantive testimony.

5. If an expert is unquestionably qualified, you may consent to his being qualified and offer to waive the testimony as to his qualifications. This may prevent the jury from being impressed by the expert. Don't consent to this with your expert unless he is only marginally qualified.

4. Presentation of Expert Testimony

1. Bring out the details of a witness's pedigree which are helpful to your case or to which a particular juror may relate.

2. Establish how many times the expert has performed the tasks at issue. (How many similar audits has he performed or supervised?)

3. How many times has the expert been qualified as an expert in court? In which courts? On which issues?

4. If the witness testifies for both plaintiffs and defendants, bring that out.

5. Get the expert to speak in non technical terms. Make sure your witness does not condescend to the jury.

6. Generally bring out on direct that the expert is being paid for his time and the amount. (Whatever it is, the amount will seem large to the jurors).

7. Encourage the expert to bring visual aids, slides, charts, models, etc.

8. Hypothetical questions can be asked on direct or cross. This may be the one area where you should write out and read your questions.

9. Mark for ID, and read into the record important passages in critical supporting articles. Then ask expert to explain what the language means.

10. Get your expert to explain the relevant general principles to the jury and then deliver his opinion broken down into bite-sized pieces.

III. CROSS EXAMINATION OF ACCOUNTANT FACT AND EXPERT WITNESSES

A. Cross-Examination of a Fact Witness

Cross-examination is probably the hardest thing for a lawyer to do well. It requires not only a knowledge of the law applicable to the case, but a complete knowledge of the facts, knowledge of human psychology, a good sense of theatre, an ability to think under pressure, and hopefully a sense of humor. It is the study of a lifetime, and the more you do it, the better you will get. That being said, self-confidence is probably half the battle.

The late Irving Younger promulgated the "Ten Commandments of Cross-Examination." These commandments have all been violated almost as many times as the Commandments announced by Moses. Nonetheless, they provide a good set of guidelines:

I BE BRIEF. Younger believes that you should never make more than three points about a witness' credibility.

II SHORT QUESTIONS, PLAIN WORDS. Don't use legalese or technical terms if they can be avoided.

III NEVER ASK ANYTHING BUT LEADING QUESTIONS.

IV ASK ONLY QUESTIONS TO WHICH YOU ALREADY KNOW THE ANSWER.

V LISTEN TO THE ANSWER.

VI DON'T ARGUE WITH THE WITNESS.

VII DON'T PERMIT A WITNESS ON CROSS-EXAMINATION TO SIMPLY REPEAT HIS DIRECT TESTIMONY.

VIII DON'T LET THE WITNESS EXPLAIN.

IX AVOID ASKING ONE QUESTION TOO MANY.

X SAVE IT FOR SUMMATION.

There are, however, many other considerations and techniques:

1. Decide whether a fact witness is a liar or simply mistaken, and conduct your cross accordingly. If someone is mistaken, your manner of approach should be fairly gentle. You are trying to get the witness to admit to some doubt about whether they are correct. A hostile cross-examination will probably make the witness stick more closely to his or her story and may backfire with a jury who thinks the witness is trying to be truthful.

2. Different styles may be applicable to different witnesses - sledgehammer or "velvet dagger" - "death of a thousand cuts."

3. DON'T READ YOUR QUESTIONS. Engage in a dialogue which you control through leading questions. Work from notes which remind you of the areas you want to hit in your examination but don't read the questions.

4. Ideally, all questions in a cross-examination should be answered yes or no.

5. If witness answers a yes-no question by going beyond yes or no, move to strike the extra material as non-responsive. Keep doing this as long as necessary.

6. Don't ask your questions in a monotone. Use your voice, inflection, and body language to convey your feelings. Act bewildered or angry depending upon what seems appropriate. Roll your eyes or shake your head subtly.

7. Don't be afraid to break the rules if you know what you are doing or are completely desperate.

8. Begin and end strongly if possible.

9. Draw out the best impeachment with multiple questions.

10. Proceed in a logical order that the jury will be able to follow.

11. Do not ask a witness questions which begin "Do you remember______?" unless you are really testing their recollection. Virtually all questions should be posed as statements e.g., "Isn't it a fact that _____?" Similarly, don't phrase the question as "I assume. . ."

12. Do not ask a witness to "explain" or ask a witness "why." Don't allow a witness to "explain." (The only possible exception to this rule is "when you know the witness cannot possibly give a good explanation." Asking the question is still living dangerously.)

13. If you have depositions, you will be reading for impeachment, copy the key section and tape or electronically paste it into your notes. This way you don't have to look for it.

14. Always try to get a hostile witness to adopt as much of your story as you can. However, questioning designed to elicit admissions should precede questions designed to discredit the witness.

15. If the witness is testifying differently on a particular point than another plaintiff's witness, emphasize that discrepancy. Ask the witness if the other version is incorrect or even a lie. "If someone else testified to that version of events, would that person be wrong [be lying]?" You cannot, however, impeach one witness with another's deposition testimony.

16. If a witness is being evasive, ask the court to direct him to answer and keep trying the same question until you get an answer. Presumably the evasiveness will become evident to the jury.

17. **Prior Inconsistent Statements**. Witnesses can be impeached for prior inconsistent statements. See F.R.E. 801(d) (1); C.P.L.R. R. 4514. To find those inconsistent statements, you must compare the witness' previous statement in a deposition, complaint or correspondence on the same topic.

    Impeachment by prior inconsistent statement must be done properly. First, wed the witness to his present testimony. "Are you sure that __________?" "There is no doubt in your mind that _______?" "The rest of your testimony is as true and accurate as this statement?" You can also ask "And you want this jury to believe you when you say happened? And you want this jury to give you a large sum of money based on this having happened?" Next, get the witness to say that any different statement would be "false" or even a "lie." Then, ask the witness whether he ever gave a different version. After he answers that he did not, then confront him with his previous answer. First, you should get him to acknowledge he was under oath when he was questioned previously[15]:

"Q: You testified at my office on _________?

A: Yes.

Q: And your lawyer Mr. Jones was present the whole time?

A: Yes.

Q: And you had an opportunity to consult with him?

A: Yes.

Q. And he sat next to you during the deposition?

A: Yes.

Q: And you were under oath to tell the truth?

A: Yes.

Q: The same oath you took before this jury?

A: Yes.

Q: And a court reporter was present to take down the questions you were asked and the answers you gave?

A: Yes.

Q. In the same way that a court reporter is present here today to down the questions you are asked and the answers you give?

A: Yes.

Q. And your testimony was put in the form of a book like the one I am holding now?

A: Yes.

Q. And you were given it by your attorney and asked to read it?

A: Yes.

Q: And you had a chance later to make corrections in the testimony that you gave on ________?

A: Yes.

---

15. If the witness was not under oath, then get the witness to acknowledge that circumstances under which the statement was made were such that he should have told the truth (e.g., police statement, insurance claim, claim against the government.)

Q: And you corrected anything that was incorrect?

A: Yes.

Q. And you signed your name on the correction sheets?

A. Yes.

Q. And you swore again to the truth of the statements made in your deposition?

A. Yes.

Then to impeach the witness correctly, you must cite the page and line of the testimony and read the testimony back in Q and A form.

Q "Isn't it a fact that you were asked the following questions and gave the following answers at page ___, line______?

Q. "What color was the light?"

A. "Red."

Q. "Did you give those answers to those questions then?"

A. Yes.

When the witness concedes giving those answers at his deposition, you then ask which testimony is correct, the previous testimony or the testimony he just gave the jury. If the witness says that the previous testimony was correct, then ask the witness: "So your present testimony was unreliable [incorrect] [a lie] [a mistake]?" Ask the witness whether there is anything else in his present recollection that is incorrect [that he is unsure of]. Use phrases like: "You are telling this jury now ______" or "It is your present testimony [your testimony today] that _______."

If the witness says that his present testimony is correct and the earlier testimony is wrong, then the classical follow-up is:

Q. So your recollection of these events is better today than it was ______ years ago?

A. Yes.

If you have more prior inconsistent statements, then follow more or less the same procedure. The exact way in which you proceed depends upon whether you want to suggest that the witness is merely mistaken and unreliable or is lying. If you want to suggest that the witness is merely unreliable, you can ask (gently):

> Q. So, you really aren't too sure what happened, are you? [Your recollection isn't really completely accurate? You might be wrong?]

Alternatively, you can ask (angrily):

> Q. Isn't it a fact that you just made up this explanation and you can't keep your lies straight?

The tone of the questions is important. If you want to suggest that the witness is all mixed up, your tone should become increasingly pitying that the witness is such a dolt. Conversely, you can become increasingly angry at the witness' attempts to fool the jury. A combination of the two techniques might be that you show disdainful contempt that the witness is such a bad liar. Other variations are, of course, available.

18. **Interest**. If the accountant witness stands to gain or lose, directly or indirectly, from the result in the action, then the witness can be impeached for interest. Thus, with a corporation, determine whether the witness will obtain any of the proceeds of the recovery by way of bonuses. Alternatively, if the action threatens the continuing existence of the corporation, it may also threaten the witness' job or income.

19. **Bias**. You can always impeach a witness by showing bias for or against a party. You will not get a witness to admit that he or she is lying, so the point of this is to suggest it to the jury in summation. If the accountant witness has strong ties (family, business, personal) to the entity on whose behalf he or she is testifying, you can suggest bias.

B. Cross-Examination of an Expert Witness

The cross-examination of the accounting expert will be built principally on the information obtained through investigation and discovery and any statements made at the expert's deposition.

1. Update the searches done prior to the deposition to find out if there have been subsequent developments.

2. Look at the information obtained in investigation and the statements made at the deposition to see what can be used for impeachment.

3. Plan the cross out with your expert.

4. Determine what lines of cross were successful in other proceedings.

5. Bear in mind that experts can also be cross-examined in the same manner as other witnesses. Thus, evidence which would effect the credibility of a non-expert witness may be admissible.

6. Ask whether the witness' opinion is based upon information given him by the plaintiff. If the expert answers yes, then get him to acknowledge that, if the plaintiff has lied or is mistaken, his expert opinion is no longer valid.

7. Bring out factors which the expert was not told, did not consider or did not investigate carefully and ascertain whether those factors might change the expert's opinion.

8. Possibly ask whether this is an issue upon which reasonable accountants or auditors might disagree.

9. Break the expert's opinion up into its components. Thus, if one of the factual components is discredited by the jury, the whole opinion may collapse.

10. If the expert's opinion turns upon his judgment, ask the witness whether he could be wrong. If he says no, ask him if he has ever been wrong in the past. If he says he has never been wrong, stop and point out his arrogance to the jury in summation. If he says he has been wrong, save it for summation and argue that, since he has been wrong before, he could be wrong now.

11. Listen carefully to your adversary's hypothetical questions to see if they contain facts not proven or invalid assumptions.

12. Highlight tests or observations that your expert did, that the opposing expert did not do.

13. See if you can get the expert to criticize some aspect of the plaintiff's performance or conduct.

NOTES

10

ETHICAL ISSUES AND FINANCIAL DATA

Daniel J. Leffell

Paul, Weiss, Rifkind, Wharton & Garrison LLP

I. WHO IS COVERED?

A. Section 307, 15 U.S.C. § 7245: Rules of Professional Responsibility for Attorneys

"minimum standards of professional conduct for attorneys appearing and practicing before the Commission in any way in the representation of issuers"

— report evidence of a material violation to the chief legal counsel or the chief executive officer of the company

— report the evidence to the audit committee, another independent committee or the board of directors

B. "Appearing and Practicing Before the Commission"

17 C.F.R. § 205.2 (a)(1):

— Transacting any business with the Commission. . .

— Representing an issuer in an SEC proceeding, investigation, inquiry, information request, or subpoena

— Providing advice in respect of the securities laws or SEC rules regarding any document that. . .will be filed with. . . .the SEC

— Advising an issuer as to whether information. . .is required under the securities laws or SEC rules to be filed with. . .the SEC

17 C.F.R. § 205.3 (b)(5):

— An attorney retained or directed by an issuer to investigate evidence of a material violation reported under [these rules] shall be deemed to be appearing and practicing before the Commission.

II. WHAT IS REQUIRED?

A. Duty to Report Evidence of a Material Violation (17 C.F.R. § 205.3 (b))

(1) Attorney who "becomes aware of evidence of a material violation" must "report such evidence to the issuer's chief legal officer. . .or to both the issuer's chief legal officer and its chief executive officer. . .forthwith. . ."

(2) CLO "shall cause such inquiry. . .as he or she reasonably believes is appropriate"

If CLO determines there is no material violation, CLO must advise the reporting attorney of the basis for the determination

Otherwise, CLO must

(A) Take all reasonable steps to cause the issuer to adopt an appropriate response, and "advise the reporting attorney thereof"

or

(B) Refer the report to a qualified legal compliance committee

B. "Material Violation" (17 C.F.R. § 205.2 (i))

"a material violation of an applicable United States federal or state securities law, a material breach of fiduciary duty arising under United States federal or state law, or a similar material violation of any United States federal or state law"

C. "Evidence of a Material Violation" (17 C.F.R. § 205.2 (e))

"credible evidence, based upon which it would be <u>un</u>reasonable, under the circumstances, for a prudent and competent attorney <u>not</u> to conclude that it is reasonably likely that a material violation has occurred, is ongoing, or is about to occur"

D. "Up the Ladder" (17 C.F.R. § 205.3 (b))

(3) "Unless an attorney. . .reasonably believes that the chief legal officer or the chief executive officer of the issuer. . .has provided an appropriate response within a reasonable time, the attorney shall report the evidence of a material violation to:

— "(i) The audit committee. . .;

— "(ii) Another committee. . . consisting solely of directors who are not employed, directly or indirectly, by the issuer. . .;

or

— "(iii) The issuer's board of directors [if there is no committee of independent directors]"

E. "Appropriate Response" (17 C.F.R. § 205.2 (b))

The attorney reasonably believes that:

— (1) There is no material violation

— (2) The issuer has adopted appropriate remedial measures

or

4

— (3) The issuer has retained or directed an attorney to review the reported evidence. . .and either

(i) Has substantially implemented any remedial recommendations. . .

or

(ii) Has been advised that such attorney may. . .assert a colorable defense

F. Attorney's Response (17 C.F.R. § 205.3 (b)(9))

> An attorney who does not reasonably believe that the issuer has made an appropriate response within a reasonable time. . .shall explain his or her reasons therefor to the chief legal officer. . ., the chief executive officer. . .), and directors to whom the attorney reported the evidence of a material violation. . .

G. Futility (7 C.F.R. § 205.3 (b)(4))

> If an attorney reasonably believes that it would be futile to report evidence of a material violation to the issuer's chief legal officer and chief executive officer. . .the attorney may report such evidence [to the audit committee]

III. ALTERNATIVE REPORTING PROCEDURES (17 C.F.R. § 205.3(c))

A. Procedures Apply to Attorneys for an Issuer with a Qualified Legal Compliance Committee

(1) Attorney may, as an alternative to the reporting requirements of paragraph (b), report such evidence to a qualified legal compliance committee

(2) CLO may refer a report to a previously established qualified legal compliance committee in lieu of causing an inquiry to be conducted

B. Qualified Legal Compliance Committee (7 C.F.R. § 205.2(k))

(1) At least one member of the audit committee and two or more independent directors

(2) Written procedures

(3) Authority and responsibility

— (i) To inform the CLO & CEO of any report of evidence of a material violation

— (ii) To determine whether an investigation is necessary. . .and, if it determines an investigation is necessary or appropriate, to:

(A) Notify the audit committee or the full board of directors;

(B) Initiate an investigation, which may be conducted either by the chief legal officer (or the equivalent thereof) or by outside attorneys;

and

(C) Retain such additional expert personnel as the committee deems necessary

— (iii) At the conclusion of any such investigation, to:

(A) Recommend. . .that the issuer implement an appropriate response to evidence of a material violation;

and

(B) Inform the CLO, CEO and board of directors of the results of any such investigation and the appropriate remedial measures to be adopted

IV. EXCEPTIONS TO DUTY TO REPORT

A. 17 C.F.R. § 205.3 (b)(6)

No duty to report if:

— (i) Attorney was retained or directed to investigate

and

(A) Attorney reports the results of the investigation to the CLO

and

(B) CLO reports the results of the investigation to the board of directors

or

— (ii) Attorney was retained or directed to assert a colorable defense, and CLO provides reasonable and timely reports on such proceeding to the board of directors. . .

B. 17 C.F.R. § 205.3 (b)(7)

No duty to report if the attorney was retained or directed by a qualified legal compliance committee:

— (i) To investigate such evidence of a material violation;

or

— (ii) To assert. . .a colorable defense. . .in any investigation or. . . proceeding relating to such evidence of a material violation.

V. ISSUER CONFIDENCES (17 C.F.R. § 205.3(d))

A. Reports Under Sarbanes-Oxley

(1) "Any report under this section (or the contemporaneous record thereof) or any response thereto (or the contemporaneous record thereof) may be used by an attorney in connection with any investigation, proceeding, or litigation in which the attorney's compliance with this part is in issue."

B. Disclosure to SEC

(2) Attorney <u>may reveal</u> to the SEC, without the issuer's consent, confidential information to the extent the attorney reasonably believes necessary:

— (i) To prevent a material violation likely to cause substantial injury to the financial interest or property of the issuer or investors;

— (ii) To prevent the issuer, in a Commission investigation or administrative proceeding from committing perjury. .

or

— (iii) To rectify consequences of a material violation that caused, or may cause, substantial injury to the financial interest or property of the issuer or investors in the furtherance of which the attorney's services were used.

VI. SANCTIONS AND DISCIPLINE (17 C.F.R. § 205.6)

— civil penalties and remedies for a violation of the federal securities laws available to the Commission in an action brought by the Commission thereunder

— an administrative disciplinary proceeding initiated by the SEC with possibility of censure or temporary permanent bar against appearing or practicing before the Commission

— An attorney who complies in good faith is not subject to discipline or liable under inconsistent standards

— An attorney practicing outside the US is not required to comply to the extent prohibited by foreign law

VII. NOISY WITHDRAWAL

Initially Proposed Section 205.3(d):

(1) Where an attorney. . .does not receive an appropriate response, or has not received a response in a reasonable time, to his or her report, and the attorney reasonably believes that a material violation is ongoing or is about to occur and is likely to result in substantial injury to the financial interest or property of the issuer or of investors:

— (i) An attorney retained by the issuer shall:

(A) Withdraw forthwith from representing the issuer, indicating that the withdrawal is based on professional considerations;

(B) Within one business day of withdrawing, give written notice to the Commission of the attorney's withdrawal, indicating that the withdrawal was based on professional considerations;

and

(C) Promptly disaffirm to the Commission any opinion, document, affirmation, representation, characterization, or the like in a document filed with or submitted to the Commission, or incorporated into such a document, that the attorney has prepared or assisted in preparing and that the attorney reasonably believes is or may be materially false or misleading;

— (ii) An attorney employed by the issuer <u>shall</u>:

(A) Within one business day, notify the Commission in writing that he or she intends to disaffirm some opinion, document, affirmation, representation, characterization, or the like in a document filed with or submitted to the Commission,. . .that the attorney has prepared or assisted in preparing and that the attorney reasonably believes is or may be materially false or misleading; and

(B) Promptly disaffirm to the Commission, in writing, any such opinion, document, affirmation, representation, characterization, or the like

— (iii) The issuer's chief legal officer. . .<u>shall</u> inform any attorney retained or employed to replace the attorney who has withdrawn that the previous attorney's withdrawal was based on professional considerations.

(2) Where an attorney. . .does not receive an appropriate response, or has not received a response in a reasonable time,. . .and the attorney reasonably believes that a material violation has occurred and is likely to have resulted in substantial injury to the financial interest or property of the issuer or of investors but is <u>not ongoing</u>:

— (i) An attorney retained by the issuer <u>may</u> [take all the steps specified in Section 205.3(d)(1)]

— (ii) An attorney employed by the issuer <u>may</u> [take all the steps specified in Section 205.3(d)(1)]

— (iii) The issuer's chief legal officer. . .<u>shall</u> inform any attorney retained or employed to replace the attorney who has so withdrawn that the previous attorney's withdrawal was based on professional considerations.

(3) The notification to the Commission prescribed by this paragraph (d) <u>does not breach the attorney-client privilege</u>.

NOTES

11

ETHICAL ISSUES AT THE INTERSECTION OF LAW AND ACCOUNTING

Lori Lynn Phillips

Heller Ehrman LLP

In cases and investigations involving accounting issues, lawyers should be mindful of not just their own ethical obligations, but also the ethical rules applicable to accountants. Whether the accountants are witnesses, the client, or the opposing party, lawyers will benefit from an understanding of the rules of professional conduct governing the accounting profession. This outline provides a brief overview of ethical issues that may arise at the intersection of law and accounting.

I. DOCUMENTS RELATING TO ACCOUNTING ISSUES IN INVESTIGATIONS AND LITIGATION

A. Preservation of Accounting Documents

In many cases, accounting documents are crucial evidence. Damages analysis and forensic accounting procedures often depend on careful preservation of company financial information, and electronic information is rarely static as the company continues to operate its business. Accordingly, at the outset of any litigation or investigation, or when litigation is reasonably anticipated, attorneys should ensure that the client preserves all potentially relevant documents — in particular, electronic documents that could be altered easily, either intentionally or unintentionally. Hon. Lee H. Rosenthal, *A Few Thoughts On Electronic Discovery After December 1, 2006*, 116 Yale L.J. Pocket Part 167 (Nov. 30, 2006) ("Although the Civil Rules do not define preservation obligations — statute, regulation, or common law supplies the substantive standards — the rules recognize that applying preservation obligations to electronically stored information is uncertain and risky."). Counsel should interview IT personnel and accounting staff promptly regarding computerized information and consider engaging an electronic discovery consultant at the earliest stage of any proceeding or investigation.

B. Auditors' Workpapers

Accountants' workpapers are often important evidence in investigations and litigation involving financial and/or accounting issues. The SEC defines workpapers as "documentation of auditing or review procedures applied, evidence obtained, and conclusions reached by the accountant in the audit or review engagement, as required by standards established or adopted by the Commission or by the Public Company Accounting Oversight Board." 17 CFR § 210.2-06(b). California law defines them as "the licensee's records of the procedures applied, the tests performed, the information obtained and the pertinent conclusions reached in an audit, review, compilation, tax, special report or other engagement." Cal. Code Regs. tit. 16, § 68.1(a). "Audit documentation shall include, but is not limited to, programs, analyses, memoranda, letters of confirmation and representation, copies or abstracts of company documents, and schedules or commentaries prepared or obtained by the licensee." Cal. Bus. & Prof. Code § 5097(a).

Workpapers may shed light on the scope of the accountants' engagement (engagement letters, continuance materials, opinion letters), the work performed (planning memos, engagement checklists, status memos), and the nature and quality of the accountant-client relationship (permanent file, management representation letters, documents provided to accountants for testing, notes of client interviews, client questionnaires). They provide contemporaneous evidence of the client's financial circumstances, which can be key evidence in cases where the audit client's solvency is in question. They may also reflect communications from the audit client that could be relevant to investigations of potential fraud.

- **Auditors' Duty to Preserve Workpapers:** Auditors for publicly traded companies are required by SEC regulation to retain workpapers for seven years. 17 CFR § 210.2-06(a). California law (and the law in most other states) similarly imposes a minimum seven-year retention period on auditors. *See* Cal. Bus. & Prof. Code § 5097(e). This does not mean that the auditor must retain a copy of every piece of paper that was reviewed by the audit team. Rather, the auditor is required to preserve "records relevant to the audit or review, including workpapers and other documents that form the basis of the audit or review, and memoranda, correspondence, communications, other documents, and records (including electronic records), which: (1) Are created, sent or received in connection with the audit or review, and (2) Contain conclusions, opinions, analyses, or financial data related to the audit or review." 17 CFR § 210.2-06(a).
- **Access to Workpapers:** The workpapers belong to the auditor, not the audit client. An audit client's right to access workpapers is determined by state law. *See, e.g.*, Ariz. Rev. Stat. § 32-744, -749; Cal. Code Regs. tit. 16, § 68; Fla. Stat. § 473.318; N.J. Stat. § 45:2B-66; Wash. Rev. Code § 18.04.390.

- **Prohibition on Disclosure of Confidential Information:** Accountants are typically prohibited by law from disclosing their clients' confidential information. *See, e.g.*, 26 U.S.C. § 7216 (tax preparer who knowingly or recklessly discloses information provided for preparation of a return may be charged with a misdemeanor); Cal. Code Regs. tit. 16, § 54.1 (with certain limited exceptions, prohibiting disclosure of confidential information obtained by a licensee in his or her professional capacity). Accordingly, without the client's express permission, accountants usually should not release confidential information regarding their clients without a subpoena.

II. WITNESSES

A. Percipient Witnesses

- **If the witness wishes to be compensated, do not agree to pay more than the witness's usual hourly rate:** Accountants who are asked to provide testimony as percipient witnesses may ask to be compensated for their time. In some engagements, auditors may insist that the engagement letter include a clause providing for such compensation if they are required to provide testimony relating to their audit work. If the witness is to give testimony, it is important to avoid the appearance that the witness is being paid for his or her testimony. Accordingly, they should be paid for their time at their standard hourly rate and no more.

B. Expert Witnesses

Any litigation involving financial or accounting issues is almost certain to involve accounting experts. Accounting experts can assist counsel in understanding accounting issues, interpreting workpapers and other technical documents, identifying and describing relevant professional standards, ascertaining potential failures by a company's accounting personnel and outside accountants, analyzing damages, proving fraud, and generally assisting counsel in preparing the client's case. Testifying experts may also be critical to presenting accounting issues to a judge or jury. Counsel should bear in mind the following considerations:

- **As with any expert, assure that your expert's opinion meets Daubert standards:** Be sure the individual's credentials are current and his or her experience pertinent. *See, e.g.*, *Seatrax, Inc. v. Seabock Int'l, Inc.*, 200 F.3d 358, 371 (5th Cir. 2000) (affirming district court's finding that plaintiff's accounting expert was unqualified).

- **Before questioning an expert on accounting issues, determine whether the expert's opinion complies with the applicable standards of professional conduct.** Because juries often find it difficult to understand complex issues of accounting, which may come down to a "battle of the experts," jurors may be significantly influenced by their perception of the integrity of the witness. If the opposing party can point to ethical transgressions — even relatively minor ones such as improper use of the "CPA" credential while on inactive status or failure to complete all Continuing Professional Education standards — the expert's credibility can be called into question.

- **Be careful to keep separate the role of testifying experts and consulting experts on accounting issues.** *See, e.g.*, *Trigon Ins. Co. v. United States*, 204 F.R.D. 277 (E.D. Va. 2001) (allowing discovery from consulting experts where owner of consulting firm was designated as testifying expert and consulting firm appeared to have "ghost written" report of testifying expert).

III. PRIVILEGE ISSUES

A. Accountant-Client Privileges

A number of states have recognized an accountant-client privilege, and some of those have expressly extended the privilege to independent auditors on theories that suggest that sharing information with an auditor who can be considered to carry common interests with the client does not constitute waiver. *See*, *e.g.*, Colo. Rev. Stat. § 13-90-107(1)(f); 225 Ill. Comp. Stat. 450/27; Md. Code Ann., Cts. & Jud. Proc. § 9-110; Mich. Comp. Laws § 339.713; Nev. Rev. Stat. § 49.185, .205; N.M. Stat. § 38-6-6. Several other states recognize an accountant-client privilege in some form. *See*, *e.g.*, Ariz. Rev. Stat. § 32-749; Fla. Stat. § 473.316; Ga. Code § 43-3-32; Idaho Code § 9-203A; Ind. Code §§ 25-2.1-14-1 to 14-2; Mo. Rev. Stat. § 326.151; 63 Pa. Cons. Stat. § 9.11a; Tenn. Code. § 62-1-116. The federal courts and most other states have not recognized an accountant-client privilege.

B. Attorney-Client Privilege and the Common Interest Doctrine: Disclosures to Auditors and Government Enforcement Agencies

Particularly in states where no accountant-client privilege applies, attorneys should be careful about sharing confidential client information with accountants. Unless the accountants have been retained to assist the attorneys in litigation, the disclosure could be deemed a waiver of the privilege.

- *See*, *e.g.*, *Gutter v. E.I. DuPont De Nemours & Co.*, No. 95-CV-2152, 1998 WL 2017926, at *3 (S.D. Fla. May 18, 1998) ("disclosure to outside auditors may waive the attorney-client privilege").
- *United States v. Kovel*, 296 F.2d 918 (2d Cir. 1961) (extending attorney-client privilege to accountants retained to assist attorneys).

In the wake of major corporate scandals and the passage of Sarbanes-Oxley, the relationships between auditors and clients changed. Under increasing pressure from the SEC and PCAOB, auditors have had to seek a wider range of documentation and information from clients in conducting their audits, including documentation of the results of internal investigations. *See*, *e.g.*, SEC Deputy Chief Accountant Scott A. Taub, Remarks at the University of Southern California Leventhal School of Accounting SEC and Financial Reporting Conference (May 27, 2004) (transcript available at http://www.sec.gov/news/speech/spch052704sat.htm) ("If a company's outside counsel is unwilling or unable to provide its expert views, the auditor should consider whether sufficient alternate procedures can actually be performed to allow the audit to be completed."). Accordingly, counsel conducting internal investigations and their clients must be wary of the risk that disclosure of such documents to auditors may waive the attorney-client privilege or work product protections that ordinarily would apply to documents produced during an investigation.

In some situations, communications with accountants and regulators are protected by the "common interest" doctrine. That doctrine is an exception to the general rule that disclosure of privileged materials to a third party waives the privilege. Under the common interest doctrine, communications among parties with a common interest about a legal matter and their respective attorneys remain privileged.

- *In re Grand Jury Subpoena: Under Seal*, 415 F.3d 333, 341 (4th Cir. 2005) (purpose of the privilege is to allow persons with a common legal interest to "communicate with their respective attorneys and with each other to more effectively prosecute or defend their claims" (internal quotation marks omitted)), *cert. denied*, 126 S. Ct. 1114 (Jan. 9, 2006).

- *Cavallaro v. United States*, 284 F.3d 236, 249-50 (1st Cir. 2002) ("The common-interest doctrine prevents clients from waiving the attorney-client privilege when attorney-client communications are shared with a third person who has a common legal interest with respect to those communications, for instance, a codefendant." The common interest exception applies "where (1) the communication is made by separate parties in the course of a matter of common interest; (2) the communication is designed to further that effort; and (3) the privilege has not been waived.").

- *Lectrolarm Custom Sys., Inc. v. Pelco Sales, Inc.*, 212 F.R.D. 567 (E.D. Cal. 2002) (holding that common interest doctrine applied to communications between insured and insurer, because they had a "commonality of interest" in underlying suit).

- *Roush v. Seagate Tech., LLC*, No. H030212, — Cal. Rptr. 3d —, 2007 WL 1202558 (Cal. Ct. App. April 25, 2007) (narrowly confining common interest doctrine in California to situations in which sharing of privileged information "furthers the attorney-client relationship"; "sharing destroys the privilege where the parties simply have 'overlapping interests'").

Companies who have shared work product with auditors have argued that they share a common interest — determining whether irregularities have occurred and should be addressed. The case law is not uniform on these issues, however, and therefore the disclosure of work product to auditors involves some degree of risk of waiver.

- *S. Scrap Material Co. v. Fleming*, No. Civ.A. 01-2554, 2003 WL 21474516, at *9 (E.D. La. June 18, 2003) (finding no waiver where client disclosed work product to auditors because case was not "one of those cases where a party deliberately disclosed work-product in order to obtain a tactical advantage or where a party made testimonial use of work-product and then attempted to invoke the work-product doctrine to avoid cross-examination").

- *In re Pfizer Inc. Sec. Litig.*, No. 90 Civ. 1260, 1993 WL 561125, at *6 (S.D.N.Y. 2003) (litigation case reserves, while disclosed to auditors, were protected work product because auditors shared common interest with client and could not reasonably be "viewed as a conduit to a potential adversary").
- *Medinol, Ltd. v. Boston Scientific Corp.*, 214 F.R.D. 113 (S.D.N.Y. 2002) (disclosure to auditors of special litigation committee minutes reflecting results of internal investigation constituted waiver because company and auditor did not share common interest in litigation).

Companies conducting internal investigations on accounting issues must also determine the degree to which they will share potentially privileged information with enforcement officials. Sharing information may assist in persuading government officials that an enforcement action against the company is not warranted, but it increases the risk of a finding in subsequent litigation that the privilege has been waived. Counsel should consider entering into a "non-waiver" agreement with regulators prior to sharing any potentially privileged information as a precautionary measure.

- **McNulty Memorandum:** The McNulty Memorandum sets forth principles to be applied by Department of Justice officials in prosecutions involving business organizations. It requires federal prosecutors seeking privileged attorney-client communications or work product from a corporation to obtain written approval from the Deputy Attorney General. It also instructs prosecutors not to consider a corporation's advancement of attorneys' fees to employees when making a charging decision, except in extraordinary circumstances where the advancement of fees, combined with other significant facts, shows that the corporation intended to impede the government's investigation. *See* http://www.usdoj.gov/dag/speech/2006/mcnulty_memo.pdf.
- *In re Cardinal Health, Inc. Sec. Litig.*, No. C2 04 575, 2007 WL 495150 (S.D.N.Y. Jan. 26, 2007) (sharing of audit committee report with SEC did not waive work product protections because audit committee and SEC shared "common interest" of determining what had occurred and addressing irregularities).

- *In re Qwest Commc'ns Int'l Inc. Sec. Litig.*, 450 F.3d 1179, 1195 (10th Cir. 2006) (denying writ of mandamus on district court's decision that Qwest waived privilege by releasing privileged materials to federal agencies), *cert. denied*, 127 S. Ct. 584 (Nov. 13, 2006).
- *In re McKesson HBOC, Inc. Sec. Litig.*, No. C-99-20743, 2005 U.S. Dist. LEXIS 7098, at *36 (N.D. Cal. Mar. 31, 2005) (common interest doctrine did not apply to prevent waiver of privilege when McKesson provided documents to SEC investigators, because interests of McKesson and government were potentially adverse); *see also United States v. Bergonzi*, 216 F.R.D. 487, 495-96 (N.D. Cal. 2003) (common interest doctrine did not apply to prevent waiver of privilege when McKesson provided documents to SEC investigators, because interests of McKesson and government were potentially adverse).

IV. INDEPENDENCE OBLIGATIONS

Auditors are required to be independent of their audit clients throughout the audit engagement. *See, e.g.*, Public Company Accounting Oversight Board, Bylaws and Rules, § 3, Rule 3520. Cases brought against auditors often involve allegations that the auditor failed to maintain independence.

Independence can be impaired by a variety of circumstances, including, *inter alia*: acceptance of a contingent fee or commission arrangement with the audit client; investment in the client; provision of a non-audit service to the audit client related to marketing, planning, or opinion in favor of the tax treatment of certain transactions; provision of tax services to a person in a financial reporting oversight role at the audit client during the engagement period; acceptance of employment with the audit client by a former partner, principal, shareholder, or professional employee of an accounting firm who has a continuing financial interest in the accounting firm or is in a position to influence the firm's operations or financial policies; provision of bookkeeping or other services related to the accounting records or financial statements of the audit client; and provision of legal services to the client. Public Company Accounting Oversight Board, Bylaws and Rules, § 3, Rules 3521-3523; 17 CFR § 210.2-01; AICPA Code Prof. Conduct § 101. It is not feasible to summarize here all of the relevant independence standards applicable to auditors. Where auditor independence is in issue, expert witnesses will likely be called upon to speak to the relevant standards.

V. REPORTING OBLIGATIONS ARISING FROM INVESTIGATIONS AND LITIGATION

When defending a CPA or CPA firm in litigation or an investigation, counsel should be aware and advise the client regarding reporting obligations that may apply relating to the litigation. Many states and jurisdictions require accountants practicing or licensed there to report any involvement in litigation or government investigations relating to the practice of accounting. For example:

- A number of states require individual accountants and/or accounting firms who are sued in a civil action relating to accounting to notify the state board of accountancy upon judgment or settlement (or in some cases, upon filing) of such a claim. Such states include Arizona, California, Hawaii, Michigan, Nevada, New York, North Carolina, Oregon, Rhode Island, Washington, Wisconsin, and Wyoming.
- Certain states (California, Rhode Island, Washington) require individual accountants and accounting firms to notify the state board of accountancy of government investigations relating to the practice of accountancy.
- The precise details of these reporting obligations differ depending upon where the accounting work was performed and the nature of the incident. Individual state statutes and regulations should be consulted to determine the precise requirements. *See* Appendix A, attached, listing state statutes and regulations governing the licensing of accountants.

APPENDIX A
State Accountancy Acts and Accountancy Board Regulations
(as of September 2006)

State	State Accountancy Act	State Accountancy Board Regulations
Alabama	Ala. Code §§ 34-1-1 *et seq.*	Ala. Admin. Code r. 30-X-1 *et seq.*
Alaska	Alaska Stat. §§ 08.04.005 *et seq.* (through 12/31/2007)	Alaska Admin. Code tit. 12, §§ 04.005 *et seq.*
Arizona	Ariz. Rev. Stat. §§ 32-701 *et seq.*	Ariz. Admin. Code §§ R4-1-101 *et seq.*
Arkansas	Ark. Code Ann. §§ 17-12-101 *et seq.*	Ark. St. Bd. of Pub. Accountancy Rules 1-16
California	Cal. Bus. & Prof. Code §§ 5030 *et seq.*	Cal. Code Regs. tit. 16, Div. 1, §§ 1 *et seq.*
Colorado	Col. Rev. Stat. §§ 12-2-101 *et seq.*	Rules of the Col. State Bd. of Accountancy, Chapters 1-9
Connecticut	Conn. Gen. Stat. §§ 20-279b *et seq.*	Conn. St. Bd. of Accountancy Regs. §§ 20-280-15a *et seq.*
Delaware	Del. Code Ann. tit. 24, §§ 101 *et seq.*	24-100 Del. Code Regs. §§ 1 *et seq.*
District of Columbia	D.C. Code §§ 47-2853.01 *et seq.* (regulation of public accountancy); D.C. Code §§ 47-2853.41 *et seq.* (accountants in particular)	D.C. Mun. Regs. tit. 17, §§ 2500 *et seq.*
Florida	Fla. Stat. §§ 473.301 *et seq.*	Fla. Admin. Code Ann. r. 61H1-19.006 *et seq.*
Georgia	Ga. Code Ann. §§ 43-3-1 *et seq.*	Rules of Ga. State Bd. of Accountancy Chapter 20-1 *et seq.*

State	State Accountancy Act	State Accountancy Board Regulations
Guam	Guam Code Ann. tit. 22, §§ 35101 *et seq.*	25 Guam Admin R. & Regs. §§ 2101 *et seq.*
Hawaii	Haw. Rev. Stat. §§ 436B *et seq.* (all licensees); Haw. Rev. Stat §§ 466 *et seq.* (accountants)	Haw. Code R. §§ 16-71-1 *et seq.*
Idaho	Idaho Code Ann. § 54-201 *et seq.*	Idaho Admin. Code r. 01.01.01 *et seq.*
Illinois	225 Ill. Comp. Stat. 450/0.01 *et seq.*	Ill. Admin. Code tit. 68, §§ 1420-1430 *et seq.*
Indiana	Ind. Code §§ 25-2.1 *et seq.*; Ind. Code § 25-1-11 (Uniform Standards of Practice)	872 Ind. Admin. Code 1-.05-1 *et seq.*
Iowa	Iowa Code §§ 542 *et seq.*	Iowa Admin. Code r. 193A-1.1 et seq.
Kansas	Kan. Stat. Ann. §§ 1-201 *et seq.*	Kan. Admin. Regs. §§ 74-1 *et seq.*
Kentucky	Ky. Rev. Stat. Ann. §§ 325 *et seq.*	201 Ky. Admin. Regs 1:015 *et seq.*
Louisiana	La. Rev. Stat. Ann. §§ 37:71 *et seq.*	La. Admin. Code tit. 46, §§ 101 *et seq.*
Maine	Me. Rev. Stat. Ann. tit. 32, §§ 12201 *et seq.*	02-280-1 Me. Code. R. *et seq.*
Maryland	Md. Code Ann., Bus. Occ. & Prof. § 2-101 *et seq.*	Md. Code Regs. 09-24.01.00 *et seq.*
Massa-chusetts	Mass. Gen. Laws ch. 13, §§ 33 *et seq.* (Board of Public Accountancy); Mass. Gen. Laws ch. 112, §§ 87A *et seq.* (Registration of Certified Public Accountants)	252 Mass. Code Regs. §§ 1.00 *et seq.*

State	State Accountancy Act	State Accountancy Board Regulations
Michigan	Mich. Comp. Laws §§ 339.101 *et seq.* (Occupational Code); Mich. Comp. Laws §§ 339.720 *et seq.* (Public Accounting)	Mich. Admin. Code r. 338.5101 *et seq.*
Minnesota	Minn. Stat. Ann. §§ 326A.01 *et seq.*	Minn. R. 1105.0100 *et seq.*
Mississippi	Miss. Code Ann. §§ 73-33-1 *et seq.*	50-022-001 Miss. Code R. § 1.1 *et seq.*
Missouri	Mo. Ann. Stat. §§ 326.250 et seq.	Mo. Code Regs. Ann. tit. 20, §§ 2010 *et seq.*
Montana	Mont. Code Ann. §§ 37-50-101 *et seq.*	Mont. Admin. R. §§ 24.201.101 *et seq.*
Nebraska	Neb. Rev. Stat. §§ 1-105.01 *et seq.*	288 Neb. Admin. Code §§ 1-001 *et seq.*
Nevada	Nev. Rev. Stat. §§ 628.002 *et seq.*	Nev. Admin. Code §§ 628.010 et. seq.
New Hampshire	N.H. Rev. Stat. Ann. §§ 309-B:1 *et seq.*	N.H. Code R. Ac 100.01 *et seq.*
New Jersey	N.J. Stat. Ann. §§ 45:2B-54 *et seq.*	N.J. Admin. Code §§ 13:29-1.1 *et seq.*
New Mexico	N.M. Stat. Ann. §§ 61:28B *et seq.*	N.M. Code R. §§ 16.60 *et seq.*
New York	N.Y. Educ. Law §§ 5408 *et seq.*	N.Y. Comp. Codes R. & Regs. tit. 8, §§ 29 *et seq.*
North Carolina	N.C. Gen. Stat. §§ 93 *et seq.*	21 N.C. Admin. Code 08A.0100 *et seq.*
North Dakota	N.D. Cent. Code §§ 43.02 *et seq.*	N.D. Admin. Code 01-01 *et seq.*
Ohio	Ohio Rev. Code Ann. §§ 4701.01 *et seq.*	Ohio Admin. Code 4701:1-1 *et seq.*

State	State Accountancy Act	State Accountancy Board Regulations
Oklahoma	Okla. Stat. Ann. tit. 59, §§ 15.1 *et seq.*	Okla. Admin. Code §§ 10:1-1-1 *et seq.*
Oregon	Or. Rev. Stat. §§ 673.010 *et seq.*	Or. Admin. R. 90-001-000 *et seq.*
Pennsyl-vania	63 Pa. Stat. Ann. §§ 9.1 *et seq.*	49 Pa. Code §§ 11.1 *et seq.*
Puerto Rico	P.R. Laws Ann. tit. 20, §§ 771 *et seq.*	No P.R. Board of Accountancy regulations available online in English.
Rhode Island	R.I. Gen. Laws §§ 5-3.1-1 *et seq.*	02-020-001 R.I. Code R. §§ 1.0 *et seq.*
South Carolina	S.C. Code Ann. §§ 40-2-5 *et seq.*	S.C. Code Ann. Regs. 1-01 *et seq.*
South Dakota	S.D. Codified Laws §§ 36-20B-1 *et seq.*	S.D. Admin. R. 20:75:01 *et seq.*
Tennessee	Tenn. Code Ann. §§ 62-1-101 *et seq.*	Tenn. Comp. R. & Regs. 0020-1-.01 *et seq.*
Texas	Tex. Occ. Code Ann. §§ 901 *et seq.*	22 Tex. Admin. Code §§ 501 *et seq.*
Utah	Utah Code Ann. §§ 58-1-101 *et seq.*	Utah Admin. Code r. 156-1-101 *et seq.*
Vermont	Vt. Stat. Ann. tit. 26, §§ 73 *et seq.*; Vt. Stat. Ann. tit. 3, §§ 129 *et seq.*	04-030-010 Vt. Code R. §§ 1.1 *et seq.*
Virginia	Va. Code Ann. §§ 54.1-4400 *et seq.*	18 Va. Admin. Code §§ 5-21-10 *et seq.*
Virgin Islands	V.I. Code Ann. tit. 27, §§ 230 *et seq.*	No V.I. Board of Accountancy regulations currently available online.
Washington	Wash. Rev. Code §§ 18.04 *et seq.*	Wash. Admin. Code 4-25-00 *et seq.*

State	State Accountancy Act	State Accountancy Board Regulations
West Virginia	W. Va. Code §§ 30-9-1 *et seq.*	W. Va. Code R. §§ 1-1-1 *et seq.*
Wisconsin	Wis. Stat. §§ 442.001 *et seq.*	Wis. Admin. Code Accy §§ 1.001 *et seq.*
Wyoming	Wyo. Stat. §§ 33-3-101 *et seq.*	006-061-001 Wyo. Code R. §§ 1 *et seq.*

NOTES

12

OUTLINE FOR FRAUD AND FINANCIAL DISASTER: A FORENSIC ACCOUNTANT'S OVERVIEW

A. Christine Davis, CPA

Hemming Morse, Inc.

1. Definition of Financial statement Fraud

"Fraud is an intentional act that results in a material misstatement in financial statements that are the subject of an audit."[1] This is also known as an "accounting irregularity." The term "irregularities" is the predecessor of the term "fraud" in the auditing standards.

> "Financial statement fraud is the *deliberate misrepresentation* of the financial condition of an enterprise accomplished through the *intentional misstatement* or *omission* of amounts or disclosures in the financial statements to *deceive* financial statement users."[2]

2. But first, what does "material" mean?

   a. Materiality is "the magnitude of an omission or misstatement of accounting information that, in light of surrounding circumstances, makes it probable that the judgment of a reasonable person relying on the information would have changed or influenced by the omission of misstatement."[3]

   b. Quantitative vs. Qualitative Thresholds – From the SECs Staff Accounting Bulletin No. 99, MATERIALITY:

   > "This staff accounting bulletin expresses the views of the staff that exclusive reliance on certain quantitative benchmarks to assess materiality in preparing financial statements and performing audits of those financial statements is inappropriate; misstatements are not immaterial simply because they fall beneath a numerical threshold."

   SAB 99 sets forth certain situations where quantitatively small misstatements may be considered material, such as when the "immaterial" misstatement has caused the entity to meet analyst expectations, or changed a loss into income, or vice versa.

3. Two types of financial statement misstatements arising from fraud [AU 316.06]:

   a. Misstatements arising from fraudulent financial reporting

   b. Misstatements arising from misappropriation of assets

---

1. CONSIDERATION OF FRAUD IN A FINANCIAL STATEMENT AUDIT, AICPA AU Section 316.05. Statements on Auditing Standards are codified into various "AU Sections."
2. FRAUD EXAMINERS MANUAL, VOL. 1, Association of Certified Fraud Examiners, Inc.
3. QUALITATIVE CHARACTERISTICS OF ACCOUNTING INFORMATION, Financial Accounting Standards Board Statement of Financial Accounting Concepts No. 2.

4. Misstatements arising from fraudulent financial reporting:

   a. "...are intentional misstatements or omissions of amounts or disclosures in financial statements designed to deceive financial statement users where the effect causes the financial statements not to be presented, in all material respects, in conformity with generally accepted accounting principles (GAAP);" [AU 316.06]

   b. are usually accomplished through:

      i. manipulation, falsification, or alteration of accounting records or supporting documents from which financial statements are prepared

      ii. misrepresentation in or intentional omission form the financial statements of events, transactions, or other significant information

      iii. intentional misapplication of accounting principles relating to amounts, classification, manner of presentation, or disclosure; [AU 316.06]

   c. do not include unintentional accounting errors, although a restatement of the financial statements would be required if the unintentional errors are material.

5. Examples from this presenter's actual forensic, consulting and expert witness case work involving misstatements arising from fraudulent financial reporting:

   a. Revenue Recognition

      i. Premature or improper revenue recognition

         a. Improper "Bill-and-hold" sales

         b. Multiple-element arrangements in software contracts

         c. Consignment sales

         d. Side agreements

      ii. Fictitious revenues

   b. Manipulating reserves

      1. Bad debt reserve

      2. Loan loss reserves

3. Inventory reserve

4. Reserve for sales returns

5. "Cookie-jar" reserves (such as "restructuring" reserves)

c. Other

1. Lack of disclosures

2. Top-side adjustments

6. Misstatements arising from misappropriation of assets "involve the theft of an entity's assets where the effect of the theft causes the financial statements not to be presented, in all material respects, in conformity with GAAP." [AU 316.06]

a. More common examples include:

i. Skimming

1. Cash

2. Receivables – concealed through

a. Lapping

b. Debits to expense accounts

ii. Fraudulent disbursements

7. The following three conditions are generally present within the entity when fraud occurs [AU 316.07]:

a. Incentive and pressure – for example, pressure on management to meet analysts' expectations

b. Opportunity – for example, the opportunity to perpetrate the fraud is present due to the entity's weakness in internal controls or management's ability to override the controls

c. Rationalizing – committing the fraudulent act is justified, in the mind of the perpetrator(s), by the intense pressure placed on them.

8. Risk factors relating to misstatements arising from fraudulent financial reporting [AU 316.85]

a. The following are some examples of risk factors within the entity indicating that there may be **incentive and/or pressure** to commit fraud in financial reporting (not all risk factors are listed):

i. Issues revolving around the entity's financial stability or profitability

   1. High degree of competition or market saturation, accompanied by declining margins

   2. Significant declines in customer demand

   3. Recurring negative cash flows from operations and an inability to generate cash flows from operations while reporting earnings and earnings growth

   4. Rapid growth or unusual profitability, especially as compared to that of other companies in the same industry

ii. Excessive pressure for management to meet the requirements or expectations of third parties due to

   1. Profitability or trend level expectations (especially if unduly aggressive or unrealistic) of investment analysts, institutional investors, significant creditors, including expectations created by management in, for example, overly optimistic press releases or annual report messages

   2. Need to obtain additional debt or equity financing to stay competitive (or obtain cash)

   3. Marginal ability to meet debt repayment or other debt covenant requirements

   4. Perceived or real adverse effects of reporting poor financial results on significant pending transactions, such as business combinations.

iii. Information available indicates that management or the board of directors' personal financial situation is threatened by the entity's negative financial results because of:

   1. Significant interests in the entity

   2. Significant portions of their compensation are contingent upon achieving aggressive targets for stock price, operating results, financial position, cash flow, or selected accounts or activities

iv. There is excessive pressure on management or operating personnel to meet financial targets, including sales or profitability incentive goals.

b. The following are some examples of risk factors within the entity indicating that there may be **opportunities** to commit fraud in financial reporting (not all risk factors are listed):

i. The nature of the industry or the entity's operations provides such opportunities, such as:

1. Significant related-party transactions no in the ordinary course of business or with related entities not audited or audited by another firm

2. Assets, liabilities, revenues or expenses based on significant estimates that involve subjective judgments or uncertainties that are difficult to corroborate

3. Significant, unusual, or highly complex transactions, especially those close to period end that pose difficult "substance over form" questions

4. Significant bank accounts or subsidiary or branch operations in tax-haven jurisdictions for which there appears to be no clear business justification

ii. There is ineffective monitoring of management as a result of the following:

1. Domination of management by a single person or small group without compensating controls

2. Ineffective board of directors or audit committee oversight over the financial reporting process and internal control

iii. There is a complex or unstable organizational structure, as evidenced by the following:

1. Overly complex organizational structure involving unusual legal entities or managerial lines of authority

2. High turnover of senior management, counsel, or board members

iv. Internal control components are deficient as a result of the following:

1. Inadequate monitoring of controls, including automated controls and controls over interim financial reporting

2. High turnover rates or employment of ineffective accounting, internal audit, or information technology staff

3. Ineffective accounting and information systems, including situations involving significant deficiencies or material weaknesses in internal control

c. The following are some examples of risk factors within the entity indicating that there may be **attitudes/rationalizations** by board members, management or employees, that allow them to engage in and/or justify fraudulent financial reporting:

i. Ineffective communication, implementation, support, or enforcement of the entity's values or ethical standards by management, or the communication of inappropriate values or ethical standards

ii. Nonfinancial management's excessive participation in or preoccupation with the selection of accounting principles or the determination of significant estimates

iii. Known history of violations of securities laws or other laws and regulations

iv. Excessive interest by management in maintaining or increasing the entity's stock price or earnings trend

v. A practice by management of committing to analysts, creditors, and other third parties to achieve aggressive or unrealistic forecasts

vi. Management failing to correct known significant deficiencies or material weaknesses in internal control on a timely basis

vii. An interest by management in employing inappropriate means to minimize reported earnings for tax-motivated reasons

viii. Recurring attempts by management to justify marginal or inappropriate accounting on the basis of materiality

ix. The relationship between management and the current or predecessor auditor is strained, as exhibited by the following:

1. Frequent disputes on accounting, auditing, or reporting matters

2. Unreasonable demands on the auditor, such as unreasonable time constraints regarding the completion of the audit or the issuance of the auditor's report

3. Formal or informal restrictions on the auditor that inappropriately limit access to people or information or the ability to communicate effectively with the board of directors or audit committee

4. Domineering management behavior in dealing with the auditor, especially involving attempts to influence the scope of the auditor's work or the selection or continuance of personnel assigned to or consulted on the audit engagement

9. Risk factors relating to misstatements arising from misappropriation of assets [AU 316.85]

a. The following are some examples of risk factors within the entity indicating that there may be **incentive and/or pressure** to misappropriate assets:

i. Personal financial obligations may create pressure on management and employees with access to cash or other assets susceptible to theft to misappropriate those assets

ii. Adverse relationships between the entity and employees with access to cash or other assets susceptible to theft may motivate those employees to misappropriate those assets. For example, adverse relationships may be created by:

1. Known or anticipated future layoffs

2. Recent or anticipated change to employee compensation or benefit plans

3. Promotions, compensation, or other rewards inconsistent with expectations

b. The following are some examples of risk factors within the entity indicating that there may be **opportunities** to misappropriate assets (not all risk factors are listed):

i. Certain characteristics or circumstances may increase the susceptibility of assets to misappropriation, such as:

1. Large amounts of cash on hand or cash processed

2. Inventory items that are small in size, of high value, or in high demand

ii. Inadequate internal control over assets may increase the susceptibility of misappropriation of those assets because of the following:

1. Inadequate segregation of duties or independent checks
2. Inadequate management oversight of employees responsible for assets
3. Inadequate job applicant screening of employees with access to assets
4. Inadequate recordkeeping with respect to assets
5. Inadequate system of authorization and approval of transactions (for example, in purchasing)
6. Inadequate physical safeguards over cash, investments, inventory, or fixed assets
7. Lack of complete and timely reconciliation of assets
8. Lack of timely and appropriate documentation of transactions, for example, credits for merchandise returns.
9. Lack of mandatory vacations for employees performing key control functions
10. Inadequate management understanding of information technology, which enables information technology employees to perpetrate a misappropriation
11. Inadequate access controls over automated records, including controls over and review of computer systems event logs.

c. The following are some examples of risk factors within the entity indicating that there may be **attitudes/rationalizations** by board members, management or employees, that allow them to engage in and/or justify the misappropriation of assets:

i. Disregard for the needs for monitoring or reducing risks related to misappropriation of assets

ii. Disregard for internal control over misappropriation of assets by overriding existing controls or by failing to correct known internal control deficiencies

iii. Behavior indicating displeasure or dissatisfaction with the company or its treatment of the employee

iv. Changes in behavior or lifestyle that may indicate assets have been misappropriated

10. Highlights of "Management Antifraud Programs and Controls" commissioned by the Fraud Task Force of the AICPA's Auditing Standards Board [AU 316.86]

a. Identifies measures entities can implement to prevent, deter, and detect fraud

b. The three fundamental elements are:

i. Creating a culture of honesty and high ethics

1. Setting the tone at the top – Directors, officers and senior management

2. Creating a positive workplace environment

3. Hiring and promoting appropriate employees

4. Training – regarding the entity's values and its code of conduct

5. Confirmation – periodic confirmation by employees of their responsibilities

6. Discipline

ii. Evaluating antifraud processes and controls

1. Identifying and measuring fraud risks

2. Mitigating fraud risks

3. Implementing and monitoring appropriate internal controls

iii. Developing an appropriate oversight process.

1. Audit Committee or Board of Directors – evaluate management's identification of fraud risks, implementation of antifraud measures, creation of the appropriate "tone at the top," and oversee the activities of senior management

2. Senior Management – overseeing the activities carried out by employees, implement and monitor processes

3. Internal Auditors – can be extremely helpful in performing aspects of the oversight function

4. Independent Auditors – can assist management and the board by providing an assessment of the entity's process for identifying, assessing, and responding to the risks of fraud

5. Certified Fraud Examiners – may assist the audit committee and board of directors with aspects of the oversight process either directly or as part of a team of internal auditors or independent auditors.

11. What Usually Follows, Among other Things, When Fraud is Suspected or Detected

a. Internal investigation - oversight by board and audit committee, retain outside counsel, retain forensic accountants and/or consultants

b. Press release and Form 8-K – generally, when the entity's board, officers, and/or outside auditor concludes that any previously issued financial statements should not be relied upon, the entity has four days to file a Form 8-K report disclosing such determination.

c. Restatement of the financial statements, if the fraud caused the financial statements to be materially misstated

12. Overview of Suggested Responses Involving Forensic Consultants When Fraud is Suspected or Detected

a. Benefits of Immediately Consulting with a Forensic Accountant

An experienced forensic accountant will have the accounting, auditing, regulatory and analytical expertise to:

1. identify the potential GAAP and GAAS issues in the case

2. explain what documents would be meaningful in evaluating the merits of the case

3. properly evaluate available evidence to assist counsel in discovery, request for additional documents, and sift through the myriad of documents to identify which ones are more significant than others

4. assist in developing interview questions and suggested deposition questions

5. explain generally accepted accounting principles (GAAP) and generally accepted auditing standards (GAAS)
6. identify the GAAP misstatements, including missing disclosures and notes to the financial statements
7. develop an understanding of an entity's accounting system, including its accounting controls, or lack thereof
8. understand and explain the underlying accounting records and develop an understanding of what reports an entity's accounting system is expected to generate
9. understand the correlation among various system reports, the underlying supporting documents and the resulting amounts appearing in the financial statements
10. understand the various roles of an entity's accounting personnel and the tasks they likely performed
11. identify and explain what accounting reports and transaction documents would assist in reconstructing transactions
12. understand the events that had transpired, reconstruct the transactions and identify the related paper trail
13. understand and explain what the appropriate accounting for a transaction should have been, and the actual "accounting" performed
14. analyze and evaluate the financial statements, including identifying meaningful financial ratios that convey unexpected or unusual relationships among financial statement accounts and balances
15. review, understand and evaluate audit working papers, including proprietary audit software, audit work programs and external working papers that "link" to the computer-generated audit work programs
16. understand and explain the appropriate audit and/or procedures in accordance with professional standards, and why the actual audit and/or review procedures performed were inadequate
17. understand and explain specialized accounting relating to certain industries

18. research and obtain the appropriate and relevant accounting, auditing and regulatory standards, and last but not least,

19. quantify the misstatements contained in the previously issued financial statement misstatements, conclude as to their materiality, and, if required, prepare a thorough report that is supported by appropriate evidence and relevant professional standards.

b. Benefits of Immediately Consulting with a Computer Forensics Specialist

Obtaining a forensic image as soon as possible in the life of a case is vital as it obviously provides the litigator with a snapshot of relevant data for possible future analysis and searches. This step should be taken regardless of the strength of the case and whether or not it moves forward, as preservation of evidence is made possible by a forensic image, and data corruption or inadvertent spoliation is avoided.

Cases that involve electronic evidence will greatly benefit from the early involvement of an experienced computer forensics specialist. A computer forensics specialist has the specialized training and experience to, among other things:

1. provide guidance as to the best practices for obtaining, searching and gathering electronic evidence

2. perform court-approved forensic sector-by-sector images of workstation, server or offline hard drives and other storage media.

NOTES

NOTES

13

FRAUD, FINANCIAL REPORTING AND PROFESSIONAL ACCOUNTABILITY: NEW AND (RE)EMERGING ISSUES

Karen Kincaid Balmer, CPA, CrFA

Kincaid Consulting LLC

Reprinted from the PLI Course Handbook, *Basics of Accounting & Finance: What Every Practicing Lawyer Needs to Know — Summer 2006* (Order #8650).

FRAUD

WHAT'S NEW?

- AUDITORS ARE REQUIRED TO LOOK FOR FRAUD TO A GREATER EXTENT. AUDITORS ARE NOT REQUIRED ABSOLUTELY TO FIND FRAUD DURING AN AUDIT.
- MANAGEMENT IS NOW REQUIRED TO CERTIFY FINANCIAL STATEMENTS AND INTERNAL CONTROL SYSTEMS.
- LAWYERS AND OTHER PROFESSIONALS HAVE A GREATER DEGREE OF RESPONSIBILITY TO IDENTIFY AND REPORT FRAUD.

WHAT'S OLD?

- GREED
- TEMPTATION
- OPPORTUNITY
- INTERNAL CONTROL WEAKNESSES
- TRUST
- A LIMITLESS NUMBER
- OF SCHEMES
- FRAUD

FRAUD = INTENTIONAL MISSTATEMENTS OF ACCOUNTING RECORDS VIA:

- MANIPULATION
- FABRICATION
- ALTERATION

FRAUD = MISREPRESENTATION IN OR INTENTIONAL OMISSION FROM THE FINANCIAL STATEMENTS:

- EVENTS
- TRANSACTIONS
- OTHER SIGNIFICANT INFORMATION

FRAUD = INTENTIONAL MISAPPLICATION OF ACCOUNTING PRINCIPLES RELATING TO:

- AMOUNTS
- CLASSIFICATION
- MANNER OF PRESENTATION
- DISCLOSURES IN FINANCIAL STATEMENTS, PRESS RELEASES, OR OTHER COMMUNICATIONS

IS FINANCIAL FRAUD INCREASING?

- THERE HAVE BEEN SIGNIFICANT INCREASES IN REPORTED OCCURRENCES AND DOLLAR IMPACT IN RECENT YEARS.
- REVENUE RECOGNITION = 70% OF NEW CASES
- EXPENSE UNDERSTATEMENT = 30% OF NEW CASES

HIGHLY PUBLICIZED FINANCIAL MISREPORTING PROBLEMS

CENDANT
LUCENT
XEROX
MICROSTRATEGIES
LERNOUT & HAUSPIE
McKESSON
RITE AID
BOSTON SCIENTIFIC
INFORMIX
SUNBEAM
PARMALAT
KPMG
MICRO WAREHOUSE
ENRON
BANKERS TRUST
TENET HEALTHCARE
PHYSICIAN COMPUTER NETWORK
HEALTHSOUTH
WORLDCOM
DYNEGY
MUTUAL FUNDS
ADELPHIA
ADECCO. . .AND MANY OTHERS

THE NUMBER OF RESTATEMENTS HAVE ACCELERATED OVER THE YEARS

	% Increase per year
■ 116 – 1997	—
■ 158 – 1998	36%
■ 216 – 1999	37%
■ 233 – 2000	8%
■ 270 – 2001	16%
■ 330 – 2002	42%
■ 323 – 2003	-2%

	% Increase per year
■ 414* – 2004	28%
1997 vs 2004*	257%

*NOTE: THE 2004 NUMBER IS AN INCOMPLETE NUMBER DUE TO NON-FILINGS OF 235 COMPANIES AS OF THE DATE THIS PRESENTATION WAS PREPARED.

STUDIES SHOW POTENTIAL REASONS FOR THE INCREASES IN FRAUD

- AN ANONYMOUS SURVEY OF CFO'S FOUND THAT TWO THIRDS HAD BEEN SUBJECTED TO PRESSURE WITHIN THEIR COMPANIES TO MISREPRESENT FINANCIAL RESULTS.
- A SURVEY OF TOP 10 GRADUATING HIGH SCHOOL SENIORS ACROSS THE COUNTRY SHOWED THAT 80% FELT THAT IT WAS OK TO CHEAT ON EXAMS OR PAPERS.
- THE PROBABILITY OF LOWER LEVEL MANAGEMENT OR STAFF CHEATING OR STEALING IF SENIOR MANAGEMENT IS DISHONEST? NEARLY 100%

REASONS BEHIND THE INCREASE

- INCREASED PRESSURE TO MEET ANALYSTS EXPECTATIONS
- MANAGEMENT COMPENSATION TIED TO EARNINGS
- BOOM MARKET CONDITIONS
- NOTHING SEEMED TOO GOOD TO BE TRUE
- STARTS SMALL
- JUSTIFICATION ON GRAY AREAS OF ACCOUNTING
- DOMINOS AS EACH QUARTER IS MISSED
  - **I PERSONNALLY DON'T BELIEVE THAT MOST FINANCIAL STATEMENT FRAUDS START OUT WITH THE INTENT TO DEFRAUD.**

OTHER SIGNIFICANT FRAUD FACTS:

- APPROXIMATELY 39% OF ALL FRAUD OCCURS IN COMPANIES WITH FEWER THAN 100 EMPLOYEES.
- FRAUD CAN BE PARTICULARLY HARMFUL TO ENTITIES OF THIS SIZE, WHERE FINANCIAL RESOURCES ARE LESS FLEXIBLE. SEE TWO ARTICLES THAT I WROTE INCLUDED IN THE HANDBOOK REGARDING FRAUD AT SMALL COMPANIES.

FINDING FINANCIAL STATEMENT FRAUDS IS EXTREMELY UNLIKELY SIMPLY BY READING PUBLICLY FILED FINANCIAL STATEMENTS.

FINDING FRAUD - MOST LIKELY METHODS:

- EMPLOYEE TIPS – 50%
- EXTERNAL AUDITORS – 12%
- INTERNAL AUDITORS – 12%
- CLUES/UNUSUAL BEHAVIOR OR DOCUMENTS – 26%

NOTE: NUMBERS ARE APPROXIMATE AND BASED ON ACFE STATISTICS

SOME OF THE SIGNIFICANT ATTRIBUTES THAT A FORENSIC ACCOUNTANT MUST HAVE ARE:

- SKEPTICISM
- CURIOUSITY
- PERSISTENCE
- KNOWLEDGE
- ABLE TO COMMUNICATE

DON'T UNDERESTIMATE WHAT CLUE OR CLUES MAY LEAD TO THE DISCOVERY OF A FRAUD. SOME TIMES THE ONLY CLUES ARE SMALL. KEEP A SKEPTICAL MIND AND FOLLOWUP ON THINGS THAT DON'T MAKE SENSE.

SIMPLE THINGS THAT LEAD ME TO THE DISCOVERY OF A FRAUD (TITLES ARE MINE):

- IF THE CHECK DOESN'T FIT – AT THE BEGINNING OF MY CAREER I HAD FINISHED A PROPERLY CONSTRUCTED STATISTICAL SAMPLING OF A COMPANY'S PAYROLL AND LATE ON A FRIDAY NIGHT WAS PREPARING TO RETURN THE DOCUMENTS TO THEIR FILE CABINETS WHEN I NOTICED THAT ONE CHECK WAS ABOUT AN EIGTH OF AN INCH BIGGER THAN ALL OF THE OTHER CHECKS IN THE BOX. (THE CHECKS WERE STORED IN LONG KEYPUNCH CARD BOXES STANDING FRONT TO BACK, SO I COULD SEE THE SIZE OF APPROXIMATELY 2,500 CHECKS AT ONE TIME.) THE CHECK WAS MADE OUT TO THE PAYROLL SUPERVISOR. AT FIRST I DIDN'T SUSPECT FRAUD. HOWEVER, WHEN I WENT TO THE SECOND AND THIRD BOXES AND FOUND AN ADDITIONAL OFF-SIZED CHECK IN EACH OF THESE BOXES, ALSO MADE OUT TO THE PAYROLL SUPERVISOR, I KNEW THAT SOMETHING WAS WRONG.

  GIVEN THAT I WAS JUST STARTING MY CAREER AND HAD NO TRAINING IN FRAUD (THERE WAS NO EMPHASIS OR SPECIFIC TRAINING ON FRAUD DETECTION BACK THEN) I WAS CONCERNED ABOUT "CRYING WOLF" UNTIL I WAS ABSOLUTELY SURE. I PUT ALL OF THE DOCUMENTS AWAY, WENT HOME FOR THE WEEKEND AND CALLED A COLLEGE PROFESSOR TO VET MY FINDINGS AND CONCERNS. BASED ON THAT CONVERSATION, I RETURNED TO THE OFFICE ON MONDAY AND AFTER REVIEWING MY FINDINGS, TOOK MY FINDINGS TO MY MANAGER. ADDITIONAL WORK REVEALED THAT THE FRAUD HAD OCCURRED FOR TEN YEARS UNDETECTED.

VARIOUS INTERNAL CONTROL WEAKNESSES ALLOWED THE FRAUD TO OCCUR AND REMAIN UNDETECTED. THE PRIMARY WEAKNESS WAS THAT THE PAYROLL SUPERVISOR RECEIVED AND RECONCILED THE PAYROLL BANK STATEMENT HIMSELF. NO ONE EVER REPLACED HIM ON THIS FUNCTION. HE ALSO WAS PERMITTED TO REQUEST THE AMOUNT OF MONIES FROM THE OPERATING ACCOUNT TO BE TRANSFERRED TO THE PAYROLL ACCOUNT WITHOUT ANYONE MATCHING THE PAYROLL REGISTER TO THE REQUESTED AMOUNT.

THE REASON FOR THE CHECK SIZE DIFFERENCE WAS BECAUSE THE PAYROLL SUPERVISOR HAD GONE TO A PRINTING COMPANY AND HAD A COMPLETE SECOND SET OF COMPANY CHECKS MADE SO THAT HE COULD SUBSTITUTE THE CORRECT NUMBERED CHECK INTO THE CHECKS CASHED. HE HAD NOT WANTED TO ALTER THE ORIGINAL CHECK, SO HE SET ABOUT TO COMPLETELY SUBSTITUTE EACH ONE.

HE WAS FIRED AND MADE FULL RESTITUTION. THE COMPANY DECLINED TO PRESS CRIMINAL CHARGES.

- GRAMMA'S BREAD AND JAM – IN THIS CASE, EARLY IN MY CAREER I BEFRIENDED THE HEAD BOOKKEEPER, WHO LOVED TO BRING HOMEMADE BREAD AND JAM TO THE OFFICE. ABOUT A WEEK INTO THE AUDIT SHE HAD GAINED ENOUGH CONFIDENCE IN ME, BASED ON OUR FRIENDLY CONVERSATIONS, TO LITERALLY HAND ME A FILE CONTAINING ALL OF THE DOCUMENTS THAT SHE HAD COLLECTED OVER THE YEARS REGARDING IMPROPER PAYMENTS MADE THROUGH THE ACCOUNTS PAYABLE DEPARTMENT.

  SHE HAD BEEN AFRAID TO BRING THIS FORWARD EARLIER FOR FEAR OF LOSING HER JOB. SHE HAD NOT HAD THE CONFIDENCE THAT COMPANY MANAGEMENT WOULD BELIEVE HER. SHE WAS FRUSTRATED ABOUT THE PAYMENTS TO SUCH AN EXTENT THAT SHE KEPT COPIES OF ALL THE TRANSACTIONS WITH NOTES TO DESCRIBE WHAT WAS WRONG WITH EACH. ESSENTIALLY, SHE WAS WAITING FOR THE RIGHT MOMENT IN HER MIND TO COME FORWARD. MY COMMUNICATIONS WITH HER GAVE HER THE COMFORT THAT WAS NEEDED... WITHOUT MY KNOWING IT. THIS IS A SKILL THAT I LATER LEARNED IS ESSENTIAL IN MANY INVESTIGATIONS.

- "I THINK I LEFT THAT RECEIPT AT HOME" – DURING A ROUTINGE CASH COUNT OF A PETTY CASH BOX, I FOUND A SMALL SHORTAGE ($26.25). THE CLERK WAS CONCERNED AND STATED THAT SHE MUST HAVE LEFT A RECEIPT AT HOME FOR A BIRTHDAY CAKE THAT SHE HAD PURCHASED THE WEEK BEFORE FOR AN OFFICE PARTY. DUE TO THE SMALL AMOUNT I WASN'T EXTREMELY CONCERNED AND COUNSELED HER TO LOOK FOR THE RECEIPT AND TO BRING IT IN THE NEXT DAY.

  WHEN SHE CAME IN THE NEXT DAY SHE TOLD ME THAT SHE COULD NOT FIND IT. I THEN PROCEEDED TO SHOW HER HOW TO USE THE "OVER AND SHORT" FORM TO REPLACE LOST RECEIPTS OR UNEXPLAINED DIFFERENCES. I EXPLAINED THAT ANY OVERAGES OR SHORTAGES MUST BE REPORTED TO HER SUPERVISOR AND AFTER REVIEW APPROVED PRIOR TO REPLENISHMENT OF THE PETTY CASH. I FURTHER EXPLAINED THAT THIS PRACTICE WAS TO ENABLE THE SUPERVISOR TO KNOW HOW THE CASH WAS MANAGED AND TO ENABLE THE PETTY CASH TO REMAIN AT AN IMPRESSED (SAME) AMOUNT.

  SHE RETURNED TO ME LATER IN THE DAY WITH THE COMPLETED OVER AND SHORT FORM WHICH SHOWED A DIFFERENCE OF $31.25. WHEN I ASKED WHY THE FORM WAS $5 MORE THAN THE ORIGINAL SHORTAGE, SHE BECAME AGGITATED AND STATED THAT THE ORIGINAL SHORTAGE WAS $31.25. WHEN I SHOWED HER THE CASH COUNT SHEET THAT SHOWED A SHORTAGE OF $26.25, WHICH SHE HAD ACKNOW-LEDGED EARLIER IN THE DAY, THE DAY BEFORE AND WITH HER SIGNATURE, SHE IMMEDIATELY STATED THAT THE ADDITIONAL SHORTAGE MUST HAVE BEEN STOLEN BY ME!!!!!!!

  NOT TAKING THIS WITH MUCH ENTHUSIASM, I CALLED IN HER BOSS AND HER BOSS' BOSS FOR A CONFRONTATION. UPON STATING THE FACTS NOTED ABOVE, SHE IMMEDIATELY CONFESSED TO HAVING STOLEN THE MONEY AND MUCH MORE OVER A PERIOD OF YEARS FOR VARIOUS LUNCHES, GIFTS AND OTHER ITEMS.

THANK GOODNESS FOR THE STANDARD AUDIT PRACTICE OF PREPARING A SIGNED CASH COUNT SHEET.

I COULD GO ON WITH WAR STORIES, BUT I SELECTED THESE AS SIMPLE EXAMPLES OF THE USE OF CURIOSITY, COMMUNICATION SKILLS, AND PERSISTENCE.

FINANCIAL STATEMENT FRAUDS

MOST FRAUDS START SMALL WITH THE PERPETRATOR(S) PLANNING TO OFFSET THE "MISSTATEMENT" WITH INCREASED REVENUES IN THE NEXT QUARTER. OFTEN THE FOLLOWING QUARTER IS NOT SUCCESSFUL ENOUGH TO "COVER" THE MISSTATEMENT, SO THE MISSTATEMENT GETS ROLLED INTO THE NEXT QUARTER. MANY TIMES THE SUBSEQUENT QUARTER IS ALSO BELOW EXPECTATIONS AND THE PERPETRATOR(S) FEEL COMPELLED TO CREATE AN ADDITIONAL MISSTATEMENT IN ORDER TO KEEP FROM BEING FOUND OUT. THIS PROCESS CAN BE APPROPRIATELY CALLED THE TREADMILL EFFECT, BECAUSE THE COMPANY AND THE PERPETRATOR(S) LITERALLY ARE ON A TREADMILL FROM WHICH THEY CANNOT GET OFF.

SOME OF THE MOST COMMON METHODS OF "COOKING THE BOOKS" FRAUDS ARE LISTED BELOW:

- SHIPMENTS ARE ACCELERATED
- QUARTERS ARE KEPT OPEN
- RESERVES ARE REDUCED
- REVENUE ARE RECOGNIZED ON ANTICIPATED ORDERS
- CONSIGNMENT SALES ARE IMPROPERLY RECOGNIZED
- BILL-AND-HOLD SALES IMPROPERLY RECOGNIZED
- CHANNEL STUFFING
- OVERVALUATION OF INVENTORY
- ACCOUNTS RECEIVABLE MANIPULATION
- EXPENSE RECOGNITION DELAYED
- INTERCOMPANY CREDITS USED
- ACQUISITION RESERVES ADJUSTED
- FALSE INVENTORY "IN TRANSIT" RECORDED
- PHANTOM INVENTORY CREATED
- PHONY SHIPMENTS RECORDED
- BAD FAITH ESTIMATES

- ONE-TIME CHARGES
- RELATED PARTY TRANSACTIONS
- UNSUPPORTABLE GENERAL LEDGER REVISIONS MADE
- UNSUPPORTABLE TOP-SIDE ADJUSTMENTS MADE
- SOURCE: ACCOUNTING IRREGULARITIES AND FINANCIAL FRAUD, SECOND EDITION

THERE IS AN INCREASED RISK TO ALL OUTSIDE PROFESSIONAL SERVICE PROVIDERS TO IDENTIFY AND REPORT FRAUD IN TODAY'S WORLD. IT IS NOT JUST AUDITORS WHO HAVE AN INCREASED RESPONSIBILITY. WE ARE SEEING LAWYERS, BANKERS, BANKS, BROKERS, AND OTHER PROFESSIONALS BEING HELD ACCOUNTABLE FOR HAVING KNOWLEDGE OF A FRAUD, OR BEING IN A POSITION WHERE ONE SHOULD HAVE HAD KNOWLEDGE, BUT FOR. . .

ACCOUNTANTS RESPONSIBILITY FOR FINDING AND REPORTING FRAUD HAS CHANGED SIGNIFICANTLY AS A RESULT OF SARBANES-OXLEY. ONE OF THE KEY TOOLS RECOMMENDED VIA SOX FOR USE IN HELPING AUDITORS DETECT FRAUD WAS A STUDY PREPARED IN 1987 BY THE TREADWAY COMMISSION.

- THIS STUDY WAS OFFICIALLY KNOWN AS THE NATIONAL COMMISSION ON FRAUDULENT FINANCIAL REPORTING (COSO FOR SHORT).
- IT ACTUALLY COMPRISED 20 SEPARATE STUDIES.
- ITS PURPOSE WAS TO IDENTIFY CAUSES OF FRAUDULENT FINANCIAL REPORTING.
- IT EXAMINED THE ROLE OF AUDITORS.

ACCOUNTANTS RESPONSIBILITY FOR FINDING AND REPORTING FRAUD HAS BEEN STUDIED BY OTHER GROUPS AND CODIFIED AS FOLLOWS:

- THE AICPA ISSUED THE STATEMENT OF AUDITING STANDARDS NUMBER 53 (SAS NO. 53) WHICH DISCUSSED THE AUDITOR'S RESPONSIBILITY TO DETECT AND REPORT ERRORS AND IRREGULARITIES. THIS STATEMENT DID NOT REQUIRE AN AUDITOR TO DETECT FRAUD DURING AN AUDIT ENGAGEMENT.

- SAS NO 82 CONSIDERATION OF FRAUD IN A FINANCIAL STATEMENT AUDIT – SUPERCEDED SAS NO. 53. THIS STATEMENT ALSO DID NOT REQUIRE AN AUDITOR TO DETECT FRAUD DURING AN AUDIT ENGAGEMENT. IT DID NOT SEEK TO ALTER THE AUDITOR'S RESPONSIBILITY FOR DETECTING FRAUD, RATHER TO INCREASE THE AUDITOR'S AWARENESS OF THAT RESPONSIBILITY.
- SAS NO 82 WAS SUPERCEDED BY SAS NO 99. AGAIN, THIS STATEMENT DID NOT REQUIRE AN AUDITOR TO DETECT FRAUD DURING AN AUDIT ENGAGEMENT.
- SAS 99 – ENTITLED "AUDITOR RESPONSIBILITY FOR DETECTING FRAUD" IS STILL EMPLOYED BY AUDITORS, BUT AGAIN DOES NOT REQUIRE THE DETECTION OF FRAUD DURING AN AUDIT ENGAGEMENT.
- NOW WE HAVE THE SARBANES-OXLEY ACT, WHICH ESTABLISHED MANY NEW REQUIREMENTS, SUCH AS MANAGEMENT AND AUDITOR CERTIFICATIONS OF INTERNAL CONTROLS EFFECTIVENESS AND MORE. AGAIN, HOWEVER, THIS ACT DOES NOT EXPLICITLY REQUIRE THE AUDITOR TO DETECT FRAUD.

ARTHUR LEVITT, WHO HEADED THE SEC DURING MUCH OF THE 90'S STARTED WARNING ABOUT MANIPULATED EARNINGS AGGRESSIVELY IN 1998. HE IS CREDITED WITH COINING THE PHRASE "COOKIE JAR RESERVES" WHICH LEVITT FELT WERE USING RESERVES FOR LIWBILITIES TO INAPPROPRIATELY MANAGE EARNINGS. LEVITT WARNED THAT THE SEC WAS STARTING TO INVESTIGATE MORE COMPANIES.

LEVITT WAS SEVERELY CRITICIZED BY A NUMBER OF ADVERSARIES, WHO ALLEGEDLY TRIED TO HAVE HIM REPLACED BY CONGRESS. UNFORTUNATELY, LEVITT'S CONCERNS AND WARNINGS WERE PROVEN TO HAVE A LOT OF MERIT DURING THE EARLY 2000'S.

DOES MANAGEMENT HAVE THE RIGHT TO "SMOOTH" OR "MANAGE" EARNINGS? WHILE THIS MAY REDUCE SHARP SWINGS IN STOCK PRICES DUE TO EARNINGS VOLITILITY, IT ALSO MAY "HIDE" THE TRUTH ABOUT EARNINGS FROM INVESTORS.

- LEVITT'S RECOMMENDATIONS WERE BASED PRIMARILY ON THE TREADWAY COMMISSION'S RECOMMENDATIONS 13 YEARS EARLIER.

- ONE OF THE TREADWAY COMMISSION'S RECOMMENDATIONS RESULTED IN THE FORMATION OF THE BLUE RIBBON COMMITTEE ON IMPROVING THE EFFECTIVENESS OF CORPORATE AUDIT COMMITTEES, WHICH RECOMMENDED NEW RULES FOR THE SEC, AICPA, NYSE, NASD AND THE ASE.

- THE SEC BASICALLY ADOPTED THE BLUE RIBBON COMMISSIONS RECOMMENDATIONS IN 1999.

- THE ACCOUNTING PROFESSION'S PUBLIC OVERSIGHT BOARD ISSUED A REPORT ENTITLED "PANEL ON AUDIT EFFECTIVENESS" MEANT TO ENHANCE AUDIT EFFECTIVENESS IN 2000.

- THE PUBLIC OVERSIGHT BOARD WAS REPLACED BY SARBANES-OXLEY'S MANDATED PUBLIC COMPANY ACCOUNTING OVERSIGHT BOARD (PCAOB). IT FURTHER DETAILS ACCOUNTANTS' AND MANAGEMENTS' RESPONSIBILITIES FOR FINDING AND REPORTING FRAUD.

- PCAOB: Section 404 – INTERNAL CONTROL – AUDITOR ATTESTATION REQUIRES INCREASED REPORTING RESPONSIBILITIES REGARDING AN ENTITY'S SYSTEM OF INTERNAL CONTROLS, SPECIFICALLY REQUIRING THE IDENTIFICATION AND CLASSIFICATION OF WEAKNESSES IN THOSE CONTROL SYSTEMS.

- <u>MANAGEMENT</u> MUST NOW CERTIFY QUARTERLY AND ANNUAL FINANCIAL RESULTS (SARBANES-OXLEY - 2002) AND INTERNAL CONTROL SYSTEMS.

- <u>AUDITORS</u> MUST NOW CERTIFY ANNUALLY MANAGEMENTS' ASSERTION THAT INTERNAL CONTROLS ARE EFFECTIVE (SEC – MAY 2003).

- <u>ATTORNEYS</u> FACE A NEW ABA REQUIREMENT REGARDING POTENTIAL REPORTING OF MALFEASANCE - BREAKING ATTORNEY CLIENT PRIVILEGE (ABA – AUGUST 2003). THERE HAS BEEN A SIGNIFICANT RESPONSE FROM THE LEGAL COMMUNITY REGARDING THIS MATTER. THIS GENERALLY IS DISCUSSED IN GREATER LENGTH IN THE ETHICS SECTION OF THIS PROGRAM.

WHAT DO THE SECURITIES ACTS SAY ABOUT FRAUD? SECTION 10(b) AND Rule 10B-5

- SECTION 10(b) OF THE SECURITIES EXCHANGE ACT OF 1934, AND A CORRESPONDING SEC RULE KNOWN AS RULE 10b-5, MAKE IT UNLAWFUL FOR ANY PERSON DIRECLY OR INDIRECTLY "TO USE OR EMPLOY, IN CONNECTION WITH THE PURCHASE OR SALE OF ANY SECURITY," ANY "MANIPULATIVE OR DECEPTIVE DEVICE OR CONTRIVANCE" IN VIOLATION OF SEC REGULATIONS.
- SECTION 10(b) MAKES IT UNLAWFUL TO DELIBERATELY SAY ANYTHING OF CONSEQUENCE THAT IS FALSE OR MISLEADING IN CONNECTION WITH THE PURCHASE OR SALE OF A SECURITY, INCLUDING SIGNIFICANT INACCURACIES IN A COMPANY'S FINANCIAL STATEMENTS FILED AS PART OF ITS FORM 10-K OR FORMS 10-Q.
- MUST PROVE "INTENT TO DECEIVE"
- DOES NOT IMPOSE LIABILITY FOR ACCIDENTS OR NEGLIGENCE
  - SOURCE: ACCOUNTING IRREGULARITIES AND FINANCIAL FRAUD (SECOND EDITION)
  - SEE ERNST & ERNST V. HOCHFELDER, UNITED STATES SUPREME COURT, 1976

INTERNAL CONTROLS PLAY A KEY ROLE IN ALL COMPANIES WHO DO AND DO NOT HAVE FRAUDS.

- ONE THING THAT ALL FRAUDS HAVE IN COMMON IS A BREAKDOWN IN INTERNAL CONTROLS.
- INTERNAL CONTROLS ARE THE CAPSTONE OF FRAUD PREVENTION. WHAT I MEAN BY THIS IS IF THEY ARE SET UP PROPERLY THEY WILL PREVENT A FRAUD FROM OCCURRING IN THE BEGINNING. EXAMPLES OF CAPSTONE CONTROLS (CAPSTONE IS MY NOMINCLATURE – NOT AN INDUSTRY STANDARD DESCRIPTION) ARE REQUIRING BLANK CHECKS TO BE LOCKED UP, REQUIRING TWO SIGNATURES ON CHECKS OVER A CERTAIN AMOUNT, REQUIRING ORIGINAL INVOICES TO BE ATTACHED TO EACH CHECK PRIOR TO SIGNING FOR THE SIGNATOR'S REVIEW, ETC.
- INTERNAL CONTROLS ALSO ARE THE BACKSTOP FOR DETECTING FRAUD. WHAT I MEAN BY THIS IS (AGAIN THIS IS MY NOMINCLATURE), CONTROLS THAT ARE SET UP TO CATCH AN IRREGULARITY AFTER IT HAS HAPPENED, SUCH AS REVIEWING ALL OF THE CANCELLED CHECKS RETURNED BY THE BANK TO SEE IF AMOUNTS OR PAYEES HAVE BEEN ALTERED.

TODAY'S PUBLICLY TRADED COMPANIES HAVE MOST IF NOT ALL OF THE FOLLOWING:

- INTERNAL CONTROLS
- INTERNAL AUDITORS
- AUDIT COMMITTEE
- EXTERNAL AUDITORS
- ETHICS POLICIES
- "TONE AT THE TOP"

STILL THERE ARE FRAUDS AND ALWAYS WILL BE. WHY? BECAUSE NO CONTROL SYSTEMS ARE PERFECT. THERE IS ALWAYS A COST BENEFIT EVALUATION THAT MUST BE DONE TO DETERMINE IF THE ESTIMATED RISK ASSOCIATED WITH A CONTROL WEAKNESS IS WORTH THE COST OF THE "FIX".

NEVERTHELESS, INTERNAL CONTROLS HAVE BECOME INCREASINGLY MORE IMPORTANT. INTERNAL CONTROL SYSTEMS ARE NOT WELL UNDERSTOOD IN THEIR TOTALITY BY MOST PEOPLE. EVEN WITH THE ADDED EMPHASIS ON PROPER CONTROLS AND ENHANCED EVALUATION OF CONTROLS, THEY ARE STILL EASIER TO CIRCUMVENT THAN MOST WOULD GUESS.

INTERNAL CONTROLS SHOULD NOT BE CONSTRUED TO BE JUST A TECHNICAL COMPUTER FUNCTION. A PROPER SYSTEM ENCOMPASSES NOT ONLY COMPUTER SYSTEMS, BUT ALL OF THE MANUAL (HUMAN) INTERFACES AND INTERACTIONS.

IN ORDER TO PROPERLY EVALUATE A SYSTEM OF INTERNAL CONTROLS, ONE MUST VIEW THE BIG PICTURE. WHY? BECAUSE THERE MAY BE MULTIPLE WAYS TO CIRCUMVENT PROCEDURES AND/OR MULTIPLE WAYS TO PROVIDE MITIGATING CONTROLS TO FORESTALL A FRAUD.

MANAGING A FRAUD

WHILE MOST OF YOU HAVE NOT HAD TO DEAL WITH A FRAUD IN YOUR BUSINESS ENVIRONMENT, THE LIKELIHOOD THAT YOU WILL AT SOME TIME DURING YOUR CAREER, OR THE LIKELIHOOD THAT YOU WILL BE ASKED FOR ADVICE BY A CLIENT OR ASSOCIATE IS SIGNIFICANTLY GREAT. FOLLOWING ARE THE ABSOLUTE MINIMUM MUST DO'S FOR MANAGING A FRAUD.

- ISOLATE THE SUSPECT – DO NOT LET SENTIMENTALITY OR FRIENDSHIP PERMIT YOU TO BE COMPASSIONATE ON THIS POINT. IF A FRAUD HAS OCCURRED, THE LIKELIHOOD THAT THE SUSPECT WILL ATTEMPT TO DESTROY DOCUMENTS OR COMPUTER FILES IF PERMITTED CONTINUED ACCESS TO THE PREMISES IS TOO GREAT. EVEN IF THE FRAUD IS NOT CONFIRMED, STAY FIRM ON THIS POINT. THERE ARE ACCEPTABLE WAYS TO ISOLATE THE PERSON(S) WITHOUT ACCUSING THEM IMMEDIATELY OF WRONG DOING.
- CONTROL THE DOCUMENTS AND COMPUTER SYSTEMS – IMMEDIATELY SHUT DOWN THE SUSPECT'S ACCESS TO ALL DOCUMENTS AND COMPUTER SYSTEMS.
- NOTIFY MANAGEMENT AND/OR THE BOARD – AS APPROPRIATE
- NOTIFY APPLICABLE INSURANCE CARRIER(S) – FAILURE TO NOTIFY CARRIERS IN A TIMELY FASHION MAY CREATE COVERAGE ISSUES.
- ESTABLISH THE FORENSIC TEAM – INTERNAL AND/OR EXTERNAL – RAPIDLY
  - DECIDE IF THIS INCLUDES THE CURRENT EXTERNAL AUDITORS OR IF AN INDEPENDENT AUDITOR SHOULD BE HIRED
  - THE SAME APPLIES TO COUNSEL
- THE FORENSICS TEAM GENERALLY SHOULD BE HIRED BY COUNSEL TO PRESERVE PRIVILEGE IF NEEDED IN THE FUTURE.

- ESTABLISH PR PLAN/RELEASES FOR BOTH INTERNAL AND EXTERNAL RELEASE. FRAUDS ARE IMPOSSIBLE TO KEEP QUIET. BETTER TO CONTROL THE FLOW OF INFORMATION THAN TO COMBAT IT.
- I HAD A CASE WHERE A SUSPECT WAS PERMITTED TO "STAY TO HELP SORT OUT THE PROBLEM". ON A WEEKEND DURING THE INVESTIGATION, BUT BEFORE HIS CULPABILITY WAS VERIFIED, THE SUSPECT REMOVED TWO PICKUP TRUCK LOADS OF BOXES OF DOCUMENTS FROM THE PREMISES. THE LOSS OF THESE DOCUMENTS WAS NOT DISCOVERED UNTIL SOME TIME INTO THE INVESTIGATION. DESPITE THE EFFORTS OF THE FBI AND THE LANDFILL OWNERS, THE DOCUMENTS WERE NOT FOUND. AS A RESULT, MANY OF THE ORIGINAL DOCUMENTS NEEDED TO VERIFY THE FRAUD WERE GONE. THE INSURANCE COMPANY INITIALLY TOOK THE POSITION THAT THEY WOULD COVER ONLY THOSE LOSSES SUPPORTED BY ORIGINAL DOCUMENTS. ULTIMATELY, LENGTHY SUBSEQUENT DISCUSSIONS YIELDED A BETTER RESULT FOR THE CLIENT, HOWEVER, AT AN ADDITIONAL COST.

HOW CAN ATTORNEYS FIND OR DETER FRAUD?

- AS COUNSEL TO A COMPANY, WHETHER IN-HOUSE OR EXTERNAL, YOU MAY BE IN A POSITION TO SEE MORE "CLUES" FROM MANAGEMENT THAN MOST OTHERS. IT IS NOW IMPORTANT THAT ATTORNEYS UNDERSTAND MORE ABOUT:
  - FINANCIAL STATEMENTS
  - REPORTING AND DISCLOSURE REQUIREMENTS
  - MANAGEMENT PRESSURES AND INCENTIVES
  - SUBSTANCE OF SIGNIFICANT TRANSACTIONS
    - BY UNDERSTANDING THE NATURE OF TRANSACTIONS IN WHICH THEY BECOME INVOLVED, SUCH AS:
    - CONTRACTS
    - BORROWINGS
    - ACQUISITIONS
    - SALES
    - LEASES
    - DISCLOSURES
  - QUESTIONING WHEN THE SUBSTANCE OF A TRANSACTION APPEARS TO BE DIFFERENT THAN ITS LEGAL FORM
  - DISCUSSIONS WITH MANAGEMENT, EMPLOYEES, INVESTMENT BANKERS, INTERNAL AUDITORS, EXTERNAL AUDITORS, OTHERS

A FEW BASIC INTERNAL CONTROL RECOMMENDATIONS

- BALANCE THOSE BOOKS
- RECONCILE CASH INDEPENDENTLY
- SEGREGATE DUTIES
- ROTATE AUDITORS
- TALK WITH THE AUDITORS ABOUT ANY CONCERNS

- EMPHASIZE THAT AUDITORS TALK WITH YOU AND THE BOARD
- "TONE AT THE TOP"

WHILE WE HAVE CONCENTRATED OUR DISCUSSIONS ON PUBLICLY TRADED COMPANIES, IT SHOULD BE NOTED THAT THE SAME INTERNAL CONTROL CRITERIA APPLY TO SMALL BUSINESS, GOVERNMENTAL AND NOT FOR PROFIT ENTITIES. SMALLER BUSINESSES GENERALLY DO NOT HAVE THE STAFF TO PROVIDE AN ADEQUATE SEGREGATION OF DUTIES FOR VARIOUS REASONS, PRIMARILY COST. THEREFORE, CERTAIN CONTROLS BECOME INCREASING MORE IMPORTANT TO PERFORM IN A CONSISTENT AND CONSCIENCIOUS MANNER. PLEASE SEE THE TWO ARTICLES WRITTEN BY ME WHICH ARE ALSO INCLUDED IN THIS BOOK.

AUDITORS' RESPONSIBILITIES ARE NOT LESS ON AUDITS OF NON-PUBLICLY TRADED ENTITIES.

THE RESPONSIBILITIES OF THE SARBANES-OXLEY ACT DO NOT BY LAW APPLY TO NON-PUBLICLY TRADED ENTITIES, HOWEVER, SOX REQUIREMENTS ARE INCREASING BEING DRIVEN DOWN TO SUCH ENTITIES.

SELECT MINI CASE STUDIES

OVERVIEW

- GOALS
  - BECOME FAMILIAR WITH EXAMPLES OF FRAUD
  - DISCUSS METHODS OF DETECTING, PREVENTING AND DEALING WITH FRAUD
- TYPES OF FRAUD
  - GOOD OL' FASHION FRAUD
  - SWAPPING
  - CHANNEL STUFFING
  - RELATED PARTIES

PART I:
GOOD OL' FASHIONED FRAUD

SELECTED EXAMPLES

- CHECK FRAUD
  - FORGING INSTRUMENTS
  - ALTERING INSTRUMENTS
- EXPENSE REIMBURSEMENT
- PONZI SCHEME

CHECK FRAUD: FORGED ENDORSEMENTS

TYPES:

- FORGING THE ENTIRE INSTRUMENT.
- ALTERING PAYEE OR AMOUNT.

EXAMPLE

COMPTROLLER OF CORPORATION EMBEZZLES $4.5 MILLION OVER A PERIOD OF SIX YEARS BY ALTERING THE PAYEE AND (SOMETIMES) THE AMOUNT OF AUTHENTICALLY SIGNED CHECKS.

HOW FRAUD WAS DETECTED

- ALERT BANK TELLER NOTICED COMPTROLLER'S PATTERN OF CHECK CASHING.
- SUPERVISOR REVIEWED ACCOUNT HISTORY AND ALERTED THE COMPANY'S ADMINISTRATIVE DIRECTOR.
- THE ADMINISTRATIVE DIRECTOR CONFRONTED THE COMPTROLLER, WHO IMMEDIATELY CONFESSED.

RECOURSE

- AVAILABLE AGAINST THE WRONGDOER (USUALLY LONG GONE AND/OR JUDGMENT PROOF).
- AVAILABLE AGAINST ONE OF THE BANKS THAT HANDLED THE CHECK, ACCORDING TO A CERTAIN HIERARCHY.
- ALTHOUGH RECOURSE IS SOMETIMES AVAILABLE AGAINST SOLVENT WRONGDOERS OR CORPORATE INSURANCE POLICIES, THE BEST CASE SCENARIO IS ALWAYS TO PREVENT THE FRAUD.
- IN THIS CASE, THERE WERE INSURANCE POLICIES THAT PAID FOR NEARLY THE ENTIRE LOSS.
- THE COMPTROLLER IS IN PRISON.

PREVENTING CHECK FRAUD

- INTERNAL CONTROLS:
  - MULTIPLE SIGNATURES FOR CHECKS OVER A CERTAIN AMOUNT.
  - LIMIT THE NUMBER OF AUTHORIZED SIGNERS.
  - MANDATORY TWO-WEEK VACATIONS FOR PERSONS WHO HANDLE LARGE AMOUNTS OF CASH.
  - SPOT CHECKS OF BANK RECORDS BY PERSONS OTHER THAN THOSE RESPONSIBLE FOR KEEPING THE BOOKS.
- EXTERNAL CONTROLS:
  - BANKING RELATIONSHIP WHEREIN BANKERS CAN SPOT ODD CHECK CASHING PATTERNS.
  - EFFECTIVE EXTERNAL AUDIT.

EXPENSE REIMBURSEMENT

- SIMPLE, LUCRATIVE AND COMMON.
- CAN BE PERPETRATED BOTH BY PERSON BEING REIMBURSED AND PERSON PREPARING REIMBURSEMENTS.

EXAMPLE:

- COMPANY PERMITTED CASH REIMBURSEMENT OF SEVERAL THOUSAND DOLLARS.
- EXECUTIVE'S ASSISTANT PREPARED EXPENSE REPORTS AND GOT THE MONEY FOR THE EXECUTIVE.

PREVENTIVE MEASURES

- LIMIT THE AMOUNT OF CASH THAT CAN BE OBTAINED.
- REQUIRE EMPLOYEES TO OBTAIN CASH IN PERSON.
- ROUTINE INTERNAL AUDITS.
- IF YOU SUSPECT SOMEONE'S ENGAGED IN FRAUD – *LOCK THEM OUT* WHILE YOU INVESTIGATE.

PONZI SCHEME

- INVESTMENT PROGRAM WHICH IS NOT SUPPORTED BY A REVENUE-PRODUCING BUSINESS IN WHICH INVESTORS ARE ATTRACTED BY PROMISES OF ENORMOUS RETURNS.
- NEW INVESTOR DOLLARS PAY PROFITS AND REPAY PRINCIPAL TO PREVIOUS INVESTORS.
- COLLAPSE INEVITABLE WHEN PERPETRATOR CANNOT ATTRACT SUFFICIENT INVESTORS TO PAY THE RETURNS AND/OR PRINCIPAL TO PREVIOUS INVESTORS.
- A BRIEF HISTORY: CHARLES PONZI.

EXAMPLE:

- YOUNG INVESTMENT ADVISOR ATTRACTS CLIENTS WITH PROMISE OF 50% PLUS RETURNS. HIS APPETITE FOR A LAVISH LIFE GROWS WITH HIS REPUTATION – REQUIRING MORE INVESTORS.
- TYPEWRITTEN STATEMENTS OF ACCOUNT.
- ONE MAN OPERATION.

SOME PREVENTIVE MEASURES

- DUE DILIGENCE ON INVESTMENT FIRMS THAT OPERATE AS A "ONE-MAN SHOW." THE LACK OF AVAILABLE INFORMATION CAN SOMETIMES BE AS TELLING AS ADVERSE INFORMATION.
- CHECK ACCOUNT STATEMENTS TO VERIFY THAT BASIC INFORMATION (E.G. STOCK VALUES) IS CORRECT.

SOME WARNING SIGNS

- INVESTMENT ADVISOR DENIES ACCESS TO DOCUMENTS THAT PROVIDE BACK UP FOR INFORMATION PROVIDED ON BARE-BONES MONTHLY STATEMENTS.
- INVESTMENT ADVISOR PROVIDES EXCUSES AS TO WHY BACK-UP DOCUMENTS ARE UNAVAILABLE OR DIFFICULT TO OBTAIN.
- RED FLAGS INCLUDE ACCOUNT STATEMENTS THAT:
  - ARE HAND-TYPED.

- CONTINUALLY CONTAIN ERRORS.
- ARE ROUTINELY SENT OUT LATE.

PART II: "SWAPS"

"SWAPS"

- LOOSELY DEFINED AS A VARIETY OF DEALS WHICH EMPLOY A QUID PRO QUO ARRANGEMENT.
- PRINCIPALLY USED TO DESCRIBE INSURANCE CONTRACTS TO COVER BANK LOANS, OTHER COMMERCIAL OBLIGATIONS AND SIMILAR AGREEMENTS.
- ALSO INCLUDE AGREEMENTS THAT HAVE CONTRA-SIDE LETTERS, I.E. GIVING SOMETHING BACK TO THE PRIMARY ENTITY EVEN IF IT IS NOT OF EQUAL VALUE.
- SOME OF THE LARGEST CURRENT ACCOUNTING SCANDALS HAVE INVOLVED SWAPS.

SELECTED EXAMPLES:

- THE "SIDE LETTER"
- EQUAL BUT UNEQUAL SERVICES

EXAMPLE # 1: THE "SIDE LETTER"

THE TRANSACTION

- ALPHA AGREES TO PURCHASE BETA FOR $100 MILLION.
- BOTH COMPANIES ANNOUNCE THE DEAL AS A $100 MILLION TRANSACTION.

THE "SWAP"

- BOTH COMPANIES AGREE IN A SIDE LETTER THAT $50 MILLION OF THE PURCHASE PRICE IS TO BE IMMEDIATELY PLACED INTO AN ESCROW ACCOUNT WITH AN INDEPENDENT AGENT WHO WILL TRANSFER THAT SUM BACK TO ALPHA OVER A SCHEDULED PERIOD OF TIME.
- THIS FACT IS NOT PUBLICLY DISCLOSED.
- BETA HAS NO RIGHTS UNDER ANY CONDITIONS TO RECEIVE THE MONIES HELD IN ESCROW.

BOOK-KEEPING

- ALPHA BOOKS THE ENTIRE PURCHASE PRICE AS VARIOUS ASSETS ON THEIR BALANCE SHEET, WITH MORE THAN $90 MILLION RECORDED AS GOODWILL.

- THE AMORTIZATION PERIOD FOR THIS AMOUNT IS 40 YEARS; OR $2.25 MILLION PER YEAR.

RESULTS

- WHEN MONIES HELD IN ESCROW ARE TRANSFERRED BACK TO ALPHA, THE INCOMING FUNDS ARE RECORDED AS A DEBIT TO CASH AND A CREDIT TO REVENUE.
- THE TOTAL PERIOD OF RECOVERY IS THREE YEARS RESULTING IN SIGNIFICANTLY HIGHER REVENUE VERSUS EXPENSE DURING THAT THREE YEAR PERIOD: APPROXIMATELY $25 MILLION IN THE FIRST YEAR; $17.5 MILLION IN THE SECOND YEAR; AND $7.5 MILLION IN THE THIRD YEAR.

ODDITIES

- ALPHA MUST PAY INCOME TAXES ON THE FICTITIOUS REVENUE DURING THE THREE YEAR PERIOD WHILE THE EXPENSES WILL NOT RESULT IN A TAX SET-OFF FOR A TOTAL OF FORTY YEARS.
- THE TIME VALUE OF MONEY CAUSES ALPHA TO LOSE SIGNIFICANT VALUE BASED ON THIS TRANSACTION.
- ALPHA PAYS TAXES ON NON-TAXABLE FUNDS THAT WERE MERELY MOVED BACK AND FORTH.

CONCLUSION

- A FRAUDULENT MISSTATEMENT OF THE FINANCIAL STATEMENTS.
- PURCHASED BUSINESS IS OVERVALUED.
- REVENUE AND CASH INFLOW ARE OVERSTATED.
- EXPENSES ARE OVERSTATED.
- A FALSE REPRESENTATION FROM BOTH COMPANIES REGARDING THE PURCHASE/SALE OF THE ENTITY.

EXAMPLE # 2: EQUAL BUT UNEQUAL SERVICES

THE TRANSACTION

- CHARLIE AND DELTA ENTER INTO TWO SEPARATE BUT EQUAL VALUE SERVICE AGREEMENTS:
  - CHARLIE AGREES TO PROVIDE ADVERTISING SERVICES.
  - DELTA AGREES TO PROVIDE REPAIR SERVICES.

THE TERMS

- BOTH AGREEMENTS ARE:
  - FOR FIVE YEAR PERIODS.
  - FOR EQUAL AMOUNTS ($10 MILLION) EACH YEAR DUE TO THE OTHER PARTY.
  - DUE AND PAYABLE ON THE SAME DAY EVERY YEAR BY WIRE TRANSFER OF FUNDS ONLY.
  - DO NOT REQUIRE EITHER PARTY TO USE THE SPECIFIED SERVICES – EVER!

IN PRACTICE

- BOTH PARTIES WIRE THE MONEY BACK AND FORTH.
- BOTH PARTIES RECORD REVENUE FROM THE EXCHANGE.

THE RESULT:

- ON A CASHFLOW BASIS, THE TRANSACTION IS CASH NEUTRAL: THERE IS BOTH A $10 MILLION DEBIT AND CREDIT TO THE CASH ACCOUNT.
- AT THE SAME TIME, THE REVENUE ACCOUNT RECEIVES A $10 MILLION CREDIT, AND A PREPAID ADVERTISING OR PREPAID REPAIRS AND MAINTENANCE SERVICES ACCOUNT RECEIVES A $10 MILLION DEBIT.
- THE RESULT IS THAT REVENUES APPEAR TO BE $10 MILLION GREATER THAN THEY ACTUALLY ARE.
- EXECUTIVES CAN BE FUNNY PEOPLE
- WHEN ONE COMPANY EXECUTIVE WAS ASKED WHY THEY CHOSE THE AMOUNT PROVIDED FOR IN THE CONTRACTS INSTEAD OF AN AMOUNT MUCH GREATER, HIS

REPLY WAS THAT THEY KNEW THEY HAD TO SET THE AMOUNT AT A LEVEL THAT WOULD SEEM BELIEVABLE.

LESSONS:

- GIVEN SARBANES-OXLEY, WHEN DRAFTING OR REVIEWING CONTRACTS, ATTORNEYS MUST CONSIDER THE ACCOUNTING IMPLICATIONS OF A TRANSACTION.

- IN EXAMPLE #1, A RED FLAG SHOULD HAVE BEEN RAISED FOR AN ATTORNEY DRAFTING THE SALES AND ESCROW AGREEMENT EVEN THOUGH THE CONTRACTS THEMSELVES WERE PERFECTLY LEGAL.

- IN EXAMPLE #2, THE ACCOUNTING IS MORE COMPLICATED, BUT THE RECIPROCAL NATURE OF THE SERVICE CONTRACTS AND THE FACT THAT THEY DID NOT REQUIRE SPECIFIC SERVICES SHOULD HAVE RAISED RED FLAGS.

PART III: CHANNEL STUFFING

- "CHANNEL STUFFING" HAS BEEN DEFINED AS A SELLER INDUCING A PURCHASER TO INCREASE SUBSTANTIALLY ITS PURCHASES BEFORE IT OTHERWISE WOULD WITH THE RESULT OF SHIFTING EARNINGS INTO EARLIER QUARTERS.

LEGAL TREATMENT – BRIEF OVERVIEW

- "CHANNEL STUFFING" IS TYPICALLY PLEAD UNDER THE SECURITIES LAWS AS A FORM OF ACCOUNTING FRAUD, E.G., A COMPANY IS MISSTATING ITS EARNINGS BY FALSELY PORTRAYING SALES.
- "THERE IS NOTHING INHERENTLY IMPROPER ABOUT PRESSING FOR SALES EARLIER THAN IN THE NORMAL COURSE. . ."
- A SUCCESSFUL COMPLAINT WILL TYPICALLY ALLEGE THAT A DEFENDANT KNEW OF DECLINING DEMAND, INDUCED THE DISTRIBUTOR OR CUSTOMER TO PURCHASE PRODUCT THEY DID NOT OTHERWISE NEED AND THAT THE RESULTING REVENUE MATERIALLY IMPACTED THE DEFENDANTS' REPORTED EARNINGS.

EXAMPLE: SUNBEAM

- "CHAINSAW AL" – REQUIRED DISTRIBUTORS TO "PURCHASE" ITEMS AT THE END OF A REPORTING PERIOD.
- DISTRIBUTORS HAD A SEPARATE SIDE AGREEMENT ALLOWING THEM TO RETURN UNSOLD ITEMS SUBSEQUENTLY AT THEIR DISCRETION.
- UNDER GAAP THE SALE OF THE ABOVE ITEMS WAS NOT "COMPLETE" – REVENUE SHOULD NOT HAVE BEEN RECOGNIZED

A FINAL WORD: RELATED PARTIES – THE POTENTIAL FOR ABUSE

- "SWAPPING"
- "CHANNEL STUFFING"

- CONSOLIDATION
- HIDING COSTS
- HIDING DEBT

CASE 1: RELATED COMPANY OWNERSHIP

- COMPANY D SELLS PRODUCT TO COMPANY C AT FULL MARKET VALUE
- COMPANY D IMMEDIATELY RECOGNIZES REVENUE ON SALES
- COMPANY C HOLDS PRODUCT FOR 6-12 MONTHS
- THE PRODUCT IS SOFTWARE WITH AN AVERAGE SHELF LIFE OF USUALLY 12 MONTHS
- COMPANY A PROVIDED FINANCING TO COMPANY C USING B AS AN INTERMEDIARY FOR PRODUCT PURCHASES FROM COMPANY D
- DISCLOSURE IS MADE BY COMPANY D OF RELATED PARTY RELATIONSHIP BETWEEN D AND C ONLY
- NO DISCLOSURE IS MADE OF COMPANY C'S SALES OF INVENTORY HELD

NOTES

14

FRAUD: PROTECT YOUR CLIENT & BUSINESS

Karen Kincaid Balmer, CPA, CrFA

Kincaid Consulting LLC

Reprinted from the PLI Course Handbook,
*Basics of Accounting & Finance:
What Every Practicing Lawyer Needs to Know —
Summer 2006* (Order #8650).

No one likes to think fraud can happen on their watch. However, owners, managers, directors or counsel are likely to encounter a fraud situation at some point in each of their careers.

The implications for a company can be more than just financial. Fraud results from a major breach of trust. This breach of trust can lead to feelings of remorse, guilt and/or anger toward the perpetrator. Co-workers and managers begin to question why they didn't see what was happening and often doubt their own judgment and abilities.

First reactions to the discovery of fraud are generally shock and inaction. Too often management is surprised to learn that controls were not sufficient to prevent significant losses.

Unfortunately, trusted employees often have the advantage of relationships and positions where they can still influence management and directors immediately after being caught in order to let them " stay to help correct the problem." While the offer may sound genuine, it is most often made so that the perpetrator can continue to manipulate the process and destroy important documents and computer records.

This can happen, because companies can and do stay in business for years with honest employees who do not take advantage of long standing weaknesses.

Some of the "must do" steps that we recommend to prevent fraud, particularly for our smaller business clients, include:

- Review the physical controls over cash receipts and expenditures;
- Review how entries are made to the company's books and records and by whom;
- Implement necessary improvements to existing controls;
- Require thorough pre-hiring background checks of all new employees who will handle cash assets or prepare the company's books;
- Have the owner or external auditor periodically receive unopened bank statements and review all returned checks and other outflows to ensure that there are no suspicious or improper disbursements (companies that receive check copies on electronic medium should be subject to the same type of review);

Simple steps that management should take once a fraud is suspected include:

- Remove the suspected perpetrator from the site immediately for the duration of the investigation;

- Shut down the perpetrator's access to computers, documents and other employees;
- Notifying counsel or the company's insurance carrier immediately (failure to notify the carrier may invalidate the policy);
- Through counsel, engage the proper financial expert to conduct the forensic investigation, to ensure that all investigative work will withstand the scrutiny of the insurance company, potential civil or criminal enquiries, etc.

[Neither of the above lists should be deemed to be all inclusive of recommended steps during an actual investigation.]

All frauds have one element in common; lack of adequate internal controls. Knowing this and taking the steps to react swiftly and minimize losses can be invaluable.

Management and owners are often reluctant to have someone come into their business with the express purpose of checking controls when they have never knowingly had a fraudulent employee. The old adage, "if it ain't broke, don't fix it" often comes into play. The unfortunate result of not evaluating and improving controls is that the longer a fraud goes undetected, the more damaging the consequences.

Routine, annual financial statement audits may not provide and in-depth review of internal controls. While auditors' responsibilities to detect fraud have increased in recent years, testing procedures for a financial statement audit are designed to provide "reasonable assurance" that the financial statements taken as a whole are fairly presented. Many small and mid-sized businesses usually do not have an audit, rather, they have less rigorous procedures performed to complete financial statements, such as reviews or compilations.

Small businesses also have a more difficult time implementing comprehensive controls due to their limited ability to segregate critical duties, such as cash collection and record keeping. In cases like these we always tell our clients the following: If you can implement only one control, we strongly recommend that the owner, manager or external auditor periodically receive the bank statements unopened directly from the bank.

These statements should be opened promptly and all cancelled checks or other disbursements reviewed to ensure each payee and payment have a valid business purpose. Any questionable items should be investigated promptly. This action will alert employees that the company does double-check their cash expenditures – prior to and subsequent to payment. This simple act can save millions of dollars simply by identifying and ending fraud while losses are still small.

Internal control breakdowns and their consequences, particularly during the recent accounting scandals involving major public companies, have led the Securities and Exchange Commission to adopt enhanced rules, beginning effective May 27, 2003, which require public company executives to certify that their companies have adequate controls to prevent and detect accounting violations and fraud, and to evaluate and report at the end of each quarter any substantial change in their internal controls.

The accounting firm that audits a company's books will also have to attest in the company's annual report that company officials consider the internal controls over financial reporting to be adequate. (New York Times article date May 28, 2003)

While these rules do not specifically apply to small and mid-sized companies, the issue of internal control has reached an unprecedented level in U.S. businesses. No small or mid-sized firm, whether for profit or not for profit will not feel the effects of this internal control push. Businesses seeking to borrow money, not for profit boards and many others are being asked about their systems of control.

Businesses that have good internal controls lessen their economic risk of loss, as well as the fiduciary risk to management and board members.

So, whether it's a) an employee stealing cash from the register, b) a loan officer setting up fictitious loans, c) a manager booking fictitious sales, or 4) any number of other nefarious schemes, businesses can significantly deter or prevent fraud by periodically verifying that controls are in place and functioning. They can prevent additional losses by knowing how to handle the situation once a fraud has been found.

NOTES

15

SMALL BUSINESSES, TRUST AND INTERNAL CONTROL WEAKNESSES

Karen Kincaid Balmer, CPA, CrFA

Kincaid Consulting LLC

Reprinted from the PLI Course Handbook,
Basics of Accounting & Finance:
What Every Practicing Lawyer Needs to Know —
Summer 2006 (Order #8650).

The Association of Certified Fraud Examiners estimates that 6% of all revenues generated in 2004 will be lost as a result of fraud. They further state that small businesses are the most vulnerable to fraud and abuse, averaging $127,500 in losses per scheme as compared to $97,000 in the largest companies. I agree, based on my client experiences. The reason for the substantially smaller amount lost at large entities has to do with a greater level of internal controls. More frauds are prevented and more are stopped at an earlier stage due to good internal controls.

I recently had the opportunity to work on a bank fraud case involving a small, well-capitalized regional bank. The bank had suffered a sizable loss over a period spanning more than ten years that wiped out more than 50% of the shareholders' equity in the bank.

An external audit discovered the first clues of an elaborate scheme in which millions of dollars had been stolen by shifting monies between existing customers' loan accounts rather than creating new loans under fictitious names.

The external audit firm had limited forensic accounting experience, while the bank's board and management had none. As is typical of many complex frauds, it took some time to pull together enough information to verify that a fraud had in fact occurred and to start to put together the audit trail required for the insurance company, the regulatory bank examiners and other investigative agencies. This detailed and elaborate scheme entailed thousands of false transactions to obscure the true nature of the actual transactions.

When initially questioned, the officer convinced the board and management that all of the problems were due to a lack of training and an over burdensome workload. He was permitted to remain at the bank.

Hundreds of documents disappeared: A typical, nearly tragic mistake in judgment. Fortunately, the officer was unable to undo the thousands of complicated transactions that remained in the computer database.

The internal control weaknesses that allowed this to happen and continue to happen without detection for such a long period were numerous: The officer had the authority to sign money orders for any amount; there was no limit that required a second signature; the officer had responsibility for overseeing the analysis and reconciliations performed each month on the activity in that account; he access to the computer systems that block loan statements from being prepared and sent to individual loan customers; he had sole responsibility for resolving all customer questions or problems with loan balances, which included processing the transactions to "clean up the books."

Viewing these weaknesses articulated in such a concise manner begs the question, "How did no one at the bank, their auditors or any of the myriad regulatory auditors not know or suspect the potential for foul play?"

The answer is Trust mixed with a healthy dose of obfuscation. People want to trust people in positions of responsibility, especially if they are well spoken, respectful and hardworking. For the most part we are right to do so. No company wants to create an atmosphere of paranoia and distrust.

However, many frauds are perpetrated by long term, trusted employees. In this case, a number of bank employees and board members subsequently questioned and blamed themselves for not having seen what was happening. Their money was gone, but more importantly, so was their trust, comfort and sense of stability.

By implementing an effective system of internal controls, fraud can be more easily exposed or prevented by co-workers employing simple methods. It is critical to have a good set of controls in place and to review and update them on a regular basis.

Internal Controls help small and large entities in many ways:

First, they let all employees know that there are controls and that someone is monitoring them. Having highly valued and trusted employees does not remove the factor of temptation. Circumstances may arise in any employee's life that puts enormous stress on personal financial resources, providing the person with a rationalization for "borrowing" funds. Without proper preventative internal controls in place, an employee has the opportunity to take funds or other property. Once they have motive and opportunity, fraud is much more likely to occur.

In this case, the bank or its auditors could have caught and prevented the fraud much earlier by simply doing one of two things: 1) assigning the responsibility for independently resolving all customer questions and disputes to another employee, or 2) assigning the responsibility to reconcile the money order account on a frequent basis and investigating any unusual transactions to another employee. This list is by no means inclusive of all the possible controls that could be put into place.

Second, with strong controls in effect, the bank and its shareholders will have a higher degree of certainty that the bank's financial reports are accurate and reliable. Even if the board or a bank's officers are unaware of fraudulent activities, they can be held responsible for payment of civil money and other penalties if fraudulent activity materially impacts the reports filed for regulatory purposes.

Third, it costs small businesses far more to clean up after a fraud than to prevent one. In the case discussed herein, the costs for investigating, reporting, implementing corrective actions, legal costs, increased insurance costs, associated penalties and fines far exceeded the amount recoverable under the Bank's insurance policy.

As experienced accountants we have been involved in investigating "What went wrong?" and how it should be fixed to make businesses more secure. Many businesses view internal controls as cumbersome and unnecessary. However, having witnessed how financially and emotionally devastating fraud can be, the following age old saying may be appropriate:

Ben Franklin's adage, "An ounce of prevention is worth a pound of cure!" aptly applies to small businesses and the need for internal controls.

NOTES

16

PURCHASE PRICE DISPUTES, HOW THE FINANCIAL EXPERT CAN HELP YOU AVOID LEGAL LANDMINES

Glenn Newman, CPA/ABV, CFE, MBA

Robert Gray, CPA/ABV, CFE, FACFEI

Parente Randolph

I. PURCHASE PRICE DISPUTES THE ROLE OF YOUR FINANCIAL EXPERT

- Agenda:
  - Overview-the Process
  - Where Buyers and Sellers Collide
  - The Agreement-Pertinent Sections
  - Common Problems
  - War Stories
  - Questions/Answers
- M&A Activity for US; YTD through April:
  - 2006:
    - 3,410 deals valued at $427,234 million.
  - 2007:
    - 3,398 deals valued at $621,809 million.

  Source: *"Mergers & Acquisitions Report",* May 7, 2007

II. OVERVIEW OF THE ACQUISITION/DIVESTITURE PROCESS

- Mergers, Acquisitions and Divestitures are used by companies to meet their strategic/growth goals:
  - "The Wave Effect" - Fluctuates with economic and business cycles;
  - Common clauses in M&A contracts relate to accounting, economic, and financial reporting matters; and
  - View from the financial expert, not the legal perspective.

III. PURCHASE PRICE DISPUTES, THE "ROLE" OF YOUR FINANCIAL EXPERT

- Provide assistance during due diligence;
- Provide professional services in connection with deal disputes;
- Not for the "Faint of Heart";
- Usually requires a combination of GAAP, professional standards, valuation, finance, industry knowledge and experience, etc.

IV. THE PROCESS

- Typically begins with a negotiated price and contract terms for all or part of a business. Resulting in:
  1. A signed Letter of Intent ("LOI"), generally broad and non-binding, then. . . .
  2. Execution of Purchase and Sale Agreement, (due diligence by buyer, internal approvals by both parties including Board of Directors);
  3. What about seller's due diligence?
  4. How much due diligence is enough?

V. THE DEAL IS DONE. . .NOW WHAT?

Preclosing Period:

1. The length of time between the signing of the Agreement and the transaction's closing.
2. Period can vary widely, but usually 1 to 3 months;
3. The seller usually manages the business being sold;
4. Typically profit or loss accrues to the seller; and
5. Adjustments made to purchase price for the interim period

VI. THE DEAL WHERE BUYERS/SELLERS COLLIDE!

- Buyer:
  1. Maximize value, pay the least for the most:
     - Purchase at the perceived value of the company;
     - Or value of the assets acquired;
  2. Conducts due diligence:
     - Evaluate the assets it will receive;
     - Evaluate the liabilities it will assume;
     - Target a reduction to purchase price;
  3. Right to perform a post closing review.

- Seller:
  1. Maximize value, maintain or increase the price to be paid
  2. Eliminate exposure after the sale:
     - Sale to absolve seller from exposure to unknown or contingent liabilities
     - Avoid unfavorable purchase price adjustments,
- Trugman: Value v. Price!
  - Valuation is a prophecy to the future;
  - Valuation is required for tax purposes and financial reporting;
  - Purchase price is allocated to underlying assets;
  - "Value" is what you hope to get!
  - "Price" is what is paid!
  - Source: "*Understanding Business Valuation*", 2nd Edition, Gary R. Trugman
- **Post Closing Adjustments:**
  - Adjusts the purchase price to account for results of operations and other transactions during the stub period.
    1. Stub Period is between X date, (date of signed agreement or other agreed upon date) and the transaction's closing date.
  - Seller provides buyer a closing balance sheet prepared as of the date of closing (or close as).
    1. Used as basis to calculate the post closing adjustment(s).
  - Buyer usually has the right to Perform Post Closing Review.
    1. May object to the closing balance sheet in accordance with the Purchase/Sale agreement.
    2. Areas that will generate disputes are identified.

VII. PURCHASE/SALE AGREEMENTS, DEVIL IN THE DETAILS

- **The Agreement:**
  - Provisions seeks to assign, allocate or indemnify the risks between the parties focusing on those related to accounting issues and financial reporting:
    - Representations and Warranties;
    - Post Closing Adjustments;
    - Covenants;
    - Indemnification Clauses;
    - Earn-Out Clauses; and
    - Arbitration Clauses.
- **Representations and Warranties – Buyer's Perspective:**
  - Assist buyer in gaining an understanding of the business and its value drivers;
  - Enables the buyer to recover damages if the seller makes inaccurate/incomplete representations;
  - Allows the buyer to abort the transaction if it finds issues with the seller's representations before closing; and
  - Buyer representations generally involve financial considerations, ability to complete the transaction.
- **Representations and Warranties:**
  - Seller's Perspective:
    1. Prepared financial statements in accordance with Generally Accepted Accounting Principles (GAAP);
    2. Is GAAP consistently applied?
    3. Prepared in accordance with historical company policy or some other basis of accounting;
    4. No contingent liabilities exist, except those disclosed in F/S's;
    5. No material adverse changes since date of financials used in negotiations; and
    6. Generally does not state the financial statements are complete, accurate, true or correct.

- **Post Closing Adjustment Clause:**
  - Necessary since the business continues and as a result financial statements change from that which buyer based purchase price.
    1. Attempts to account for changes in financial position (Balance Sheet, Revenues and/or Cash Flows.);
    2. Usually allocates to the sellers the economic risks and profits during the period from the initial financial statements until the closing date;
    3. Protects the buyer against potential seller abuses, (e.g. sale of inventory without replacement).
- **Post Closing Adjustment Clause:**
  - States a calculation of value-often a net asset value-on the closing balance sheet and compares the value to the value reflected in the financial statements upon which the buyer based the purchase price;
  - Commonly calls for a dollar-for-dollar adjustment for changes in net asset value;
  - Can call for a multiple of the change in net asset value if it affects operating earnings, inventory reduction;
  - Adjustment can add or subtract from purchase price; and
  - Escrow accounts often involved.

VIII. COMMON PROBLEM AREAS

- **Post Closing Review:**
  - Litigation most often arises out of buyers review of the post closing balance sheet and specific objections to the way seller accounted for, or did not account, for items contained in the balance sheet.
    - Since buyer now is in control of the company, increased opportunity to:
      - Gain access to information that may have not been available prior to the closing;
      - Use company personnel's knowledge of accounting systems, practices and procedures;

- By objecting to balance sheet amounts or balances, buyer is proposing adjustments; and
- There is usually a specified period buyer can object and propose purchase price adjustment.

• **Preferable v. Acceptable GAAP:**

- Often parties mistakenly believe that GAAP provides one "**right number**";
- Disputes arise between Buyer's and Seller's interpretation;

1. Buyer proposes an adjustment based on a different method from that applied by the seller. Claims seller used a method different than that buyer's understanding of the purchase agreement terms.
2. Seller may change from one acceptable GAAP method of accounting to another in the closing balance sheet to affect the purchase price.

• **GAAP v. Consistency:**

- Does GAAP or consistency take precedence when applying an accounting method to a particular transaction or account balance?

1. While GAAP usually takes precedence over consistency, absent the specific requirements of the agreement, buyers should be wary of making a blanket overall statement concerning GAAP unless they specifically understand the ramifications to their financial statements.

- Application of term "consistent" - Does consistent mean:

1. Done repeatedly, consistently reported in the same manner;
2. Calculated in the same manner consistently; or
3. A particular amount is consistent.

• **Interim v. Year End Reporting:**

- Agreement may mandate consistency between precluding financials and final financials at closing.

1. Interim monthly financials;
2. Year end financial statements;
3. Quarter end financial statements;

- Do all of these financial statements report transactions in the same manner or are more rigorous standards applied for year end financial statements as opposed to those issued at an interim month end?
- If different sets of standard are applied and precluding financials were based on an interim statement but closing financials are at year end, audited, which methodology applies?

• **Financials Prepared Based on Company Policy:**

- An alternative to GAAP. Common situation arises when:
  1. A subsidiary does not keep its own financials;
  2. Seller is carving out a part of a business unit or division;
  3. Top level adjustments to GAAP;
  4. Materiality; or
  5. Exclusion of Footnotes.

• **Errors or Irregularities Discovered After Closing:**

- Generally not addressed in the Agreement because it is assumed that financials statements are correct. (Errors, irregularities, GAAP departures.)
  1. Circumstances to consider- when it occurred, when it became know, when it was corrected;
  2. If error occurred in financial statements purchase price was based on, seller corrects error and it results in an upward adjustment to the purchase price, buyer will argue that seller should not benefit from their own errors;
  3. If buyer detects and error that was not present in the financial statements, and it would lower the purchase price, buyer will seek a purchase price adjustment;
  4. What do you think the buyer would do if they discover an error favorable to them, company should be worth more, that were present in the closing financial statements?
     - Correct! They probably will not dispute it

- **Materiality:**
  - Concept can be applied to individual items, transactions, balance sheet or income statement line items or the financial statements taken as a whole. Large area for potential for dispute.
  - Many agreements use a threshold, specific dollar amount after which an adjustment is necessary. Adjustment can be in the form of:
    1. Gross amount is adjusted, dollar for dollar;
    2. Basket or deductible, adjustment for amount over materiality level;
  - As many agreements do not address materiality, the level may be implied from other language contained in the Agreement;
  - If materiality is not addressed, seller can have a difficult time defending purchase price adjustments buyer desires. However, if GAAP is written as the basis for closing financials, materiality can be considered.
  - ***GET IT (Purchase Price) RIGHT THE FIRST TIME!***
- **Right to Offset:**
  - Often not written into agreements, sellers may try to claim a right of offset as a defense against buyer's proposed adjustments.
    1. Buyer will most likely only identify those adjustments which are advantageous to them;
    2. Seller tries to prevent the buyer from this "selective objection" to amounts recorded in the financial statements by offsetting adjustments
       - Under accrual to offset over accrual;
  - Difficult to ascertain the intent of the parties and decide whether to adjust the purchase price if agreement is absent on this issue;
  - May be decided by agreement's specified applicability of GAAP; GAAP based on line item or GAAP for financial statements taken as a whole

- **Earn Out Provisions, Put Back Provisions and Hindsight:**
  - Commonality of these three areas involve future performance and/or knowledge gained after the transaction's closing date.
    1. Earn Outs: Complicated because buyer may not run the business in the same manner the seller did, combined with other entities, segment divested;
    2. Put Backs: Relates to adequacy of various allowance accounts, A/R, inventory;
       - Interpretation, did buyer make sufficient effort to collect accounts receivable in the ordinary course of business?
       - How is ordinary course of business standard applied?
    3. Hindsight: Do the events that occurred post closing support the amounts reflected on financial statement?
       - Generally not persuasive for buyer if no persuasive evidence the information or knowledge existed prior to the closing financial statements being prepared in accordance with GAAP.
       - Seller has a persuasive argument if buyer claimed adjustment for account subsequently collected.
- **Issues of Control:**
  - Involves the manipulation of accounting and financial reporting by the party in control through the postclosing adjustment process.
    1. In a management buyout, buyer runs the company between the signing of agreement and postclosing adjustment. Opportunity exists for the accounting and financial reporting to be manipulated.
    2. Seller, if in control, may attempt to "clean up" the balance sheet to buyer's detriment during the stub period.
  - Control can also be a factor related to Earn Out and Put Back Provisions.

IX. HELP, WE NEED AN ACCOUNTANT/CONSULTANT!

- What can the Accountant/Consultant Offer?
  - Independent and unbiased advice in approaching disputes and can identify alternative, strategic options;
  - Outside party does not carry an emotional attachment to the transaction; and
  - Often can enhance and expedite the dispute resolution process.
- What Services can the Accountant/Consultant Offer?
  - Dispute Formulation, working for one of the parties involved.
    - Identifying objections to postclosing and purchase price adjustment clauses;
    - Calculating and supporting objections under purchase price adjustments clauses;
    - Interpreting technical accounting literature to establish whether a proposed adjustment is warranted under GAAP;
    - Reporting objections in accordance with the terms of the purchase/sale agreement; and
    - Reviewing the opposing party's probable objections and support.
- Additional Services the Accountant/Consultant May Offer:
  1. Assist in discovery requests, depositions, document reviews;
  2. Conduct analyses and calculate damages;
  3. Trial presentation: testimony, preparation, cross examination;
  4. Dispute negotiation/arbitration/settlement; and
  5. Help to avoid disputes. (Assist with identifying ambiguous language in Agreements or drafting complex clauses.)

NOTES

NOTES

17

CURRENT SEC ENFORCEMENT ACTIONS, ACCOUNTING AND DISCLOSURE ISSUES

Alexander M. Vasilescu

Securities and Exchange Commission

Basics of Accounting & Finance Summer 2006: What Every Practicing Lawyer Needs to Know

Alexander M. Vasilescu

SEC Regional Trial Counsel/

Chief of Trial Unit

1

U.S. SECURITIES AND EXCHANGE COMMISSION

"We are the investor's advocate."

William O. Douglas
SEC Chairman, 1937-1939

2

Disclaimer

The views expressed in this presentation are those of Alexander Vasilescu. The SEC, as a matter of policy, disclaims responsibility for any private publication or statement by any of its employees. The views expressed herein are those of the authors and do not necessarily reflect the views of the Commission or its staff.

3

SEC Enforcement Division

Current SEC Enforcements, Accounting and Disclosure Issues

- current SEC enforcement issues
- "hot topics," such as the Sarbanes-Oxley Act of 2002,
- revenue recognition issues,
- off balance sheet investment and liabilities issues,
- auditor independence, and pro forma issues.

5

SEC
Investigations Today

6

Current SEC Enforcement Issues

- Larger Penalties and Monetary Awards
- Cooperation Means Much More Than Complying With Subpoenas Requesting Documents and Testimony
- Parallel Criminal Prosecutions Much More Frequent
- Gate-Keepers Will Be Held Accountable – attorneys, accountants and board members.

7

SEC Investigations Today

- More Investigations
- Quicker Investigations
- More Aggressive Investigations
- Casting Wider Net
- Increase in Joint DOJ-SEC Investigations
- 21(a) Cooperation
  - Privilege Waiver Generally Requested

8

SEC Investigations Today- 2

- Fraud Charges Regularly Charged Against Company
  - Conflict Between Company and Individuals
- Increased Personal Liability
  - Individuals
  - Companies
  - Audit Committee Members
  - Audit Partners
  - Lawyers

9

SEC Investigations Today- 3

- Tougher Settlements
  - Increase in Amount of Civil Penalties
  - Increase In Amount of Time-Out in Rule 102(e) Proceedings

10

Larger Penalties and Monetary Awards

- Entities
  - WorldCom - $750 million
  - Qwest -$250 million civil penalty (to be distributed)
  - Computer Associates - $225 million in restitution
  - Symbol -$37 million in civil penalty and other monetary relief
  - KPMG -$10 million civil penalty
- Individuals
  - Frank Walsh (Tyco) -- $20 million (restitution)
  - David Delainey (Enron)-- $3.74 million
  - Paul Allaire (Xerox) -- $1 million + disgorgement
  - Barry Romeril (Xerox) -- $1 million + disgorgement
- In many cases, no tax deductions; no insurance

11

Cooperation Means Much More Than Complying With Subpoena Requesting Documents and Testimony

- The Seaboard Standard
  Link on web: www.sec.gov/litigation/investreport/34-44969.htm
- The DOJ's Thompson Memo Standard
  Link on web: www.usdoj.gov/dag/cftf/corporate_guidelines.htm
- Sarbanes-Oxley SEC 307
  link on web: www.law.uc.edu/CCL/SOact/sec307.html

12

Seaboard

The SEC's enforcement allows for leniency for cooperation.

- The Seaboard § 21(a) Report sets forth the basic parameters defining the SEC's "carrot," and like the other side of a coin it shares with SOX 307 (discussed below), it seeks cooperation from the public company. The Commission gave Seaboard a lenient resolution, no action, for the fraud committed by the controller of its subsidiary based on the company's break-neck internal investigation and unfettered access it provided to the SEC. A public company's cooperation with the SEC, does not mean that the public company or other respondent or defendant will necessary obtain a free pass.

13

DOJ's Thompson Memo and SEC's Seaboard

On January 20, 2003, the then-Deputy Attorney General, Larry Thompson, issued a revised version of a previous DOJ memorandum concerning the prosecution of corporations. The Thompson Memo, while very similar to the previous Holder Memo, directs prosecutors to place "increased emphasis on and scrutiny of the authenticity of a corporation's cooperation" and also places greater stress on compliance programs. The memo outlines nine factors that a prosecutor should consider in deciding whether to charge the corporation:

- *1. the nature and seriousness of the offense, including the risk of harm to the public, and applicable policies and priorities, if any, governing the prosecution of corporations for particular categories of crime...;*
- *2. the pervasiveness of wrongdoing within the corporation, including the complicity in, or condonation of, the wrongdoing by corporate management...;*
- *3. the corporation's history of similar conduct, including prior criminal, civil, and regulatory enforcement actions against it...;*

14

DOJ's Thompson Memo and SEC's Seaboard

- *4. the corporation's timely and voluntary disclosure of wrongdoing and its willingness to cooperate in the investigation of its agents, including, if necessary, the waiver of corporate attorney client and work product protection...;*
- *5. the existence and adequacy of the corporation's compliance program...;*
- *6. the corporation's remedial actions, including any efforts to implement an effective compliance program or to improve an existing one, to replace responsible management, to discipline or terminate wrongdoers, to pay restitution, and to cooperate with the relevant government agencies...;*

15

DOJ's Thompson Memo and SEC's Seaboard

- *7. collateral consequences, including disproportionate harm to shareholders, pension holders and employees not proven personally culpable and impact on the public arising from the prosecution...;*
- *8. the adequacy of the prosecution of individuals responsible for the corporation's malfeasance; [and]*
- *9. the adequacy of remedies such as civil or regulatory enforcement actions....*
- The Thompson Memo takes the view that management is "responsible for a corporate culture in which criminal conduct is either discouraged or tacitly encouraged." In discussing corporate compliance programs, the memo states that the two key questions are: "Is the corporation's compliance program well designed?" and "Does the corporation's compliance program work?" It also notes that compliance programs should be tailored to detect the types of misconduct most likely to occur in the corporation's line of business.

16

Sarbanes-Oxley Section 307

Congress has charted a similar course with Section 307 of Sarbanes-Oxley (SOX).

That law and its implementing regulations not only require up-the-chain reporting within an organization, but also permit lawyers to publicly withdraw or disclose confidential information to the SEC if an issuer fails to adopt corrective action.

17

Current SEC Enforcement Initiatives

18

Newest Trends

- Options Backdating Cases

19

Brocade -- options

SEC v. Gregory L. Reyes, et al.
Litigation Release No. 19768 (July 20, 2006)
http://www.sec.gov/litigation/litreleases/2006/lr19768.htm

On July 20, 2006, the Commission announced the filing of civil securities fraud charges against Gregory L. Reyes, the former CEO, President, and Chairman of Brocade Communications Systems, Inc., and Stephanie Jensen, its former Vice President of Human Resources, alleging that the two routinely backdated stock option grants to give employees favorably priced options without recording necessary compensation expenses. The action was among the first cases involving manipulation of stock option grants in violation of the federal securities laws.

20

Brocade -- options

According to the Commission's complaint, Reyes and Jensen regularly caused Brocade to grant "in-the-money" options (i.e., the exercise price is below the stock's market price on the day of grant, giving the recipient an immediate paper gain) to both new and current employees between 2000 and 2004, but backdated documents to make it appear that the options were "at-the-money" (i.e., the exercise price is the same as the stock's market price on the day of the grant) when granted, thus concealing millions of dollars in expenses from investors. Under well-settled accounting principles applicable at the time, options granted "at-the-money" did not need to be expensed. In contrast, options granted "in-the-money" needed to be recorded as a compensation expense.

21

Brocade -- options

The complaint alleged that Reyes repeatedly used hindsight to select a date with a lower stock price from the recent past as the supposed option grant date. The complaint alleged that, to facilitate the scheme, Jensen created, or directed others to create, paperwork making it appear that the options had been granted on the earlier date. In some instances, employment offer letters and compensation committee minutes were falsified and purported to document option grants to employees before they had even been hired by the company. As a result of this practice, Brocade was able to give employees "in-the-money" stock options without having to recognize compensation expenses as required by accounting rules. When these stock option abuses surfaced, Brocade was required to restate and revise its financial statements for fiscal years 1999 through 2004.

22

Brocade -- options

The complaint also named Antonio Canova, Brocade's former CFO, who is alleged to have learned of the backdating after joining Brocade. According to the complaint, Canova was specifically warned in writing that option paperwork had been forged to enable an employee to get favorably priced options; however, he took no action and failed to advise Brocade's auditors and Audit Committee. The complaint alleged that despite this knowledge, Canova signed Brocade's false and misleading financial statements and SEC filings.

The Commission's complaint charged Reyes, Canova, and Jensen with fraud and other violations of the federal securities laws, including the books-and-records, internal controls, misrepresentations to auditors, and Sarbanes-Oxley certification provisions.

23

Comverse -- Options

- **SEC Charges Former Comverse Technology, Inc. CEO, CFO, and General Counsel in Stock Option Backdating Scheme**
- **U.S. Attorney's Office for the Eastern District of New York Files Separate Criminal Complaint**
- **FOR IMMEDIATE RELEASE**
  2006-137
- *Washington, D.C., August 9, 2006* - The Securities and Exchange Commission today filed civil charges against three former senior executives of Comverse Technology, Inc. (Comverse), alleging that they engaged in a decade-long fraudulent scheme to grant undisclosed, in-the-money options to themselves and to others by backdating stock option grants to coincide with historically low closing prices of Comverse common stock. Two of the executives, Comverse's founder and former Chairman and CEO Jacob "Kobi" Alexander, and David Kreinberg, Comverse's former Chief Financial Officer, also created a slush fund of backdated options by causing options to be granted to fictitious employees and, later, used these options to recruit and retain key personnel. The other executive charged in the SEC complaint is William F. Sorin, Comverse's former General and Senior General Counsel, and a former Comverse director.

24

Comverse -- Options

- The complaint alleges that the former executives collectively realized millions of dollars of ill-gotten compensation through the exercise of illegally backdated option grants and the subsequent sale of Comverse common stock. As part of the scheme, the former executives made material misrepresentations to investors regarding Comverse's stock option grants and concealed from investors that Comverse had not recorded compensation expenses for option grants. As a result, Comverse, a maker of software, systems, and related services for multimedia communication and information processing applications headquartered in New York, N.Y., materially overstated its net income and earnings per share between 1991 and at least 2002.

25

Comverse -- Options

- The Commission's complaint, filed in the United States District Court for the Eastern District of New York after a five-month investigation, alleges that, beginning in 1991, Alexander repeatedly used hindsight to select a date when the closing price of Comverse's common stock was at or near a quarterly or annual low. Alexander later communicated this date and closing price to Sorin in order for it to be used as the date of, and exercise price for, a grant of Comverse options. Sorin, with Alexander's knowledge, then created company records that falsely indicated that a committee of Comverse's board of directors had actually approved the option grant on the date Alexander had "cherry-picked." Kreinberg, the complaint alleges, joined the scheme no later than 1998, and assisted Alexander in selecting backdated grant dates. Kreinberg knew that company records reflected false grant dates.

26

Comverse -- Options

- Alexander and Kreinberg, according to the complaint, also created a slush fund of backdated Comverse options between 1999 and 2002 by, among other methods, secretly inserting fictitious names amid the names of actual Comverse employees on proposed option grantee lists which then were submitted to a committee of Comverse's board of directors for approval. Kreinberg instructed a Comverse employee to conceal the existence of the slush fund from Comverse's auditors and in March 2006, after learning that a special committee of Comverse's board would investigate the company's option grants, Kreinberg undertook to hide the existence of the slush fund by altering records in Comverse's electronic option-tracking system. Alexander, Kreinberg, and Sorin also made misrepresentations to Comverse's auditors in order to conceal the backdating scheme.

27

Comverse -- Options

- As a result of the scheme, the complaint alleges that Alexander realized actual gains of nearly $138 million from sales of stock underlying the exercises of backdated options that were granted during the 1991 through 2001 period. At least $6.4 million of this gain represents the in-the-money portion of the options at the time of the grant to Alexander. Kreinberg realized an actual gain of nearly $13 million from sales of stock underlying the exercises of backdated options that were granted during the 1994 to 2001 period, with at least $1 million of this gain representing the in-the-money portion of the options at the time of the grant to Kreinberg. Sorin realized an actual gain of more than $14 million from sales of stock underlying the exercises of backdated options that were granted during the 1991 to 2001 period, with approximately $1 million of this gain representing the in-the-money portion of the options at the time of the grant to Sorin.

28

Comverse -- Options

- The complaint alleges that under well-settled accounting principles in effect at the time, companies that granted in-the-money options were required to record a corresponding compensation expense and disclose such amounts in filings with the Commission. Comverse has publicly announced that it expects to restate historical financial results for multiple years in order to record additional, material non-cash charges for option-related compensation expenses.

29

Comverse -- Options

- Between fiscal year 2001 and 2002, Kreinberg, with Sorin's knowledge, is alleged to have initiated a similar backdating scheme at Ulticom, Inc., a publicly-traded, majority-owned subsidiary of Comverse. Like Comverse, Ulticom has publicly announced that it expects to restate historical financial results for multiple years in order to record additional, material non-cash charges for option-related compensation expenses.

30

Apple -- Options

- *April 24, 2007* - The Securities and Exchange Commission filed charges against two former senior executives of Apple, Inc. in a matter involving improper stock option backdating. The Commission accused former General Counsel Nancy R. Heinen of participating in the fraudulent backdating of options granted to Apple's top officers that caused the company to underreport its expenses by nearly $40 million. The Commission's complaint alleges that Heinen, of Portola Valley, Calif., caused Apple to backdate two large options grants to senior executives of Apple — a February 2001 grant of 4.8 million options to Apple's Executive Team and a December 2001 grant of 7.5 million options to Apple Chief Executive Officer Steve Jobs — and altered company records to conceal the fraud.

31

Apple -- Options

- The Commission also filed, and simultaneously settled, charges against former Apple Chief Financial Officer Fred D. Anderson, of Atherton, Calif., alleging that Anderson should have noticed Heinen's efforts to backdate the Executive Team grant but failed to take steps to ensure that Apple's financial statements were correct. As part of the settlement, Anderson agreed (without admitting or denying the allegations) to pay approximately $3.5 million in disgorgement and penalties..

32

Apple -- Options

- According to the Commission's complaint, filed in the Northern District of California, Apple granted 4.8 million options to six members of its executive team (including Heinen and Anderson) in February 2001. Because the options were in-the-money when granted (i.e. could be exercised to purchase Apple shares at a below market price), Apple was required to report a compensation charge in its publicly filed financial statements. The Commission alleges that, in order to avoid reporting this expense, Heinen caused Apple to backdate options to January 17, 2001, when Apple's share price was substantially lower. Heinen is also alleged to have directed her staff to prepare documents falsely indicating that Apple's Board had approved the Executive Team grant on January 17. As a result, Apple failed to record approximately $18.9 million in compensation expenses associated with the option grant. Anderson, who should have realized the implications of Heinen's actions, failed to disclose key information to Apple's auditors and neglected to ensure that the company's financial statements were accurate. Both Heinen and Anderson personally received millions of dollars in unreported compensation as a result of the backdating.

33

Apple -- Options

- The Commission's complaint also alleges improprieties in connection with a December 2001 grant of 7.5 million options to CEO Steve Jobs. Although the options were in-the-money at that time, Heinen — as with the Executive Team grant — caused Apple to backdate the grant to October 19, 2001, when Apple's share price was lower. As a result, the Commission alleges that Heinen caused Apple to improperly fail to record $20.3 million in compensation expense associated with the in-the-money options grant. The Commission further alleges that Heinen then signed fictitious Board minutes stating that the Board had approved the grant to Jobs on October 19 at a "Special Meeting of the Board of Directors" — a meeting that, in fact, never occurred.

34

Apple -- Options

- Heinen is charged with, among other things, violating the antifraud provisions of the Securities Act of 1933 and the Securities Exchange Act of 1934, lying to Apple's auditors, and violating prohibitions on circumventing internal controls. The Commission is seeking injunctive relief, disgorgement, and money penalties against Heinen, in addition to an order barring her from serving as an officer or director of a public company.
- Anderson, without admitting or denying the allegations in the Commission's complaint, has agreed to a permanent injunction from further violations of the antifraud, reporting, internal controls, and other provisions of the federal securities laws. Anderson also will disgorge approximately $3.49 million in ill-gotten gains and prejudgment interest, representing the in-the-money portion of the Executive Team options grant that Anderson exercised, and will pay a civil penalty of $150,000.

35

Apple -- Options

- The Commission also announced today that it would not bring any enforcement action against Apple based in part on its swift, extensive, and extraordinary cooperation in the Commission's investigation. Apple's cooperation consisted of, among other things, prompt self-reporting, an independent internal investigation, the sharing of the results of that investigation with the government, and the implementation of new controls designed to prevent the recurrence of fraudulent conduct.

36

Scientific Atlanta

SEC v. Scientific-Atlanta, Inc.

Litigation Release No. 19735 (June 22, 2006)

http://www.sec.gov/litigation/litreleases/2006/lr19735.htm

In the Matter of Wallace G. Haislip

Admin. Proc. File No. 3-12339 (June 22, 2006)

http://www.sec.gov/litigation/admin/2006/34-54031.pdf

http://www.sec.gov/litigation/admin/2006/34-54030.pdf

In the Matter of Julian W. Edison

Admin. Proc. File No. 3-154031 (June 22, 2006)

http://www.sec.gov/litigation/admin/2006/34-54031.pdf

37

Scientific Atlanta

On June 22, 2006, the Commission charged Scientific-Atlanta, Inc. with aiding and abetting certain of Adelphia Communications Corporation's violations of the reporting, books and records, and internal controls provisions of the federal securities laws. Scientific-Atlanta entered into a marketing support agreement with Adelphia in 2000 that Adelphia misused to inflate its earnings by approximately $43 million.

Scientific-Atlanta has agreed to pay $20 million in disgorgement in settlement of the charges. The SEC also announced that Wallace G. Haislip, Scientific-Atlanta's Senior Vice President, Operations, and Julian W. Eidson, Scientific-Atlanta's Senior Vice President, have consented to the issuance of cease-and-desist Orders for their respective roles in causing Adelphia's violations.

38

Scientific Atlanta

The SEC's complaint alleged that in August 2000, Adelphia requested that Scientific-Atlanta increase the price of digital cable television boxes it was selling to Adelphia and pay the amount of the price increase back to Adelphia in the form of marketing support for the stated purpose of marketing the Scientific-Atlanta cable television boxes. Adelphia did not use the marketing support payments to market Scientific-Atlanta cable television boxes, recorded the price increase as a capital expense, and recognized the marketing support payments as a contra marketing expense, thereby artificially reducing its marketing expense and increasing EBITDA. The transaction did not affect Scientific-Atlanta's public financial statements.

39

Scientific Atlanta

The complaint alleged that Scientific-Atlanta was aware of a number of facts that together demonstrated that Adelphia was misusing the marketing support agreement. Those facts included, among others, (i) a retroactive price increase on set-top boxes previously delivered to Adelphia; (ii) Adelphia's request for a commercially unreasonable high dollar amount in marketing support payments; (iii) repeated requests for higher levels of marketing support in later periods even though the major marketing push was to have occurred in earlier periods; (iv) knowledge that Adelphia's request for the marketing support agreement was driven by its desire to obtain an accounting benefit; and (v) the inclusion of a false reason for the price increase in one of the contracts documenting the marketing support agreement.

40

Scientific Atlanta

Scientific-Atlanta, without admitting or denying the allegations in the Complaint, consented to the entry of a final judgment, subject to court approval, that requires Scientific-Atlanta to pay $20 million in disgorgement and enjoins Scientific-Atlanta from violating and aiding and abetting any violations and any future violations of Sections 13(a), 13(b)(2)(A), and 13(b)(2)(B) of the Exchange Act, and Rules 12b-20, 13a-1, and 13a-13 thereunder.

The SEC's Orders against Haislip and Eidson, the most senior Scientific-Atlanta executives responsible for approving the form of the marketing support agreement, found that they should have been on notice that Adelphia was unlikely to be using the marketing support agreement to market Scientific-Atlanta boxes. Haislip and Eidson were ordered to cease and desist from causing any violations and any future violations of Sections 13(a), 13(b)(2)(A), and 13(b)(2)(B) of the Exchange Act and Rules 12b-20, 13a-1, and 13a-13 thereunder. Haislip and Eidson agreed to the settlements without admitting or denying the findings in the SEC's Orders.

41

Motorola, Inc.

On May 8, the Commission issued an Order Instituting Cease-and-Desist Proceedings, Making Findings, and Imposing a Cease-and-Desist Order Pursuant to Section 21C of the Securities Exchange Act of 1934 against Motorola, Inc.

The Order finds that, in 2001, Motorola, Inc., a vendor of digital cable television set-top boxes, entered into a round-trip cash transaction with Adelphia Communications Corporation, a cable television systems operator. Under a purported marketing support agreement, Adelphia paid money to Motorola which was immediately returned to Adelphia in the form of marketing support payments. The agreement, which was backdated and applied retroactively to the prior fiscal year, provided that Motorola would increase the price of digital cable television set-top boxes it was selling to Adelphia and pay the amount of the price increase back to Adelphia in the form of payments to market Motorola's cable television set-top boxes. Adelphia did not use the marketing support payments to market Motorola's cable television set-top boxes. Instead, Adelphia recorded the price increase it paid Motorola as a capital expense, and recognized the marketing support payments as a contra marketing expense, thereby artificially reducing its marketing expense and increasing Earnings Before Interest, Taxes, Depreciation and Amortization.

42

Motorola, Inc.

The Order also finds that Motorola employees were aware of a number of unusual and unique facts that together demonstrated that Adelphia was misusing the marketing support agreement. Those facts included:

(i) Adelphia's request to increase the cost of Motorola set-top boxes was the first time a customer had asked the Motorola executives involved in the transaction to increase the price of Motorola's products;

(ii) the marketing support agreement, which Adelphia provided to Motorola, contained a false reason for the price increase;

(iii) Motorola executives insisted as a condition to entering into the transaction that Adelphia provide a letter from its counsel that Adelphia would not use the transaction in contravention of federal regulations governing cable television rates - instead, an Adelphia finance executive who was later implicated in the fraud signed the letter;

43

Motorola, Inc.

(iv) the marketing support agreement did not contain any details of marketing to be done by Adelphia and required no input from Motorola's marketing department;

(v) the marketing support agreement was backdated and the price increase and marketing support payment obligation were made retroactive to the beginning of the prior fiscal year and applied to products that had already been sold to and paid for by Adelphia;

(vi) the transaction was a "wash" transaction with no economic impact on Motorola; and

(vii) Motorola did not treat the transaction as a marketing transaction for accounting purposes.

44

Motorola, Inc.

Based on the above, the Commission orders Motorola to cease and desist from committing or causing any violations and any future violations of Sections 13(a) and 13(b)(2)(A) of the Securities Exchange Act of 1934 and Rules 12b-20, 13a-1, and 13a-13 thereunder. The Order also requires Motorola to pay $25 million in disgorgement and prejudgment interest to the Registry of the Court for the United States District Court for the Southern District of New York, in the case captioned SEC v. Adelphia Communications Corp., et al., 02 Civ. 5776 (PKC). Such funds will be held in the Registry pending the approval of a plan to distribute the funds to the victims of the Adelphia fraud. Motorola agreed to the settlement without admitting or denying the findings in the Commission's Order. (Rel. 34-55725; AAE Rel. 2607; File No. 3-12630)

45

- Financial Fraud
  - Financial Fraud Task Force
  - Computer Associates
    www.sec.gov/litigation/litreleases/lr18891.htm
  - Symbol Technologies
    http://www.sec.gov/litigation/litreleases/lr18734.htm

46

- Disclosure v. GAAP
  - Edison Schools www.sec.gov/news/press/2002-67.htm

47

Financial Fraud

- Revenue Recognition: SAB 101
  - Bill & Hold
  - Round Trips
  - Side Agreements
  - Timing
- Managing Earnings
  - Balance Sheet Manipulation
  - Reserves
  - Writedowns

48

Disclosure v. GAAP

- Edison Schools
- Accounting OK
- Disclosure Problematic
- Relates to New Disclosure Controls Requirement

49

Materiality

- SAB 99
- Quantitative
- Qualitative
- Different Metrics
  - EPS
  - Revenue
  - Others

50

Parallel Criminal Prosecutions Much More Frequent

- Computer Associates

web link: http://www.sec.gov/litigation/litreleases/lr18891.htm

Prosecutions by the U.S. Attorney's Office for E.D.N.Y. against 7 former CA officers, including former CEO, Head of Sales, CFO, and General Counsel. Guilty Pleas from 5 of 7, including CFO and General Counsel. http://www.usdoj.gov/opa/pr/2004/September/04_crm_642.htm

Company enters into Deferred Prosecution agreement with U.S. Attorney agreeing to $225 million in restitution and numerous forward-looking undertakings, also in SEC consent judgment, such as appointment of independent examiner and corporate reforms

51

Gate-Keepers Will Be Held Accountable – attorneys, accountants and board members.

- September 22, 2004, General Counsel Steven Woghin charged in Computer Associates Case.
- October 20, 2004: KPMG agrees to pay $10 million and Rule 102(e) censure to settle charges relating to Gemstar accounting fraud.

52

Stephen Cutler's Speech Sept 20, 2004 www.sec.gov/nws/speech/spch092004smc.htm

- "On to the first of the legislation's three themes - which, you'll recall, is the importance of the gatekeeper function in our capital markets. What do I mean by 'gatekeepers?' The sentries of the marketplace: the auditors who sign off on companies' financial data; the lawyers who advise companies on disclosure standards and other securities law requirements; the research analysts who warn investors away from unsound companies; and the boards of directors responsible for oversight of company management. They're paramount in ensuring that our markets are clean. And Congress recognized that when it enacted Sarbanes-Oxley."

53

Auditor www.sec.gov/news/speech/spch092004smc.htm

- "With respect to auditors, the legislation ended the profession's self-regulatory regime and established in its place the Public Company Accounting Oversight Board. On the auditor independence front, Sarbanes-Oxley imposed significant restrictions on the sorts of relationships accounting firms could have with the companies they audit."

54

Lawyers www.sec.gov/news/speech/spch092004smc.htm

- "As for lawyers, Sarbanes-Oxley required the SEC to set minimum standards of professional conduct for those appearing and practicing before us. And the SEC has done so, requiring attorneys with evidence of material violations of federal securities laws or breaches of fiduciary duty to 'report up the ladder' to senior management and, if necessary, the board of directors. I recently read with interest about a new program at Harvard that addresses issues raised by the business of law. The professor who founded the program said in an interview that '[i]f Enron has taught us anything, it ought to be that professionals have a very important role as gatekeepers. We have to understand the market in which the professionals operate and the pressures they are under. We need to develop institutional strategies that allow firms to regulate their members better.' As law has become more of a business than a profession, it's gotten that much harder in my view for lawyers to heed the advice of lawyer and statesman, Elihu Root. He said that '[a]bout half the practice of a decent lawyer is telling his clients that they are damned fools and should stop.'"

55

Analysts www.sec.gov/news/speech/spch092004smc.htm

- Wall Street's research analysts also came under Congress' scrutiny in Sarbanes-Oxley. You're all familiar with the stories about Jack Grubman, Henry Blodget and other analysts whose fealty was to their investment banking colleagues - and the fees those colleagues were generating - rather than to the investors they were supposedly serving. Ultimately, the SEC, the New York Attorney General and other regulators addressed this problem in a global settlement with a dozen Wall Street firms that resulted in payments to date of more than $1.5 billion and significant structural reforms. The Sarbanes-Oxley Act required the adoption of rules governing securities analysts' potential conflicts of interest and in July, 2003, the SEC approved a series of New York Stock Exchange and NASD rules that further segregated the research analyst function from investment banking and required improved disclosure to customers.

56

Independent Directors

www.sec.gov/news/speech/spch092004smc.htm

- "Finally, when it comes to gatekeepers, Sarbanes-Oxley significantly increased the responsibility of independent directors - particularly, the members of a Board's audit committee - in overseeing the accounting, reporting and auditing functions. Too many times, outside directors were chosen for who they knew rather than what they knew. They weren't just disinterested; they were uninterested. But as a result of Sarbanes-Oxley, public company audit committee members now are required to meet independence and financial literacy standards; are responsible for the hiring and oversight of auditors, and must be apprised of all accounting-related complaints received by management."

57

Computer Associates

- Woghin (General Counsel)
- (1) signed a Form S-4 and a Form S-4 amendment that Computer Associates filed with the SEC in February and March 2000, while knowing, or recklessly disregarding the fact that, those filings contained materially false and misleading information regarding Computer Associates' prior revenue and earnings per share;
- (2) approved backdated contracts, including drafting a contract with misleading dates; and
- (3) allowed Computer Associates' Legal Department to approve contracts obtained by the sales force while knowing, or recklessly disregarding the fact that, those contracts contained false and misleading signature dates and that Computer Associates would recognize revenue from those contracts in the incorrect fiscal quarter.

58

Woghin's (GC) Obstruction

- Woghin obstructed the Government's investigations by allowing CA to withhold documents from the government and directing CA employees to provide false or misleading answers to questions posed by Government investigators. As to withholding documents, in response to a request from the Commission staff dated February 26, 2002, Woghin allowed CA to withhold for more than one year backdated contracts from being produced to the government or CA's outside counsel, and allowed CA's outside counsel, which did not have knowledge of the withheld documents, to falsely represent to the SEC staff, Federal Bureau of Investigation ("FBI") and United States Attorney's Office for the Eastern District of New York ("USAO") that neither the Extended Quarters Practice nor backdated contracts existed at CA.

59

GC's Obstruction.

- Later, Woghin told CA Sales Manager H to "sit tight" and Woghin did not alert CA's outside counsel, Commission staff, FBI or USAO, after Manager H told Woghin he had a draft document that showed CA's contract with Company 4 was not completed until October 4, 1999 and bore a false signature date of September 30, 1999.
- During the summer of 2002, Woghin also allowed CA's outside counsel to produce to the government a report conducted by a forensic accounting firm that falsely concluded that no Extended Quarters Practice existed at CA while Woghin knew that CA did not provide to that forensic accounting firm evidence of numerous back-dated contracts and prematurely recognized revenue.

60

GC's Obstruction.

- Similarly, Woghin encouraged CA employees to provide misleading answers to questions posed by CA's outside counsel, counsel for CA's Audit Committee, the staff of the Commission, the USAO and the FBI.
- For example, Woghin told CA Executive I to respond to questions from the Government with the answer "It's possible, anything is possible" in response to the Government's questions regarding the existence of the Extended Quarters practice even though CA Executive told Woghin he knew of the existence of the Extended Quarters practice.

61

Charges against KPMG and CPAs

KPMG and the KPMG auditors engaged in improper professional conduct by violating Generally Accepted Auditing Standards ("GAAS") through repeated instances of unreasonable conduct during their audits and reviews of Gemstar's financial statements. KPMG—through partners Bryan E. Palbaum, John M. Wong, and/or Kenneth B. Janeski and senior manager David A. Hori—audited and reviewed Gemstar's financial statements from the quarter ended September 30, 1999, through the quarter ended March 31, 2002.

62

Other KPMG respondents

Additionally, KPGM CPAs Bryan E. Palbaum, John M. Wong, Kenneth B. Janeski, and David A. Hori consented, without admitting or denying the Commission's findings, to the entry of orders pursuant to Rule 102(e) of the Commission's Rules of Practice denying each of them the privilege of appearing or practicing before the Commission as an accountant with the right to apply for reinstatement after three years (Palbaum), one year (Wong and Janeski), and eighteen months (Hori)

63

Other Undertakings

KPMG will provide (a) immediate training to its partners and managers with respect to (i) qualitative materiality; (ii) accounting for multi-element transactions; and (iii) consideration of appropriate disclosure related to complex accounting issues; and (b) continuing training to its audit personnel on such topics, as appropriate.

64

Gemstar

- SEC filed fraud charges against former CEO and CFO of Gemstar-TV Guide International, Inc., alleging they engaged in a scheme to inflate Gemstar's revenues by at least $223M.
- Complaint alleges that they manipulated revenues of and for Gemstar's interactive program guide (IPG) technology for televisions through, among other things, recording revenues from non-existent agreements and round-trip transactions and switching revenues from one business segment to the IPG advertising sector.
- The Commission's complaint seeks:
  - Antifraud injunctions
  - Civil penalties
  - Disgorgement of compensation and trading profits ($97M for the CEO alone)

65

Overview Re: Sarbanes-Oxley

- Impact of Sarbanes-Oxley on SEC Enforcement
  - New Causes of Action
  - New Remedies
  - New Regulators
- Impact of Sarbanes-Oxley Outside SEC Enforcement
  - New Criminal Claims
  - Increased Criminal Penalties
  - New Civil Claims and New Civil Remedies

66

Effect of Sarbanes-Oxley
on
SEC Enforcement

67

New Causes of Action

Weblink: http://www.law.uc.edu/CCL/SOact/toc.html

68

New Bases for SEC Enforcement Actions

- Responsibility for Financial Reports (§ 302)
  - CEO/CFO Certification
  - Internal Controls and Procedures
  - Disclosure Controls and Procedures
- Prohibitions on Personal Loans (§492(a))
- Improper Influence on the Conduct of Audits (§303)

69

New Bases for SEC Enforcement Actions-2

- Rule 102(e) Written into the Statute (§602)
  - Actions Against Attorneys
- No Insider Trading During Pension Fund Blackout Periods (§ 306)

70

Disclosure Controls and Procedures

- Designed to ensure that information required to be disclosed in Exchange Act reports is recorded, processed, summarized and reported within applicable disclosure deadlines
- Distinguish from "internal controls"
- Procedures should identify information relevant for assessing the need to disclose material developments and risks relating to the company's business, and information whose omission would make the public report misleading

71

Disclosure Controls and Procedures - 2

- SEC does not require any specific controls or procedures
- Each company's controls and procedures must be tailored to the company's specific circumstances
- Outgrowth of recent trend in SEC Enforcement Actions

72

New Remedies

73

New Remedies For SEC Enforcement Actions

- Officer and Director Bar
  - Standard reduced from substantially unfit to only unfit (§305)
  - Can obtain in administrative proceeding (§1105)
- Forfeiture of bonuses and other incentive compensation, and profits from stock sales from CEO/CFO (§304)
  - If restatement results from misconduct
- Monetary penalties now payable into disgorgement fund.

74

New Remedies For SEC Enforcement Actions – 2

- Seek temporary freeze of monies that may be subject to disgorgement (§1103)
- No discharge in bankruptcy for federal or state securities fraud claims (§803)
- Proposal: SEC impose penalties in administrative cease-and-desist proceedings (as of last session of Congress, the proposed remedy is unlikely to pass.).

75

New Regulators

76

Public Company Accounting Oversight Board

- New Regulatory Scheme
- Regulate and Discipline Public Accounting Firms
- Modeled on NASD and NYSE Oversight of Securities Brokerage Firms
- Public Companies Must Provide Testimony And Documents to Board
- Funded by Public Companies Based on Average Annual Market Capitalization and Fees from Accounting Firms

77

Revival of Existing Regulators

- State Attorney Generals
- Department of Justice
  - Parallel Proceedings

78

Impact of Sarbanes-Oxley On Non-SEC Enforcement

79

New Bases For Criminal Liability

- CEO or CFO false certification (§ 906)
  - Up to $1 million and 10 years in prison for "knowing" violations
  - Up to $5 million and 20 years in prison for "willful" violations
- Fine and/or imprisonment for up to 25 years for knowing fraud in connection with any security (§807)
- Destruction, alteration or falsification of records with intent to obstruct or influence federal investigation – up to 20 years in prison (§802)

80

New Penalties for Existing Criminal Claims

- Penalty Against Individuals for Willful Violations of Exchange Act (e.g., false certification under Section 302 of the Act) (§1106)
  - Before: fine of up to $1 million and/or up to 10 years in prison
  - Now: fine of up to $5 million and/or up to 20 years in prison
- Corporate Penalties Increased From up to $2.5M to up to $25M
- Penalty for mail fraud and wire fraud (§903)
  - Before: up to 5 years in prison
  - Now: up to 10 years in prison

81

Whistleblower Provisions

- Section 806 of Sarbanes-Oxley
- Modeled on Other Employment-Related Statutes
- Employee Must File Complaint with Department of Labor within 90 Days
- Protection from Discrimination And Retaliation
- Reinstatement, back pay, interest and compensatory damages and reasonable attorneys' fees and costs and expert witness fees
- Fines and/or prison up to 10 years for knowing retaliation (§1107)

82

Statute of Limitations For Private Securities Fraud Claims

- § 804 of Sarbanes-Oxley
- Previous: 1 yr / 2 yr
- New: 2yr / 5 yr

83

Revenue Recognition Issues

- Examples
- Computer Associates and
- Symbol Technologies

84

Computer Associates

- During the period from at least Jan. 1, 1998, through Sept. 30, 2000, Computer Associates prematurely recognized over $3.3 billion in revenue from at least 363 software contracts that Computer Associates, its customer, or both parties, had not yet executed, in violation of GAAP.
- Executives, including defendants Kumar, Richards, and Woghin, held Computer Associates' books open for several days after the end of each quarter to improperly record in that quarter revenue from contracts that were not executed by customers or Computer Associates until several days or more after the expiration of the quarter. As a result of this improper practice, Computer Associates made material misrepresentations and omissions about its revenue and earnings in SEC filings and other public statements.
- For example, in the first, second, third and fourth quarters of FY2000, respectively, Computer Associates inflated its properly recorded revenue by approximately 25%, 53%, 46%, and 22% by improperly including prematurely recognized revenue.

85

Computer Associates

- After Computer Associates substantially refrained from recognizing revenue prematurely from contracts that its customers had signed after quarter end during the first quarter of its fiscal year 2001, the company missed its earnings estimate and Computer Associates' stock price dropped over 43% in a single day.
- Computer Associates continued the improper practice of improperly recognizing revenue from contracts that Computer Associates signed after quarter end through the fiscal quarter ending September 30, 2000.

86

Computer Associates International, Inc.

- Global Settlement for Computer Associates
  - Permanent injunction from violating antifraud and other securities violations
  - Admits felony violations in deferred prosecution agreement with EDNY
  - Agrees to pay $225 million in restitution to shareholders

87

CA's cooperation

Significant additional undertakings

- the termination of CA officers and employees who were responsible for the improper accounting, inaccurate financial reporting, and obstruction of justice, as well as those who took steps to obstruct or impede CA's internal investigation;
- The appointment of new management, including, but not limited to, an Interim Chief Executive Officer, a new Chief Operating and Chief Financial Officer, a new Head of Worldwide Sales, and a new General Counsel;
- In addition to including former SEC Commissioner Laura Unger on CA's Board of Directors, adding a minimum of two new independent directors, so that no less than two-thirds of the members of CA's board will be independent directors;

88

CA's cooperation

Significant additional undertakings

- Establishing a new Compliance Committee, a new Disclosure Committee, enhanced corporate governance procedures, and a comprehensive ethics program;
- Reorganizing CA's Finance Department, including the appointment of a Corporate Controller, a Chief Accounting Officer, and a Financial Controller for each of CA's primary business functions, and the reorganizing of its Internal Audit Department.
- Under the agreement, the court will appoint an independent examiner who will be empowered to review CA's compliance with all of the terms and conditions in the agreement.

89

Computer Associates International, Inc.

- SEC and U.S. Attorney EDNY have charged 7 former executives
  - Charged Chairman and CEO Sanjay Kumar
  - Charged former CFO Ira Zar
  - Charged former General Counsel Steven Woghin
  - All 7 former executives criminally charged.
- Significantly, each of the 7 individuals charged with obstructing government's investigation

90

Symbol Technologies

- June 3, 2004, Global Settlement with SEC and U.S. Attorney for EDNY
- Symbol Consents in SEC case to Fraud Injunction, $37 million penalty and various forwarding looking undertakings, including independent examiner
- In criminal matter, Non-prosecution agreement with U.S. Attorney for EDNY

91

SEC Press Release

Charged Symbol Technologies, Inc. with securities fraud and related violations of the reporting, record-keeping and internal control provisions of the federal securities laws. The SEC also charged eleven former Symbol executives in connection with their roles in the fraud.

The SEC's complaint alleges that from at least 1998 until early 2003, Symbol and the other defendants engaged in numerous fraudulent accounting practices and other misconduct that had a cumulative net impact of over $230 million on Symbol's reported revenue and over $530 million on its pre-tax earnings. Based in Holtsville, N.Y., Symbol supplies mobile information systems using bar code scanners and related technology and its stock is publicly traded on the New York Stock Exchange.

92

SEC Press Release

The defendants engaged in a fraudulent scheme to inflate revenue, earnings and other measures of financial performance in order to create the false appearance that Symbol had met or exceeded its financial projections.

Defendant Tomo Razmilovic, Symbol's former president and CEO, and others at the company fostered a "numbers driven" corporate culture obsessed with meeting Wall Street estimates. With no regard for generally accepted accounting principles (GAAP) or their financial reporting obligations, the defendants used the following fraudulent schemes to align Symbol's reported financial results with market expectations: (a) a "Tango sheet" process through which baseless accounting entries were made to conform the unadjusted quarterly results to management's projections; (b) the fabrication and misuse of restructuring and other non-recurring charges to artificially reduce operating expenses, create "cookie jar" reserves and further manage earnings; (c) channel stuffing and other revenue recognition schemes, involving both product sales and customer services; and (d) the manipulation of inventory levels and accounts receivable data to conceal the adverse side effects of the revenue recognition schemes.

93

SEC Press Release

Together with Razmilovic, defendants Kenneth Jaeggi, Brian Burke, Michael DeGennaro and Frank Borghese comprised most of Symbol's senior management team during the relevant period and directed the fraud.

Defendants Christopher DeSantis, James Heuschneider, Gregory Mortenson, James Dean and Robert Donlon were Symbol executives during this period and implemented the schemes.

While the accounting fraud was occurring, defendant Leonard Goldner, Symbol's former general counsel, manipulated stock option exercise dates to enable certain senior executives, including himself, to profit unfairly at the company's expense. Rather than use the actual exercise date as defined by the option plans, Goldner instituted, without board approval or public disclosure, a practice of using a more advantageous date chosen from a 30-day "look-back" period so as to reduce the cost of the exercise to the executive. To create the false appearance that these exercises actually occurred on the selected dates, Goldner had his staff backdate the requisite transactional documents and use the phony exercise dates in the forms on which the executives reported their acquisitions to the Commission and the public.

94

Non-Prosecution Agreement With U.S. Attorney's Office

- Company accepted responsibility and acknowledged that the company (a) violated federal criminal law in connection with accounting practices; and (b) filed materially false and misleading financial statements with the SEC
- Including $37 million to SEC, company paid $139 million altogether with $3 million to U.S. Postal and balance in class action.

95

Forward Looking Undertakings

The termination of employees at all levels of the company whose improper activities and/or lax supervision resulted in improper accounting and inaccurate financial reporting, or who refused to cooperate with Symbol's internal investigation;

the appointment of new management, including a new president and chief executive officer, a new chief financial officer, new senior vice presidents of finance, sales, operations, global products and customer service, a new general counsel and secretary and a new chief information officer;

96

Forward Looking Undertakings

The appointment of an independent examiner to serve for three years to monitor and report to the government and Symbol's board of directors on, among other things, Symbol's internal controls and financial reporting practices.

The establishment of an ongoing training and education program for certain of its directors, officers and employees designed to minimize the possibility of future violations of the federal securities laws by Symbol.

97

Officers and Employees Criminally charged

TOMO RAZMILOVIC, former president and chief executive officer,
KENNETH JAEGGI, former senior vice president and chief financial officer,
BRIAN BURKE, former senior vice president (operations), MICHAEL DEGENNARO, former senior vice president (finance), FRANK BORGHESE, former senior vice president (worldwide sales and service),
CHRISTOPHER DESANTIS, former vice president (finance) and JAMES HEUSCHNEIDER, former director (finance)

98

General Counsel Also Charged

The indictment also alleges that an eighth defendant, Symbol's former general counsel, LEONARD GOLDNER, orchestrated a scheme in which he and other senior executives at Symbol fraudulently exploited Symbol's stock option plans to enrich the executives and illegally minimize their tax obligation at the expense of Symbol

99

Off balance sheet investment and liabilities issues

- Enron example

Background on Enron

- On December 2, 2001, Enron Corp (7th largest U.S. company) declared bankruptcy.
- Stock closed at $1 (down $83 within 1 year).
- U.S. Senate Committee concluded that Enron's Board of Directors failed in its duties:
  - Approved Off-Balance Sheet Partnerships run by Enron Employees
  - Failed to effectively monitor these partnerships
  - Failed to react to warnings about those transactions as they came to light

100

Off balance sheet investment and liabilities issues

- SEC v. Fastow:

  The complaint allegations stem from Fastow's conduct relating to six transactions. Three of the transactions, RADR, Chewco, and Southampton, were the subject of the Commission's earlier settled action against Michael Kopper. Those transactions were part of an alleged scheme to hide Fastow's and Kopper's interest in and control of certain entities in order to keep those entities off Enron's balance sheet. This was done, according to the complaint, for self-enrichment and to mislead analysts, rating agencies, and others about Enron's true financial condition. As to Fastow's role in RADR, Chewco, and Southampton, the complaint alleges that Fastow secretly nominated certain of the owners of these entities, funded certain of their investments through undisclosed loans, collected undisclosed fees, and demanded and received under-the-table payments, including payments to himself and his family members disguised as yearly $10,000 non-taxable gifts.

101

Off balance sheet investment and liabilities issues

- SEC v. Fastow:

  Two of the remaining three transactions, the Nigerian barges and the Cuiaba transactions, are alleged to have been sham sales - best described as secret asset-parking arrangements. In one of these sales, a sale of an interest in certain Nigerian barges to a financial institution, Fastow is alleged to have personally promised that the financial institution would be taken out of its so-called investment and later arranged for an entity he controlled to buy the financial institution's interest at a pre-arranged rate of return on a pre-arranged time table.

102

Off balance sheet investment and liabilities issues

- SEC v. Fastow:

  In the second sale, Enron entered into a transaction with an off-balance-sheet entity controlled by Fastow to sell an interest in a severely troubled power plant in Cuiaba, Brazil, in order to avoid consolidation of project debt and recognize earnings. In connection with this transaction, Fastow allegedly entered into an unwritten side agreement with Enron requiring Enron to buy back the interest it just sold to Fastow at a guaranteed profit

103

Off balance sheet investment and liabilities issues

- SEC v. Fastow:

  The last set of allegations included in the complaint relate to an alleged instance of backdating documents to avoid diminution in Enron's investment in the stock of a technology company. Specifically, according to the complaint, in September 2000, Fastow and others created documents that purported to lock in the value of Enron's investment in that company back in August of 2000, when that company's stock was trading at its all-time high price. Throughout the period of his alleged fraudulent conduct, Fastow sold millions of dollars worth of Enron securities.

104

Auditor Independence and Pro Forma Issues

Ernst and Young Audit for People Soft.

Litigated ALJ decision against E&Y issued April 16, 2004

http://www.sec.gov/litigation/aljdec/id249bpm.htm

Order 1) cease and desist order, 2) disgorge $1.6868 million and interest, 3) independent consultant, 4) suspended from accepting audit enagements for six months.

Trump Hotels, Pro Forma Case

www.sec.gov/news/headlines/trumphotels.htm

January 16, 2002 Commission Order Instituting Cease-And Desist Proceedings directing Trump Hotels not to cease and desist from committing or causing violations of Section 10(b) of the Exchange Act and Rule 10b-5 thereunder.

105

Auditor Independence

Ernst and Young Audit for People Soft.

The Administrative Law Judge issued an Initial Decision finding that Ernst & Young LLP (Ernst & Young) was not independent when it audited the financial statements of PeopleSoft Inc. (PeopleSoft) for fiscal years 1994 through 1999. The independence violations occurred while Ernst & Young was PeopleSoft's auditor. Ernst & Young held a PeopleSoft license, which made possible a software product for which Ernst & Young paid royalties to PeopleSoft, and Ernst & Young worked with PeopleSoft to obtain contracts to implement PeopleSoft software.

106

Ernst and Young Audit for People Soft.

The judge concluded that Ernst & Young's conduct violated Rule 2-02 of Securities and Exchange Commission's (Commission) Regulation S-X, caused PeopleSoft to violate Sections 7(a) and 10(a) of the Securities Act of 1933, Sections 13(a) and 14(a) of the Securities Exchange Act of 1934 (Exchange Act), Rules 13a-1 and 14a-3, and Section 4C of the Exchange Act and Rule 102(e) of the Commission's Rules of Practice.

107

Ernst and Young Audit for People Soft.

The Initial Decision orders Ernst & Young to: (1) cease and desist from violating and causing violations of the statutory provisions cited above; (2) disgorge audit fees of $1,686,500 and prejudgment interest; and (3) retain an independent consultant to review its procedures and practices on auditor independence in connection with business relationships with audit clients. The Initial Decision also suspends Ernst & Young from accepting audit engagements for new Commission registrants for six months. (Initial Decision No. 249; File No. 3- 10933)

108

Pro Forma Issues

Trump Hotels Cease and Desist Proceeding

- the Commission found that:

  On Oct. 25, 1999, Trump Hotels issued a press release announcing its quarterly results. The release used net income and earnings-per-share (EPS) figures that differed from net income and EPS calculated in conformity with generally accepted accounting principles (GAAP), in that the figures expressly excluded a one-time charge. The earnings release was fraudulent because it created the false and misleading impression that the Company had exceeded earnings expectations primarily through operational improvements, when in fact it had not

109

Pro Forma Issues

- the Commission found that:

  The release expressly stated that net income and EPS figures excluded a $81.4 million one-time charge. Although neither the earnings release nor the accompanying financial data used the term pro forma, the net income and EPS figures used in the release were pro forma numbers because they differed from such figures calculated in conformity with GAAP by excluding the one-time charge. By stating that this one-time charge was excluded from its stated net income, the Company implied that no other significant one-time items were included in that figure

110

Pro Forma Issues

- the Commission found that:

  Contrary to the implication in the release, however, the stated net income included an undisclosed one-time gain of $17.2 million. The gain was the result of the termination, in September 1999, of the All Star Café's lease of restaurant space at the Trump Taj Mahal Casino Resort in Atlantic City. Trump Hotels, through various subsidiaries, owns and operates the Taj Mahal and other casino resorts. The Company's executive offices are in New York City, and its business and financial operations are centered in Atlantic City.

- Not only was there no mention of the one-time gain in the text of the release, but the financial data included in the release gave no indication of it, because all revenue items were reflected in a single line item.

111

Pro Forma Issues

- The misleading impression created by the reference to the exclusion of the one-time charge and the undisclosed inclusion of the one-time gain was reinforced by the comparison in the earnings release of the stated earnings-per-share figure with analysts' earnings estimates and by statements in the release that the Company been successful in improving its operating performance. Using the non-GAAP, pro forma figures, the release announced that the Company's quarterly earnings exceeded analysts' expectations, stating:

  Net income increased to $ 14.0 million, or $ 0.63 per share, before a one-time Trump World's Fair charge, compared to $ 5.3 million or $ 0.24 per share in 1998. [Trump Hotels'] earnings per share of $ 0.63 exceeded First Call estimates of $ 0.54.

112

Pro Forma Issues

- In addition, the release quoted Trump Hotels' chief executive officer as attributing the stated positive results and improvement from third-quarter 1998 to improvements in the Company's operations.
- In fact, had the one-time gain been excluded from the quarterly pro forma results as well as the one-time charge, those results would have reflected a decline in revenues and net income and would have failed to meet analysts' expectations. The undisclosed one-time gain was thus material, because it represented the difference between positive trends in revenues and earnings and negative trends in revenues and earnings, and the difference between exceeding analysts' expectations and falling short of them.

113

Pro Forma Issues

- On Oct. 25, the day the earnings release was issued, the price of the Company's stock rose 7.8 percent; subsequently, analysts learned of the one-time gain. On Oct. 28, the day on which an analysts' report and a news article revealing the impact of the one-time gain were published, the stock price fell approximately 6 percent.
- The Commission found that Trump Hotels violated Section 10(b) of the Exchange Act and Rule 10b-5 thereunder. The Company was ordered to cease and desist from violating those provisions.

114

NOTES

18

THE BALANCE SHEET

Lawrence M. Cirelli

Hanson Bridgett

Marcus Vlahos Rudy LLP

Terry Lloyd, CPA, CFA

The Balance Sheet

by Lawrence M. Cirelli *and* *Terry Lloyd, CPA, CFA*

HANSON BRIDGETT
MARCUS VLAHOS RUDY·LLP

Telephone: (415) 298-4300
Facsimile: (925) 476-1472
Email: tlloydcpa@astound.net

San Francisco Office
425 Market St., 26th Floor, San Francisco, CA 94105-2173
Telephone: (415) 777-3200, Facsimile: (415) 541-9366
Email: lcirelli@hansonbridgett.com
http://www.hansonbridgett.com

Balance Sheet

Assets = Liabilities + Stockholders' Equity

EXHIBIT A - SAMPLE CORPORATION
STATEMENT OF ASSETS, LIABILITIES, AND STOCKHOLDERS' EQUITY DECEMBER 31, 20XX

ASSETS	***20XX***
Current Assets:	
Cash and Cash Equivalents	*$ 6,102,934*
Temporary Investments in Marketable Securities	*5,123,433*
Client Accounts Receivable, net	*4,942,365*
Inventories (at lower of cost or market)	*11,021,001*
Prepaid items	*408,637*
Total Current Assets	*$27,598,370*
Non Current Assets:	
Investment in Long Term XYZ Company Bonds	*$ 5,230,100*
Property, Plant and Equipment, net	*13,638,261*
Intangible Assets	*1,678,184*
Total Non-current Assets	*$20,546,545*
TOTAL ASSETS	***$48,144,915***
LIABILITIES	

Current Liabilities:	
Accounts payable and accrued expenses	*$16,559,993*
Current portion of long-term debt	*2,140,193*
Other current liabilities	*100,219*
Total current liabilities	*$18,800,405*
Non-current portion of long term debt	***6,213,122***
Unfunded accrued Pension Cost	***1,019,281***
TOTAL LIABILITIES	***$26,032,808***
STOCKHOLDERS' EQUITY	
Contributed Capital:	
Common Stock, $1 par	*$500,000*
Additional paid-in capital on common stock	*16,785,196*
Retained Earnings	*4,826,911*
TOTAL STOCKHOLDERS' EQUITY	***$22,112,107***
TOTAL LIABILITIES AND STOCKHOLDERS' EQUITY	***$48,144,915***

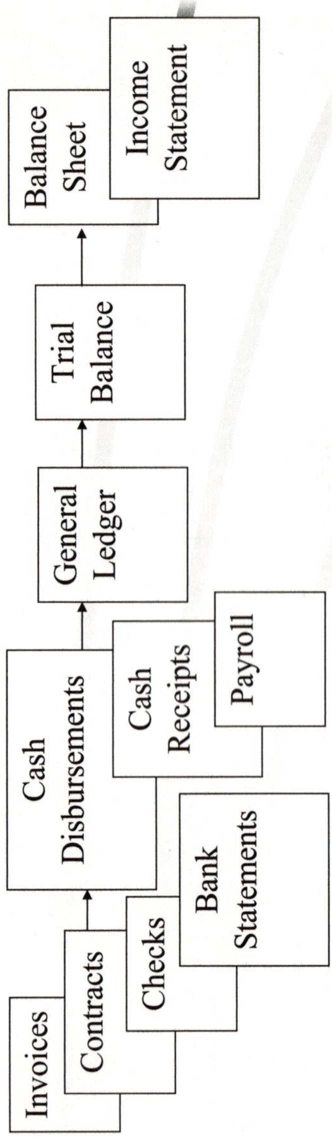

Invoices
Contracts
Checks
Bank Statements
Cash Disbursements
Cash Receipts
Payroll
General Ledger
Trial Balance
Balance Sheet
Income Statement

Definition of Assets

The economic resources used to carry out an entity's operations. They can be tangible or intangible, natural or man-made.

Current vs. Long-Term

Current Assets are:

Cash and other assets expected to be converted into cash (or sold, or consumed) within one normal operating cycle.

Current Assets

-- Cash

-- Marketable Securities

-- Receivables (net realizable value)

-- Inventory

-- Prepaid

Definition of Inventory

Tangible personal property

(i) held for sale, in the normal course of business,

(ii) in the process of production for such sale, or

(iii) held for use in the process of manufacturing products for sale.

	Date	Units	Per Unit	Total
Opening Inventory		100	$1.08	$108
Purchases:				
	1/15	150	1.10	165
	4/15	130	1.12	146
	7/11	160	1.13	181
	11/17	170	1.19	202
Total		**710**		**$802**

	Units	FIFO	LIFO	Weighted Average
Ending Inventory	130	$155	$141	$147
Net income before taxes		**$100**	**$86**	**$92**

Income Statement

	FIFO	LIFO	Weighted Average
SALES	$15,145	$15,145	$15,145
COST OF SALES			
Beginning Inventory	200	200	200
Plus Purchases	15,000	15,000	15,000
Goods Available	$15,200	$15,200	$15,200
Less Ending Inventory	155	144	147
Cost Of Sales	$15,045	$15,059	$15,053
Gross Profit	$100	$86	$92

Balance Sheet

Current Assets	FIFO	LIFO	Weighted Average
Inventory	$155	$141	$147

Observations

In times of rising costs, the FIFO method results in higher inventory value, lower costs of goods sold and, thus, higher profit.

Also, FIFO more closely approximates replacement value.

In times of rising costs, the LIFO method results in lower inventory value, higher costs of goods sold and, thus, lower profit.

If LIFO is used during times of rising costs, since profits will be lower, taxes will be lower, and there will be more cash flow.

If LIFO is used, inventory probably will be valued below market value.

Non-Current Assets

-- Long-Term Investments

-- Property, Plant and Equipment (net)

-- Intangible Assets

-- Other Assets

Definition of Liabilities

Liabilities are claims against an entity that must be satisfied with cash, other assets, new obligations or services.

Types of Liabilities

(1) Clearly Determinable Liabilities

-- Existence and amounts certain

(2) Estimated Liabilities

-- Existence certain but amount can only be estimated

(3) Contingent Liabilities

-- Existence and usually amount uncertain

Current vs. Long-Term

Current Liabilities are:

(1) Payable within one year or one operating cycle, whichever is longer, or

(2) Will be paid out of current assets or will create current liabilities.

Current Liabilities

- Short-term Notes Payable
- Current Portion of Long-Term Debt and Capital Leases
- Trade Accounts Payable
- Accrued Expenses
- Cash Dividends Payable
- Unearned Revenues
- Income Taxes Payable

Long-Term Liabilities

-- Notes Payable

-- Bonds Payable

-- Mortgages

-- Non-current Obligations under Capital Leases

-- Pension Obligations

-- Minority Interests

-- Contingent Liabilities

Contingent Liabilities

FASB Statement No. 5 defines a contingency as "an existing condition, situation or set of circumstances involving uncertainty as to possible gain or loss to an enterprise that will ultimately be resolved when one or more future events occur or fail to occur."

Contingent Liabilities

Probable -- the future event resolving the uncertainty is likely to occur

Remote -- there is only a slight chance that the event will occur

Reasonably possible -- the chance of the event occurring is more than remote, but less than probable

Stockholders' Equity

Contributed Capital:

- Capital Stock (par)
- Additional Paid-in Capital

Unrealized Capital

Retained Earnings

Contributed Capital

Capital Stock -- The legal capital retained by the company (i.e., the minimum amount the company cannot pay out in dividends).

Additional Paid-in Capital -- The additional capital contributed in excess of the legal minimum.

Example:

A company selling 100 shares of its $1 par value common stock to investors for $5 would post $100 to capital stocks, and the excess $400 to additional paid-in capital.

Unrealized Capital

The account is used to classify the receipt or usage of assets without a corresponding entry in the liability sections (i.e., donations).

A - L = SE

Retained Earnings

The total amount of entity earnings not distributed to the stockholders. That is, the retained amount of profits not distributed in the form of dividends.

Working Capital

A company's investment in short-term assets - cash, short-term securities, accounts receivable and inventory.

Net Working Capital

Current Assets - Current Liabilities

Financial Ratios

Current Ratio

Current Assets ÷ Current Liabilities

Quick Ratio

Quick Assets ÷ Current Liabilities

Quick Assets = Cash, short-term marketable securities, short-term notes and accounts receivable.

Debit Ratio

Total Liabilities ÷ Total Assets

Notes to Financial Statements

General Rule:

Disclosure is required where it is necessary to avoid a misunderstanding of the financial statements.

Of course, materiality is critical in deciding if note disclosure is required.

NOTES

19

PURCHASE PRICE DISPUTES, HOW THE FINANCIAL EXPERT CAN HELP YOU AVOID LEGAL LANDMINES

Glenn Newman, CPA/ABV, CFE, MBA

Robert Gray, CPA/ABV, CFE, FACFEI

Parente Randolph

"Purchase Price Disputes, How the Financial Expert Can Help You Avoid Legal Landmines"

Presented to: Practising Law Institute

Presenting in New York

Glenn Newman, CPA/ABV, CFE, MBA
Principal – Philadelphia, PA
(215) 972-2354
gnewman@parentenet.com

Presenting in Chicago

Robert P. Gray, CPA/ABV, CFE, FACFEI
Principal – Dallas, TX
(214) 658-6570
rgray@parentenet.com

July 10, 2007 – New York
&
August 10, 2007 - Chicago

PARENTERANDOLPH
The Power of Ideas

Purchase Price Disputes
The Role of Your Financial Expert

- Agenda:
  - – Overview-the Process
  - – Where Buyers and Sellers Collide
  - – The Agreement-Pertinent Sections
  - – Common Problems
  - – War Stories
  - – Questions/Answers

PARENTERANDOLPH
The Power of Ideas

Purchase Price Disputes
The Role of Your Financial Expert

- M&A Activity for US; YTD through April:
  - 2006:
    - 3,410 deals valued at $427,234 million.
  - 2007:
    - 3,398 deals valued at $621,809 million.

Source: *"Mergers & Acquisitions Report"*, May 7, 2007

PARENTERANDOLPH
The Power of Ideas

Overview of The Acquisition/Divestiture Process

- Mergers, Acquisitions and Divestitures are used by companies to meet their strategic/growth goals:
  - "The Wave Effect" - Fluctuates with economic and business cycles;
  - Common clauses in M&A contracts relate to accounting, economic, and financial reporting matters; and
  - View from the financial expert, not the legal perspective.

PARENTERANDOLPH
The Power of Ideas

Chronology of a Typical Deal

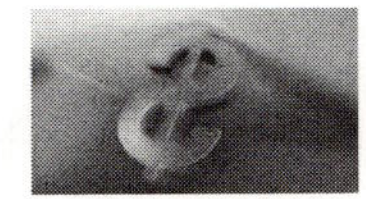

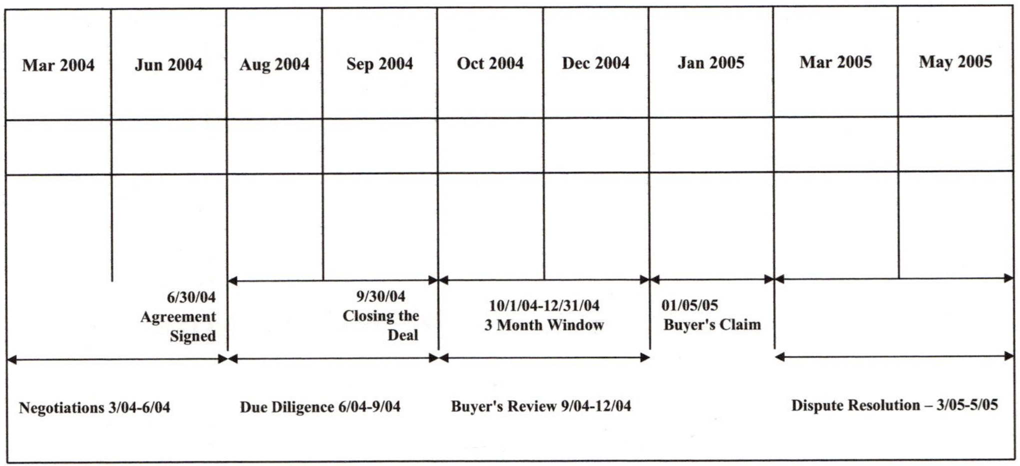

PARENTERANDOLPH
The Power of Ideas

Purchase Price Disputes, The "Role" of Your Financial Expert

- Provide assistance during due diligence;
- Provide professional services in connection with deal disputes;
- Not for the "Faint of Heart";

- Usually requires a combination of GAAP, professional standards, valuation, finance, industry knowledge and experience, etc.

PARENTERANDOLPH
The Power of Ideas

The Process

- Typically begins with a negotiated price and contract terms for all or part of a business. Resulting in:

1. A signed Letter of Intent ("LOI"), generally broad and non-binding, then….
2. Execution of Purchase and Sale Agreement, (due diligence by buyer, internal approvals by both parties including Board of Directors);
3. What about seller's due diligence?
4. How much due diligence is enough?

PARENTERANDOLPH
The Power of Ideas

The Process (continued)

The Deal is Done…Now what?

Preclosing Period:

– The length of time between the signing of the Agreement and the transaction's closing.

1. Period can vary widely, but usually 1 to 3 months;
2. The seller usually manages the business being sold;
3. Typically profit or loss accrues to the seller; and
4. Adjustments made to purchase price for the interim period

PARENTERANDOLPH

The Power of Ideas

The Deal
Where Buyers/Sellers Collide!

- Buyer:
  1. Maximize value, pay the least for the most:
     - Purchase at the perceived value of the company;
     - Or value of the assets acquired;
  2. Conducts due diligence:
     - Evaluate the assets it will receive;
     - Evaluate the liabilities it will assume;
     - Target a reduction to purchase price;
  3. Right to perform a post closing review.

PARENTERANDOLPH
The Power of Ideas

The Deal
Where Buyers and Sellers Collide! (continued)

- Seller:
  1. Maximize value, maintain or increase the price to be paid
  2. Eliminate exposure after the sale:
     - Sale to absolve seller from exposure to unknown or contingent liabilities
     - Avoid unfavorable purchase price adjustments

PARENTERANDOLPH

The Power of Ideas

The Deal Where Buyers and Sellers Collide! (continued)

- Trugman: Value v. Price!
  - Valuation is a prophecy to the future;
  - Valuation is required for tax purposes and financial reporting;
  - Purchase price is allocated to underlying assets;
  - "Value" is what you hope to get!
  - "Price" is what is paid!

Source: "*Understanding Business Valuation*", 2nd Edition, Gary R. Trugman

PARENTERANDOLPH
The Power of Ideas

The Deal Where Buyers and Sellers Collide! (continued)

- **Post Closing Adjustments:**
  - Adjusts the purchase price to account for results of operations and other transactions during the stub period.
    1. Stub Period is between X date, (date of signed agreement or other agreed upon date) and the transaction's closing date.
  - Seller provides buyer a closing balance sheet prepared as of the date of closing (or close as).
    1. Used as basis to calculate the post closing adjustment(s).
  - Buyer usually has the right to Perform Post Closing Review.
    1. May object to the closing balance sheet in accordance with the Purchase/Sale agreement.
    2. Areas that will generate disputes are identified.

PARENTERANDOLPH
The Power of Ideas

Purchase/Sale Agreements, Devil in the Details

- **The Agreement:**
  - Provisions seeks to assign, allocate or indemnify the risks between the parties focusing on those related to accounting issues and financial reporting:
    - Representations and Warranties;
    - Post Closing Adjustments;
    - Covenants;
    - Indemnification Clauses;
    - Earn-Out Clauses; and
    - Arbitration Clauses.

PARENTERANDOLPH
The Power of Ideas

Purchase/Sale Agreements, Devil in the Details (continued)

- **Representations and Warranties – Buyer's Perspective:**
  1. Assist buyer in gaining an understanding of the business and its value drivers;
  2. Enables the buyer to recover damages if the seller makes inaccurate/incomplete representations;
  3. Allows the buyer to abort the transaction if it finds issues with the seller's representations before closing; and
  4. Buyer representations generally involve financial considerations, ability to complete the transaction.

Purchase/Sale Agreements, Devil in the Details (Continued)

- **Representations and Warranties:**
  - Seller Perspective:
    1. Prepared financial statements in accordance with Generally Accepted Accounting Principles (GAAP);
    2. Is GAAP consistently applied?
    3. Prepared in accordance with historical company policy or some other basis of accounting;
    4. No contingent liabilities exist, except those disclosed in F/S's;
    5. No material adverse changes since date of financials used in negotiations; and
    6. Generally does not state the financial statements are complete, accurate, true or correct.

PARENTERANDOLPH
The Power of Ideas

Purchase/Sale Agreements, Devil in the Details (continued)

- **Postclosing Adjustment Clause:**
  - Necessary since the business continues and as a result financial statements change from that which buyer based purchase price.
    1. Attempts to account for changes in financial position (Balance Sheet, Revenues and/or Cash Flows.);
    2. Usually allocates to the sellers the economic risks and profits during the period from the initial financial statements until the closing date;
    3. Protects the buyer against potential seller abuses, (e.g. sale of inventory without replacement).

PARENTERANDOLPH
The Power of Ideas

Purchase/Sale Agreements, Devil in the Details (continued)

- **Postclosing Adjustment Clause:**
  - States a calculation of value-often a net asset value-on the closing balance sheet and compares the value to the value reflected in the financial statements upon which the buyer based the purchase price;
  - Commonly calls for a dollar-for-dollar adjustment for changes in net asset value;
  - Can call for a multiple of the change in net asset value if it affects operating earnings, inventory reduction;
  - Adjustment can add or subtract from purchase price; and
  - Escrow accounts often involved.

ParenteRandolph
The Power of Ideas

Common Problem Areas

- **Post Closing Review:**
  - Litigation most often arises out of buyers review of the post closing balance sheet and specific objections to the way seller accounted for, or did not account, for items contained in the balance sheet.
    - Since buyer now is in control of the company, increased opportunity to:
      - Gain access to information that may have not been available prior to the closing;
      - Use company personnel's knowledge of accounting systems, practices and procedures;
  - By objecting to balance sheet amounts or balances, buyer is proposing adjustments; and
  - There is usually a specified period buyer can object and propose purchase price adjustment.

PARENTERANDOLPH

The Power of Ideas

Common Problem Areas (continued)

- **Preferable v. Acceptable GAAP:**
  - Often parties mistakenly believe that GAAP provides one "**right number**";
  - Disputes arise between Buyer's and Seller's interpretation;
    1. Buyer proposes an adjustment based on a different method from that applied by the seller. Claims seller used a method different than that buyer's understanding of the purchase agreement terms.
    2. Seller may change from one acceptable GAAP method of accounting to another in the closing balance sheet to affect the purchase price.

PARENTERANDOLPH
The Power of Ideas

Common Problem Areas (continued)

- **GAAP v. Consistency:**
  - Does GAAP or consistency take precedence when applying an accounting method to a particular transaction or account balance?
    1. While GAAP usually takes precedence over consistency, absent the specific requirements of the agreement, buyers should be wary of making a blanket overall statement concerning GAAP unless they specifically understand the ramifications to their financial statements.
  - Application of term "consistent" - Does consistent mean:
    1. Done repeatedly, consistently reported in the same manner;
    2. Calculated in the same manner consistently; or
    3. A particular amount is consistent.

Common Problem Areas (continued)

- **Interim v. Year End Reporting:**
  - Agreement may mandate consistency between precluding financials and final financials at closing.
    1. Interim monthly financials;
    2. Year end financial statements;
    3. Quarter end financial statements;
  - Do all of these financial statements report transactions in the same manner or are more rigorous standards applied for year end financial statements as opposed to those issued at an interim month end?

    If different sets of standard are applied and precluding financials were based on an interim statement but closing financials are at year end, audited, which methodology applies?

PARENTERANDOLPH
The Power of Ideas

Common Problem Areas (continued)

- **Financials Prepared Based on Company Policy:**
  - An alternative to GAAP. Common situation arises when:
    1. A subsidiary does not keep its own financials;
    2. Seller is carving out a part of a business unit or division;
    3. Top level adjustments to GAAP;
    4. Materiality; or
    5. Exclusion of Footnotes.

PARENTERANDOLPH
The Power of Ideas

Common Problem Areas (continued)

- **Errors or Irregularities Discovered After Closing:**
  - Generally not addressed in the Agreement because it is assumed that financials statements are correct. (Errors, irregularities, GAAP departures.)
    - Circumstances to consider- when it occurred, when it became know, when it was corrected;

1. If error occurred in financial statements purchase price was based on, seller corrects error and it results in an upward adjustment to the purchase price, buyer will argue that seller should not benefit from their own errors;
2. If buyer detects and error that was not present in the financial statements, and it would lower the purchase price, buyer will seek a purchase price adjustment;
3. What do you think the buyer would do if they discover an error favorable to them, company should be worth more, that were present in the closing financial statements?
   - Correct! They probably will not dispute it

PARENTERANDOLPH
The Power of Ideas

Common Problem Areas (continued)

- **Materiality:**
- Concept can be applied to individual items, transactions, balance sheet or income statement line items or the financial statements taken as a whole. Large area for potential for dispute.
  - Many agreements use a threshold, specific dollar amount after which an adjustment is necessary. Adjustment can be in the form of:
    1. Gross amount is adjusted, dollar for dollar;
    2. Basket or deductible, adjustment for amount over materiality level;
  - As many agreements do not address materiality, the level may be implied from other language contained in the Agreement;
  - If materiality is not addressed, seller can have a difficult time defending purchase price adjustments buyer desires. However, if GAAP is written as the basis for closing financials, materiality can be considered.
- **GET IT (Purchase Price) RIGHT THE FIRST TIME!**

PARENTERANDOLPH
The Power of Ideas

Common Problem Areas (continued)

- **Right to Offset:**
  - Often not written into agreements, sellers may try to claim a right of offset as a defense against buyer's proposed adjustments.
    1. Buyer will most likely only identify those adjustments which are advantageous to them;
    2. Seller tries to prevent the buyer from this "selective objection" to amounts recorded in the financial statements by offsetting adjustments
       - Under accrual to offset over accrual;
  - Difficult to ascertain the intent of the parties and decide whether to adjust the purchase price if agreement is absent on this issue;
  - May be decided by agreement's specified applicability of GAAP; GAAP based on line item or GAAP for financial statements taken as a whole.

PARENTERANDOLPH
The Power of Ideas

Common Problem Areas (continued)

- **Earn Out Provisions, Put Back Provisions and Hindsight:**
  - Commonality of these three areas involve future performance and/or knowledge gained after the transaction's closing date.
    1. Earn Outs: Complicated because buyer may not run the business in the same manner the seller did, combined with other entities, segment divested;
    2. Put Backs: Relates to adequacy of various allowance accounts, A/R, inventory;
       - Interpretation, did buyer make sufficient effort to collect accounts receivable in the ordinary course of business?
       - How is ordinary course of business standard applied?
    3. Hindsight: Do the events that occurred post closing support the amounts reflected on financial statement?
       - Generally not persuasive for buyer if no persuasive evidence the information or knowledge existed prior to the closing financial statements being prepared in accordance with GAAP.
       - Seller has a persuasive argument if buyer claimed adjustment for account subsequently collected.

PARENTERANDOLPH
The Power of Ideas

Common Problem Areas (continued)

- **Issues of Control:**
  - Involves the manipulation of accounting and financial reporting by the party in control through the postclosing adjustment process.
    1. In a management buyout, buyer runs the company between the signing of agreement and postclosing adjustment. Opportunity exists for the accounting and financial reporting to be manipulated.
    2. Seller, if in control, may attempt to "clean up" the balance sheet to buyer's detriment during the stub period.
  - Control can also be a factor related to Earn Out and Put Back Provisions.

PARENTERANDOLPH

The Power of Ideas

Help, We need an Accountant/Consultant!

- What can the Accountant/Consultant Offer?
  - Independent and unbiased advice in approaching disputes and can identify alternative, strategic options;
  - Outside party does not carry an emotional attachment to the transaction; and
  - Often can enhance and expedite the dispute resolution process.

PARENTERANDOLPH
The Power of Ideas

Help, We need an Accountant/Consultant! (continued)

- **What Services can the Accountant/Consultant Offer?**
  - Dispute Formulation, working for one of the parties involved.
    1. Identifying objections to postclosing and purchase price adjustment clauses;
    2. Calculating and supporting objections under purchase price adjustments clauses;
    3. Interpreting technical accounting literature to establish whether a proposed adjustment is warranted under GAAP;
    4. Reporting objections in accordance with the terms of the purchase/sale agreement; and
    5. Reviewing the opposing party's probable objections and support.

PARENTERANDOLPH
The Power of Ideas

Help, We need an Accountant/Consultant! (continued)

- **Additional Services the Accountant/Consultant May Offer:**

  1. Assist in discovery requests, depositions, document reviews;
  2. Conduct analyses and calculate damages;
  3. Trial presentation: testimony, preparation, cross examination;
  4. Dispute negotiation/arbitration/settlement; and
  5. Help to avoid disputes. (Assist with identifying ambiguous language in Agreements or drafting complex clauses.)

ParenteRandolph
The Power of Ideas

War Story #1

- Sale of a National Construction Equipment Rental Company for $200 million: 6/30/x7 closing date; 5/31/x7 balance sheet (company audited).
  - Escrow $5 million;
  - 90 day net worth adjustment, buyer takes control;
  - CFO hates the seller!
  - Big Four firm issues white paper, $20 million claim;
  - A/R (applied to current stuff first-xx xx $5 million);
  - Inventory Computer Adjustment shortage-$7 million;
  - Accruals $1 million;
  - Taxes $7 million, passive;
  - All consultants gone!
  - What was the end result?

PARENTERANDOLPH
The Power of Ideas

War Story #2

- Advertising Company
  - $20 million revenues/volatile earnings;
  - Former sports player/attorney/great synergies;
  - GAAP issues: progress billing;
  - Importance of Due Diligence;
  - All revenue recognized as billed with no associated cost;
  - What was the end result?

War Story #3

- Vehicle dealer-public company to acquire:
  - 2 earn out periods- net income before tax;
  - Bankruptcy;
  - Simultaneous real estate deals – buyer broke it up;
  - Real estate transferred to related part(ies);
  - Dealerships, definition;
  - Sale of dealership got widow in the “money”.
  - What was the end result?

PARENTERANDOLPH
The Power of Ideas

War Story #4

- Agribusiness company:
  - Sale of stock and certain assets;
  - $100 million deal including pension plans;
  - Private company acquires subsidiary of a public company;
  - Historical financial statements 1999-2003, without footnotes;
  - What are top level adjustments?
  - Net undisclosed deferred tax liability of $5.9 million;
  - What are the damages to the buyer, if any?

PARENTERANDOLPH
The Power of Ideas

Questions & Answers

PARENTERANDOLPH
The Power of Ideas

Thank You

Glenn Newman, CPA/ABV, CFE, MBA
Principal
1880 John F. Kennedy Blvd., 17th Floor
Philadelphia, PA 19103

(215) 972-2354 (Phone)
(215) 563-5083 (Fax)

gnewman@parentenet.com
www.parentenet.com

PARENTERANDOLPH
The Power of Ideas

Thank You

Robert P. Gray, CPA/ABV, CFE, FACFEI
Principal
1717 Main Street, Suite 2230
Dallas, TX 75231

(214) 658-6570 (Phone)
(214) 658-6572 (Fax)

rgray@parentenet.com
www.parentenet.com

PARENTERANDOLPH
The Power of Ideas

Bibliography

1. *"Mergers & Acquisitions Report"*, May 7, 2007
2. "*Understanding Business Valuation"*, 2nd Edition, Gary R. Trugman
3. *"Litigation Services Handbook, The Role of the Financial Expert"*, 3rd Edition, Roman L. Weil, Michael J. Wagner and Peter B. Frank
    - Part IV: Civil Litigation
      Antitrust Business Combinations
        - *Mergers, Acquisitions, and Divestitures: The Nature of Disputes and the Role of the Financial Expert*; Mark W. Haller, Kevin D. Kreb, Benjamin W. Perks, and Thomas K. Riordan

PARENTERANDOLPH
The Power of Ideas

NOTES

NOTES

20

STATEMENT OF CASH FLOWS

Patricia A. Woodbury, CPA, CFE
FTI Consulting, Inc.

Statement of Cash Flows

Patricia Woodbury
Managing Director
Forensic and Litigation Consulting
FTI Consulting, Inc.

Statement of Cash Flows

- One of the three basic statements required by GAAP and Regulation S-X
- Authoritative Literature includes:
  - FASB Statement No. 95, *Statement of Cash Flows*
  - FASB Statement No. 117, *Financial Statements of Not-for-Profit Organizations*

Statement of Cash Flows

- Amendments to SFAS 95 include:
  - FASB Statement No. 102, *Statement of Cash Flows – Exemption of Certain Enterprises and Classification of Cash Flows From Certain Securities Acquired for Resale;*
  - FASB Statement No. 104, *Statement of Cash Flows – Net Reporting of Certain Cash Receipts and Cash Payments and Classification of Cash Flows from Hedging Transactions;*
  - FASB Statement No. 115, *Accounting for Certain Investments in Debt and Equity Securities;*
  - Statement No. 123 (Revised), *Share-Based Payments;*
  - Statement No. 140, *Transfers of Receivables;*
  - Statement No. 149, *Amendment of Statement 133 on Derivative Instruments and Hedging Activities; and*
  - Statement No. 150, *Accounting for Certain Financial Instruments With Characteristics of Both Liabilities and Equity.*

Purpose

- Explains the change in cash and cash equivalents during the period
- Provides insight into cash flows from:
    - Operations
    - Financing Activities
    - Investing Activities

Cash and Cash Equivalents

Cash

Cash Equivalents are short-term, highly liquid investments that are both:

a) Readily convertible to known amounts of cash, and
b) so near their maturity that they present insignificant risk of changes in value because of changes in interest rates.

FTI

Cash Equivalents

- Generally, investments with original maturities of three months or less qualify as cash equivalents.
- Must disclose in Notes to the Financial Statements the company's policy of investments included in cash equivalents.

Form of the Statement

- Provides reconciliation of net income to cash flow from operating activities
- Provides cash flows from each of:
  - Operations
  - Financing activities
  - Investing activities
- Provides information about non-cash financing and investing activities

FTI

Gross v. Net

- Generally gross cash flows shall be presented
- Net amounts may be presented if enterprise is essentially holding and disbursing cash on behalf of its customers
- Net amounts may also be presented if
  - Turnover is quick;
  - amounts are large; and
  - maturities are short.

FTI

Cash Flow from Investing Activities

- Include cash payments and cash receipts related to:
  - Property, plant and equipment; and
  - purchasing or selling stocks (equity) and bonds (debt) instruments issued by other companies.

FTI

Cash Flow from Financing Activities

- Include cash payments and cash receipts related to:
  - Equity and debt instruments issued by the company.
  - Receipts from contributions and investment income that are restricted for the purposes of acquiring, constructing or improving property, plant equipment.
  - Distributions to owners (i.e. dividends)

Cash Flow from Operations

- Include all cash payments and receipts related to transactions not defined as either investing or financing activities:
    - Cash receipts from sale of goods and services;
    - Cash payments to vendors
    - Cash payments to employees
    - Interest and dividends received
    - Cash paid for taxes

F T I

Non-Cash Investing and Financing Activities

- Must be separately disclosed
- Include items such as:
  - Converting debt to equity
  - Acquisition of assets financed by seller
  - Acquisition of asset through a capital lease
  - Non cash exchange transactions

Foreign Currency Cash Flow

- The reporting currency equivalent of foreign currency cash flows using exchange rates at the time of the cash flows must be used.
- The effect of exchange rate changes on cash balances held in foreign currencies should be presented as a separate line in the reconciliation of cash and cash equivalents during the period.

Presentation of Operating Cash Flows

- Direct Method – preferred by the FASB and the SEC
- Indirect Method – preferred by most financial statement preparers

FTI

Direct Method

- Preferred by the FASB and the SEC
- Includes:
  - Cash receipts from customers
  - Cash paid to suppliers and employees
  - Interest and dividends received and interest paid
  - Income taxes paid
  - Other operating cash receipts and payments

FTI

Direct Method

Cash Flow from Operations:

Cash Received from Customers	$ 4,600
Cash Paid to Suppliers and Employees	(3,200)
Interest Paid	(200)
Interest Received	80
Dividends Received	10
Income Taxes Paid	(650)
Other Payments, Net	(45)
Cash Provided By Operating Activities	**$ 595**

F T I

Indirect Method

- Preferred by preparers of financial statements
- Less difficult to prepare
- Provides in the body of the statement a reconciliation of net income to cash flows from operations by presenting the change in working capital items

FTI

Indirect Method

Cash Flows from Operations:

Net Income	$ 1,500
Items Not Requiring Current Use of Cash	
Depreciation and Amortization	180
Compensation Expense on Stock Options	15
Gain on sale of equipment	(10)
Changes in Assets and Liabilities	
Accounts Receivable, Net	(475)
Inventory	(500)
Prepaid Expenses	65
Accounts Payable and Accrued Liabilities	(180)
Cash Provided by Operating Activities	**$ 595**

FTI

Questions?

FTI

NOTES

21

STATEMENT OF CASH FLOWS

Glenn Newman, CPA/ABV, CFE, MBA

Parente Randolph

Reprinted from the PLI Course Handbook, *Basics of Accounting & Finance: What Every Practicing Lawyer Needs to Know — Summer 2006* (Order #8650).

Statement of Cash Flows

C/F from Operations

Non-Cash

Depreciation

Investing Activities

Financing Activities

IRR

Presented by:

Glenn Newman, CPA, MBA

PARENTERANDOLPH
FORENSIC & LITIGATION SERVICES
The Power of Ideas[SM]

What is a Statement of Cash Flows?

- One of three fundamental financial statements:
  - Balance Sheet
  - Income Statement
  - Statement of Cash Flows

PARENTERANDOLPH
FORENSIC & LITIGATION SERVICES
The Power of Ideas℠

Cash Flow is Critical

- **Cash is king** - Can the bills be paid?
  - Estimates and judgments are eliminated
- Assets, liabilities, revenue and expenses can be "manipulated" (legally) under GAAP
  - Cash flow allows little room for manipulation
- Cash is cash – either you have it or you don't!!

PARENTERANDOLPH
FORENSIC & LITIGATION SERVICES
The Power of Ideas℠

What is Cash?

- Cash includes:
  - Currency
  - Checks on hand
  - Deposits in banks
- Cash equivalents include:
  - Short-term, temporary investments that can be quickly and easily converted to cash

PARENTERANDOLPH
FORENSIC & LITIGATION SERVICES
The Power of Ideas℠

Statement of Cash Flows

- A summary of cash in and cash out over a period of time
  - What *generated* (increased) cash and what *consumed* (decreased) cash
- For a transaction to appear on the Statement of Cash Flows, it had to have actually been paid (or collected), not just incurred (except for changes in A/R and A/P)

PARENTERANDOLPH
FORENSIC & LITIGATION SERVICES
The Power of Ideas℠

Uses of Statement of Cash Flows

- Company
  - Predict future cash flows to build a budget
  - "Go/No-Go" on specific projects
- Lenders/Creditors
  - Determine a business's ability to pay back loans
- Investors
  - Gives insight to the company's financial health
  - Helps in assessing the "multiple"

PARENTERANDOLPH
FORENSIC & LITIGATION SERVICES
The Power of Ideas℠

Statement of Cash Flows

- Required captions
  - Net Income
  - Cash flow from operating activities/operations
  - Cash flow from investing activities
  - Cash flow from financing activities
  - Net change in cash
  - Beginning cash balance
  - Ending cash balance
  - Supplemental disclosures

PARENTERANDOLPH
FORENSIC & LITIGATION SERVICES
The Power of Ideas℠

Cash Flows from Operating Activities

- Measures the cash used or provided by a company's normal operations
- Shows the company's ability to generate positive cash flow from operations

Cash Flows from Operating Activities

- This section includes changes in:
  - Net Income (includes accruals)
  - Non-cash changes & credits
    - Depreciation/Amortization
    - Share-based compensation
  - A/R
    - Decrease in A/R – Cash comes in
  - Inventory
    - Increase in Inventory – Cash goes out
  - A/P
    - Decrease in A/P – Cash goes out

PARENTE RANDOLPH
FORENSIC & LITIGATION SERVICES
The Power of Ideas

Cash Flow from Investing Activities

- Contains all the cash used or provided by the purchase and sale of income-producing assets

- Section includes:
  - Purchase or sale of marketable securities
  - Capital expenditures (Purchase equipment)
  - Capital dispositions (Sale of equipment)
  - Other investing activities (Invest in new businesses)

PARENTERANDOLPH
FORENSIC & LITIGATION SERVICES
The Power of Ideas℠

Cash Flow from Financing Activities

- Measures the flow of cash between a firm and its owners and creditors.
- Cash outflows illustrate:
  - Company is servicing debt, or
  - Company is making dividend payments and stock repurchases
- Cash inflows illustrate:
  - Company issues stock
  - Company borrows from creditors

PARENTE RANDOLPH
FORENSIC & LITIGATION SERVICES
The Power of Ideas

Cash Flow from Financing Activities

- This sections includes:
  - Borrowings from creditors
  - Repayments to creditors
  - Issuance of common stock
  - Payment of cash dividends

ParenteRandolph
Forensic & Litigation Services
"The Power of Ideas"

Net Change in Cash

- This is the total change in cash as a result of the operating, investing, and financing activities.

- Example:

Cash provided by Operating Activities	$2.7B
Cash used in Investing Activities	(1.0B)
Cash used in Financing Activities	(1.6B)
Net Change in Cash	$0.1B
Beginning Cash Balance	0.8B
Ending Cash Balance	$0.9B

PARENTE RANDOLPH
FORENSIC & LITIGATION SERVICES
The Power of Ideas

Financial Health

- Just because a company is profitable does not mean it is generating cash, AND
- Just because a company has cash does not mean it is profitable
- Therefore, the statement of cash flows should be analyzed in conjunction with the income statement

PARENTE RANDOLPH
FORENSIC & LITIGATION SERVICES
"The Power of Ideas"

Financial Health

- Cash flow statements should always be reviewed in conjunction with the accompanying notes and MD&A
- Cash flow statements should be analyzed from one period to the next
  - A negative cash flow in one period may be the result of a business expanding its operations, which may be positive for the future

PARENTE RANDOLPH
FORENSIC & LITIGATION SERVICES
The Power of Ideas

Financial Health

- A company's cash flow is best gauged against its industry peers
  - Each industry has its own acceptable cash flow level
  - Data services exist that provide benchmarks for industry cash flows such as:
    - Risk Management Association ("RMA")
    - Integra

PARENTE RANDOLPH
FORENSIC & LITIGATION SERVICES
The Power of Ideas℠

Financial Health

- Cash flows from operating activities is important to evaluate
  - Shows how efficiently a business can produce and sell its product/services
  - Measures the potential long-term success

PARENTERANDOLPH
FORENSIC & LITIGATION SERVICES
The Power of Ideas℠

Financial Health

- ❑ Comparing the cash flows generated to the debt outstanding illustrates the ability of the company to pay its loans and interest payments

- ❑ A drop in the cash flow could effect the loan payments, and increase the company's risk

PARENTERANDOLPH
FORENSIC & LITIGATION SERVICES
"The Power of Ideas"℠

Supplemental Information

- Businesses are required to separately disclose all non-cash financing and investing activities on the statement of cash flows
  - Examples:
    - Converting debt to equity
    - Purchasing a building by acquiring a mortgage
    - Obtaining an asset (i.e. building) by receiving a gift
    - Exchange of non-cash assets or liabilities for other non-cash assets or liabilities
  - Can be included as a separate section on the statement or a narrative

PARENTE RANDOLPH
FORENSIC & LITIGATION SERVICES
The Power of Ideas℠

Supplemental Information

- Businesses should also disclose what items they are treating as cash equivalents
- Supplemental information is helpful in reconciling differences between balance sheet, income statement and statement of cash flows

PARENTE RANDOLPH
FORENSIC & LITIGATION SERVICES
The Power of Ideas℠

Examples

- ❑ Good v. Poor cash flows
- ❑ Indicators of problem children

PARENTERANDOLPH
FORENSIC & LITIGATION SERVICES
The Power of Ideas℠

Questions/Contact Information

Glenn Newman, CPA

Parente Randolph, LLC

1880 John F. Kennedy Boulevard

Philadelphia, PA 19103

gnewman@parentenet.com

215.972.2354

PARENTERANDOLPH
FORENSIC & LITIGATION SERVICES
"The Power of Ideas"

NOTES

NOTES

Program Schedule and Faculty

PROGRAM

DAY ONE: 9:00 A.M. - 5:00 P.M.

MORNING SESSION: 9:00 A.M. – 12:15 P.M.

9:00 Program Overview

NYC & CHI: Karen Kincaid Balmer

SF: Curtis Burr

9:05 Understanding Generally Accepted Accounting Principles (GAAP), Generally Accepted Auditing Standards (GAAS) and the Accounting Cycle

An overview of the fundamental principles of accounting. An overview of GAAP and GAAS and their sources, including various levels of care inherent in audits, reviews, and compilations.

NYC: David J. Zaumeyer Ph.D.

SF: Claudia P. Spencer

CHI: Karen Kincaid Balmer; Patricia A. Woodbury

11:05 Break

11:15 Understanding Balance Sheets: Assets, Liabilities and Stockholders' Equity

The elements of a balance sheet — assets, liabilities and stockholders' equity and their significance. What to look for when reading a balance sheet. Current assets such as cash, receivables, inventories, investments in debt and equity securities, and fixed and other long-term assets, including intellectual property and goodwill. Current liabilities, leases, long-term debt, pension and other post-retirement benefits, other long-term liabilities, and the components of stockholders' equity.

NYC: Christopher J. Rosetti

SF: Lawrence M. Cirelli; Terry Lloyd

CHI: Sonya Andreassen

12:15 Lunch

AFTERNOON SESSION: 1:15 P.M. – 5:00 P.M.

1:15 Understanding Balance Sheets: Assets, Liabilities and Stockholders' Equity

(Continued)

1:45 Understanding the Income Statement

The importance of revenue and expense recognition, gross margin, overhead, depreciation and tax expense. The significance of income from continuing operations, discontinued operations, changes in accounting principles, extraordinary items, and comprehensive income/loss.

NYC: Glenn Newman

SF: Brad Holsworth

CHI: Robert P. Gray

3:15 Break

3:30 Understanding the Statement of Cash Flows

How to understand and use this statement — An explanation of operating, investing and financing cash flows. What this statement can tell you about a company's financial health. The significance of supplemental information and certain non-cash information.

NYC: Felicia C. Battista

SF: Mark Ryan V. Pineda

CHI: Patricia A. Woodbury

SCHEDULE

Please plan to arrive with enough time to register before the conference begins. A continental breakfast will be available upon your arrival.

DAY TWO: 9:00 A.M. - 5:00 P.M.

MORNING SESSION: 9:00 A.M. – 12:45 P.M.

9:00 The Importance of the Notes to the Financial Statement

A guide to where to look for critical information to further explain balance sheet and income statement information.

NYC: Dan Berman

SF: Paul T. Tucci

CHI: Shirley Hudler

New York City and Chicago Programs Only:

10:00 How Lawyers Can Best Use Accountants as Experts

An attorney outlines the importance of using accountants as experts, the pros and cons, how to maintain privilege where necessary, how to properly prepare the expert for deposition, trial and cross-examination.

NYC & CHI: John P. Woods

San Francisco Program Only:

10:00 Fraud and Financial Disaster: A Forensic Accountant's Overview

Advice to attorneys for that moment when someone calls and says, "I think I have a problem."

SF: A. Christine Davis

11:00 Break

11:15 Lawyers' Use and Misuse of Financial Language: Avoiding Legal Landmines

An examination of real life pitfalls of various accounting language in legal documents.

NYC: Glenn Newman

SF: Moji Saniefar

CHI: Robert P. Gray

12:45 Lunch

AFTERNOON SESSION: 1:45 P.M. – 5:00 P.M.

New York City and Chicago Programs Only:

1:45 Fraud and Financial Disaster: A Forensic Accountant's Overview

Advice to attorneys for that moment when someone calls and says, "I think I have a problem."

NYC & CHI: Karen Kincaid Balmer

San Francisco Program Only:

1:45 How Lawyers Can Best Use Accountants as Experts

An attorney outlines the importance of using accountants as experts, the pros and cons, how to maintain privilege where necessary, how to properly prepare the expert for deposition, trial and cross-examination.

SF: James K. Lynch

2:45 Break

3:00 Current SEC Enforcement Actions, Accounting and Disclosure Issues

NYC: Alexander M. Vasilescu

SF: Robert S. Leach

CHI: Robert Burson

4:00 Legal and Accounting Ethical Issues

In any investigation or litigation matter involving accounting issues, it is often important for attorneys to understand accountants' ethics rules and regulations, as well as those of the legal profession.

NYC: Daniel J. Leffell

SF: Lori Lynn Phillips

CHI: Sally K. Sears Coder

FACULTY

CHAIR:

Karen Kincaid Balmer
Partner, Fraud & Litigation Services
Kincaid Consulting, LLC
New York City

NEW YORK CITY

Felicia C. Battista
Senior Managing Director - Forensic and Litigation Consulting
FTI Consulting, Inc.
Washington, D.C.

Dan Berman
Navigant Consulting, Inc.
Philadelphia

Daniel J. Leffell
Paul, Weiss, Rifkind, Wharton & Garrison LLP
New York City

Glenn Newman, CPA/ABV
Parente Randolph, LLC
Philadelphia

Christopher J. Rosetti
BST Valuation & Litigation Advisors LLC
New York City

Alexander M. Vasilescu
Regional Trial Counsel/Trial Unit Chief
Northeast Region Office
Securities and Exchange Commission
New York City

John P. Woods
Inspector General
New York City Department of Investigation
New York City

David J. Zaumeyer Ph.D., CPA
Marks Paneth & Shron
New York City

CHICAGO

Sonya Andreassen
Director
PricewaterhouseCoopers LLP
Chicago

Robert Burson
Senior Associate Regional Director, Securities and Exchange Commission
Chicago Regional Office
Chicago

Sally K. Sears Coder
Jenner & Block
Chicago

Robert P. Gray
Principal
Parente Randolph
Dallas, Texas

Shirley Hudler
Senior Manager
UHY Advisors FLVS, Inc.
Houston, Texas

Patricia A. Woodbury, CPA, CFE
Managing Director – Forensic and Litigation Consulting
FTI Consulting, Inc.
Washington, D.C.

John P. Woods
Inspector General
New York City Department of Investigation
New York City

CO-CHAIRS:

Curtis Burr CPA, ABV, CVA
Burr, Pilger & Mayer, LLP
San Francisco

Lawrence M. Cirelli
Hanson, Bridgett, Marcus, Vlahos, & Rudy, LLP
San Francisco

SAN FRANCISCO

A. Christine Davis
Director
Litigation and Forensic Consulting Services Group
Hemming Morse, Inc.
San Francisco

Gerry Keeler
Orrick, Herrington & Sutcliffe LLP
San Francisco

Brad Holsworth
Burr, Pilger & Mayer
San Francisco

Robert S. Leach
Branch Chief, Division of Enforcement
Securities and Exchange Commission
San Francisco District Office
San Francisco

Terry Lloyd, CPA, CFA
Cogent Valuation
San Francisco

James K. Lynch
Latham & Watkins LLP
San Francisco

Mark Ryan V. Pineda CPA
Odenberg, Ullakko, Muranishi & Co. LLP
San Francisco

Lori Lynn Phillips
Heller Ehrman
Seattle, Washington

Moji Saniefar
Orrick, Herrington & Sutcliffe
San Francisco

Claudia P. Spencer, CPA
Assurance Partner
BDO Seidman, LLP
San Francisco

Paul T. Tucci, CPA
Moss Adams LLP
San Francisco

Program Attorney: Janet L. Siegel